What the Trout Said

What the Trout Said

ABOUT THE DESIGN OF TROUT FLIES, AND OTHER MYSTERIES

REVISED AND AUGMENTED EDITION

Datus C. Proper

Drawings by BILL ELLIOTT

SWAN HILL
PRESS

First published in the UK in 1993
by Swan Hill Press
an imprint of Airlife Publishing Ltd.

ISBN 1 85310 412 4

Colour photographs by James Gilford reproduced
by permission of the photographer.

Printed in the United States of America.

Swan Hill Press

An Imprint of Airlife Publishing Ltd.
101 Longden Road, Shrewsbury SY3 9EB, England

For my father,
William Glisan Proper,
who was less interested in the trout
than in trees, flowers, and birds,
and who could have found these
without driving sixty miles,
but who spent many days of his life
getting me close to rivers.

Cada escritor es hijo de sus obras.

—CERVANTES

Acknowledgments

Major written sources are identified in the text and bibliography. I am also grateful for contributions in conversation or by letter from:

- Vincent C. Marinaro, whose written work is also of particular importance as a source (only G.E.M. Skues has made a comparable impact on my thinking)
- Scotty (William Scott) Chapman, who has been fishing the waters of the Yellowstone country since 1926 and learning something new every day
- Ned Maguire, friend of many days on Irish streams and angling scholar
- J.R. Harris, Irish fishing friend and author of an angling entomology I greatly admire

Contents

Four pages of color plates follow page 158.

Foreword

❧ ❧ ❧ In my youth I had a favorite author, one of whose books contained a preface that expressed a very beautiful sentiment. It read as follows: "Because I have known the torments of thirst I would dig a well where others might drink."

With this book I think that Datus Proper has dug such a well. Future generations of fly-fishermen may drink from it gratefully. It is a deep well, containing many treasures of knowledge concerning the craft of fly-tying and the art of fly-fishing.

For five hundred years fly-fishermen have burdened and shackled themselves with a stereotyped concept of fly imitation that kept them from understanding and enjoying the greater potential that lies in good design, as well as in pattern. This is where Datus Proper has struck at the heart of matter, and this is where he goes far beyond any other writer or researcher.

His talks with trout are more than a literary device. They are conscientious appraisals of trout's response to the many aspects of trout fly imitation. The reader may not agree with the author's conclusions. He may not agree with Proper's interpretation of the trout's reply. But he must surely agree that the problem has been clearly outlined and the important considerations stated. The reader can take it from there and build a case of his own. That is the way to progress.

Everything that Datus says in this book is authenticated by the broad base of his fly-fishing experiences in many lands and on many waters. I have had numerous opportunities, both off-stream and during our fishing excursions together, to evaluate and appreciate the depth and range of his thinking on fly-fishing matters. They are impressive. Sometimes our streamside lunches became lengthy exchanges of ideas and philosophies concerning all aspects of fly-fishing. The reader will be entertained to find many of these ideas and philosophies set forth here, enlivened by Datus Proper's pleasant humor and delightful tales of fishing episodes.

The perusal of this book by any thoughtful student of fly-fishing is bound to be a fruitful and absorbing experience. He will re-read it many times. How I would have cherished a book like this in my own formative years.

Vincent C. Marinaro
November 1981
Mechanicsburg, Pennsylvania

Introduction to the Second Edition

Fly fishing is the sport that asks why. We may release the trout, but we cling to his mysteries. Why does he take one fly and refuse others? An answer offers, until other trout come along to reject it. One after another, over at least five centuries, they have molded our sport into curious strata of science, art, and magic. This has attracted thoughtful people. They have written many books on the meeting of trout and fly. I love them, and I think that most have been wrong.

The trout's universe does not spin as we thought. He takes the fly not because its color is right—as we have wanted to believe during those centuries—but because it behaves like a natural insect. When color matters, it matters least.

We need a root change: not a revolution but a return to nature, in the form of a trout. That means throwing out an accretion of human baggage. I didn't insist on this enough in the first edition. In the little universe of fly fishing, we have the sun and the planets as mixed up as they were before Copernicus. When he suggested that the earth revolved around the sun rather than vice versa, theologians knew he was wrong. We who tie trout flies know that the way to imitate a natural insect is to match its color.

We insist on seeing the sun rise, too, though Copernicus showed that it couldn't. Real universe be damned, and real trout with it. We *want* to imitate little olive flies with little olive artificial flies. Men everywhere do it, though we English-speakers have a right to be more culture-bound than most; our ancestors made fly fishing what it is. The French enjoy straightening us out. Jean-Paul Pequegnot uses a pink fly and the trout take it as well as an olive one. But trout are barbarians. Why should fly fishing be organized to please fish when humans are in control?

Because it is getting messy. We have thousands of flies that differ hardly at all, except in color. The trout says that we need only a few, differing in behavior. This (being no more wisdom than a trout has) is barbaric.

Now you see why I was shy about moving the universe around too brusquely in the first edition. I am not ambitious of ridicule. Besides, in the seventies I wasn't sure how many readers out there would welcome an unfamiliar way of looking at trout fishing or, for that matter, how many wanted to think about fishing at all. I tried to make the book interesting for those who don't tie their own flies or know the names of each insect floating down the current. Angling shouldn't be so complex that it's a chore—or so simple that it's a bore.

People who have liked the book do seem to think of fishing as fun, which makes me happy. On the other hand, there were readers who asked whether I was writing about imitation or presentation, which shows how hard it is to break old patterns of thought. Presentation is part of imitation, not something opposed to it. The trout explains in Chapter Two.

It may also be helpful to explain where science, art, and magic fit into this book.

- Science is nature, accurately seen. An artificial trout fly that imitates nature (from the *trout's* point of view, not ours) is scientific in this broad sense.
- Art is "not imitation of nature but liberation from nature"—a definition borrowed from Professor Allan Bloom.* A fly aimed at catching humans, rather than trout, is artistic.
- Magic is supernatural, like talking trout. Do not confuse magic and art. Art escapes from the natural; magic interprets nature, venturing to explain what science cannot yet see.

---

*The Closing of the American Mind. NY: Simon & Schuster, 1987.

The time may be close when tiny electrodes implanted in the trout's brain will tell us how he thinks, scientifically. I am betting that the scientific trout will agree with my magic trout. Meanwhile, he must remain magic—not because he is cute but because he is honest. I want you to believe him, but I also want you to know that I cannot *prove* what he says.

Science, art, and magic are all good; a fishing attitude that squeezes out any of them is the worse for it. But it is up to an author to avoid confusing the three. Muddles of science and magic have produced astrology instead of astronomy, lunar tables instead of biology. Mixtures of science and art have produced ten thousand pretty flies we don't need.

Readers will have little trouble in recognizing the difference between magic and science. (The talking trout is there to help.) The difference between art and science is, to say the least, fuzzy in fishing literature. I shall try to draw attention to the confusion when we talk about color.

Fly patterns are mostly art, so I left them out of this book (and was relieved to find that few readers seemed to mind).

This is not a history, either, though I try to discover origins. (Readers care passionately about history, which says something about fly fishing.)

It looks, now, as if anglers will be talking about the design of flies for a while, so there are more sources that should be acknowledged. No one had written a book on fly design when I wrote this one, and I thought that no one had used the term with the same purpose. But of course someone had. He was W. H. Lawrie, who mentioned design in at least three books. In *Scottish Trout Flies,* published in London in 1966, he clearly had in mind what I was searching for between 1973 and 1977 (when this book was written). Lawrie analyzed the design of traditional wet flies. Further, he noted that another British angler—Henry Lamond—had referred to the design of flies in 1921. (It took Vince Marinaro to catch this and tell me about it.)

In hindsight, it was logical that the first references to design should have appeared in Britain: the British have been fishing with imitative flies for a long time. It is also logical that the first book on the subject should have appeared in the United States. The British need design, but not as badly. They have an old and attractive way with flies: they identify one that the trout likes to eat and then imitate it better and better for a few centuries. Every generation makes improvements, but few suggest departures. For this approach to work, however, anglers must concern themselves with only a few, specific, well-known insects. It turns out that the British, who live on an island, do have only a few; and the Irish, who live on an island behind an island, have even fewer. At least, there used to be only a few. These days, with new stillwater fisheries and a fair share of environmental problems, there are more times when mayflies do not rule the waves; and the sedges, midges, empids and such are not as well known.

Outside Britain and Ireland, the trout have usually been feeding on insects that I could not identify by species. Frequently even professional entomologists have been reluctant to identify these insects below generic level.

Enter design. I want to know what I'm doing. I'd like to know the name of every insect (and tree, rock, flower, and mermaid), but I don't. Without the name, I can't look up an imitation. I can see how the natural fly is behaving, though, and pick one from a fly box that behaves likewise. If it is the right size, it will probably work. If it is also the right shape, it may work better than an imitation from a book. Design does not have to be more complicated than that.

The first edition of this book did not credit fly designs appearing in books after 1977. It also omitted some writers I should have known about, but didn't. The French think readily in design terms, and Pequegnot's book—now available in English—has several designs that reached a peak of development in France. The Spanish have a fly-fishing literature that is almost as old as the British, and Spanish wet-fly designs are completely different, but there is no book on them in English yet. I cannot read German or Italian very well, and I would not venture to try Preben Torp Jacobsen in Danish. The best single set of suggestions on the first edition of this book came from a brilliant Dutch angler, Rudi van Alberda. (That says something about what fly fishing has become: they scarcely have trout in Holland.)

Mind you, the British have lost their monopoly, but they have not slowed down. Brian Clarke and John Goddard have written *The Trout and the Fly*, which proposes new designs and shows why they are useful in photographs that compare to Vince Marinaro's. Neil Patterson describes simple, innovative mayfly designs.

In America, there is a boom in fly fishing and in books about it. Gary LaFontaine's book on caddisflies contains original designs based on research. Chauncy K. Lively was one of our first purposeful fly designers, and his ideas are now available in book form. Sylvester Nemes' two books have helped to revive one of the oldest designs—the soft-hackle fly.

I have added one new wet-fly design and one dry in this edition, and in time might learn enough to want more. Most of the flies are still surface or midwater designs. The latter may help to fill a gap in the literature, which often focuses on either top or bottom. More important, it's easier to sink flies than float them, so we don't need quite as many deep-sinking designs. This is not to say that it is any easier to fish deep. I just don't want to fix things that ain't broke.

Designs aren't like patterns, which go on forever. A great many of the designs we need originated (though were not fully developed) by 1950. Even by 1920, or 1900. And, as Nelson Bryant wrote in *The New York Times*, it "would require a sabbatical or an independent income" to act on all the recent fishing books (let alone magazines). Please forgive omissions and let me know about them. Anglers who have already done so will note changes in this edition.

—DATUS PROPER
Bozeman, Montana
Spring 1988

What the Trout Said

Explanation

❊ ❊ ❊ This is called an "explanation" because no one reads introductions, and also because there are some things that need explaining.

First, this is a fishing book that is mainly about fishing. Some of my favorite fishing books are mainly about *people* who go fishing. The difference is substantial. People in this book play supporting roles; the lead actors are trout and the insects trout eat.

Now, the interesting thing about fishing people is their queer, half-primitive, half-driven behavior. They do things that trout find inexplicable and that other people find irresistibly comic. Such actions were made for writers to burlesque. I have not always resisted the temptation.

Wild creatures struggling for survival cannot afford such irrational deportment. They would be comparatively dull, except for one thing: their survival depends on their ability to hide their behavior from us predators. If we could only understand their hidden language, we would be closer to understanding the elusive lady who whispers to us sometimes from the deep current on a summer evening.

And besides, we would catch more trout.

As it happens, we trout fishermen have available to us—as one option—an attractive path toward understanding. No other sport offers anything comparable. No other fish seems to have been forced by its environment into the curiously sensitive perceptions of some trout. Fishing with live bait or lures does not reveal much about these perceptions. Even the tools of science are relatively blunt, though more reliable. We have the opportunity to get at the part of a trout's life which takes most of his time and is most important to him: his search for safe food. But to understand what we observe, we must maintain careful controls, and be as honest about our results as any scientist.

The special thing about trout fishing with an imitative fly is this: it is the only sport that proceeds from a general theory. But since half of all potential readers will be tempted to put down this book at mention of such a dull and ponderous thing as a "general theory," I had better explain that there are no more theories hereafter: some odd ideas and radical propositions, perhaps, but one theory is all we need. The one we have evolved some centuries before me. It has been repeated so often that many anglers forget it *is* a theory; others forget it even exists. It comes from the first writings on trout fishing, and it goes like this: trout take the angler's fly because it resembles a natural creature which they are accustomed to eating. All the angler must do, then, is to find what that creature is and imitate it with something containing a hook: something that looks and acts natural but is in fact contrived.

Imitating the appearance and behavior of a natural insect can sometimes be difficult. The pitfalls are what this book is about. *But we know what we are trying to do.* Having accepted the theory, we can proceed to the details. We do not have to seek blindly, fatalistically, counting only on the odds or astrology.

As to avoiding those pitfalls, this book tries an approach that has been used by only a few others, and that also needs explaining. *The trout is asked for his opinion.* The fish can, of course, be hard to hear. And not any trout will do. The degenerate, half-tame variety that inhabits many streams these days is hardly worth listening to. The mother of such fish is a hatchery pond. It is necessary to consult a special kind of high-quality fish that is described early in this book.

Having found the right trout, there is the matter of what to discuss with him. The trout and I do not share enough knowledge to sustain a good conversation on most subjects. I have found trout to be bored with fishing rods, personalities, and sunsets—all of which are things that interest me about fishing. At one time, I tried to get trout to share my interest in fly patterns, but that was only sometimes successful. So I tried to forget my preconceptions and ask trout what interested *them*. The result is that this book has been written about something I have called "fly design." The term may be new; the idea really isn't, though only a few authors have written about design. No one—to my knowledge—has tried to describe a full range of designs objectively, relating them to the insects trout eat.

In chapter 9, I suggest that we can define design *"as the way materials are chosen and assembled in order to achieve a desired structural task. That task is to control behavior above all."* This is quite different from the concept of pattern, which has traditionally emphasized color. But, as in most new concepts, the reasons for departing from tradition may not immediately make sense. I hope they will make sense by the time we reach chapter 9.

You may or may not choose to believe that I have conversations with fish. I do ask you to believe that I have looked for educated fish and interpreted their opinions as honestly as I could, and that I have not asked only the questions that suit my prejudices. Since I clearly need all the help I can get, I have also consulted a number of other people who have talked to trout over the years. I have identified these people in the text.

Many honorable fishing books have not identified sources. After all, the usual goal is to help people catch fish. That need not be complicated, and history is no help. The problem is this: when you read back through the decades and centuries of fishing books, you see ideas appearing again and again, and being twisted in the process. Occasionally the ideas are improved; sometimes they come out backwards. As a rule, originals are sharper than copies. So there are a lot of references in this book to sources that will seem ancient and foreign, especially to Americans. I do not mean to ignore or belittle the many excellent new books; it is just that original thinking is always scarce, and no one man is able to contribute more than a few scraps.

My own scraps are identified in the first person singular—not because I think they are especially good but because I fear they may not be, and I want readers to know whom to blame.

If my sources sound foreign to many, some of the rivers I cite will sound exotic to practically everybody. Please do not think that I am river-dropping, like a wealthy traveler trying to impress the girls at a cocktail party. For the most part, I have fished in these places because my work took me there. In fishing, travel is not necessarily broadening. I have fished in a number of salmon rivers without finding all that much to learn about fish. And wilderness trout do not know a great deal.

But if you seek out a special kind of stream and trout, then travel can teach you something about the universalities in fishing. I admit to a special fascination with the difficult Irish and British fishing, not because it is exotic. On the contrary, it is similar to the kinds of fishing I like best in America, and can never get enough of in one lifetime.

The Old World streams also have a lot to teach about the origins of angling. There is a special discipline involved in imitating an insect that has been described for five centuries.

But why such attention to the minutiae of fishing? Can one not just go fishing for the enjoyment and leave thinking for the office?

Well, of course, if that is what pleases. It does not please me very much, speaking only of my own taste. I could not agree with Arnold Gingrich when he depreciated "manuals" in comparison with "books." The good "manuals" include Berners, part of Walton, and most of Cotton, Ronalds, Pulman, Stewart, Halford, Skues, Harding, and Marinaro—just to take a few landmarks that do not go beyond 1950, and which I therefore hope will not get me in trouble with more recent authors. All these books deal with imitative trout fishing, unlike many other good general books that draw from broader traditions.

If dealing with problems that have fascinated men for centuries does not fascinate you, I can suggest some more convenient rationales for thoughtful fishing.

- It is as important as some of the other things men think about, like nuclear physics.
- Trout live in the world's pleasant places and are sometimes sought by pleasant people. Where and with whom would you prefer to give your best?
- Light physical exercise liberates the brain and makes *not* thinking difficult.
- The frontier was conquered generations ago, and the minutiae are what's left.
- All men are compulsive hunters, or at least I am.
- I scarcely know how to pursue enjoyment, but I am able to catch a lot of it along with my trout.

All of the above are excellent reasons, and at least the last of them clarifies the angler's compulsion. Annie Dillard, a non-fisherman, explained it to me in her *Pilgrim at Tinker Creek*:

What I call innocence is the spirit's unself-conscious state at any moment of pure devotion to any object. It is at once a receptiveness and total concentration. One needn't be, shouldn't be, reduced to a puppy. . . . It is possible to pursue innocence as hounds pursue hares: single-mindedly, driven by a kind of love, crashing over creeks, keening and lost in fields and forests, circling, vaulting all hedges and hills wide-eyed, giving loud tongue all unawares to the deepest, most incomprehensible longing, a root-flame in the heart.

Innocence is a wild trout. But we humans, being complicated, have to pursue innocence in complex ways.

PART I

What the Trout Say About Fly Design

1 ⁂ Conversations with Trout

On Imitations, Fancy Flies, Lures, and How to Tell the Difference

⁂ ⁂ ⁂ Trout can settle most angling arguments. But they don't know much about art; they just know what they like. And you have to be a good listener, because they are bashful. Anglers, on the contrary, have been shouting back and forth at each other for a few hundred years. It's hard to filter out the noise and pick up a faint whisper from the depths of running water.

Trout get through to me sometimes. I am not boasting about it. By comparison to fishermen, trout are pretty sober. But reliable.

I started receiving fishy messages at a tender age. In those days, I was inclined to argue back, so the conversations did not last long. There were a lot of trout near my home in Yellowstone Park, and I could always find a stupid one. Then I got old enough to drive. The fertile Firehole River tempted me with bigger fish. They were also smarter, and they made me listen. A few years later the trout of the Pennsylvania spring creeks had a lot to say.

But for really talkative creatures, you should listen to Irish browns. The accent can be a bit thick. The gillaroos from Mayo lose me entirely, though of course I never let on. The fat trout of the limestone midlands come through clearly. And they seldom stop talking; they have such great material to work with.

In Pennsylvania, by the time the trout have started to learn something about Hendricksons, the hatch is gone; it usually peaks on one Wednesday and Thursday while I am a hundred miles away earning my wages, and then a heavy rain floods the river Saturday. In Ireland, I can count on a perfect hatch of Large Dark Olives by St. Patrick's Day, and the hatch is still going on in May. By then there are also the Grey Flag sedge, the Iron Blue Dun, and the Black Gnat, just to mention the durable hatches. Best of all is the Blue-Winged Olive, which you can fish every fine evening from June through September. The trout learn something about these flies, with hooks or without, and they will tell you. To be sure you are getting the right message, make just one small change in your fly between trips. Then, if you really listen to what the trout say instead of to what you want to believe, you can draw some conclusions about fly design. And that is the story of this book.

My first "imitation" of the Large Dark Olives was trout-proof. I tied it from a pattern. It was too big, too bushy, and entirely the wrong color; but most of the changes it needed were obvious. Four seasons later, my Olives were pretty respectable. Mind you, I'm just repeating the trouts' opinion. I've said nothing.

The Blue-Winged Olive—a different genus—was more difficult. The trout told me clearly that what looked right to me looked wrong to them. But they would not say what looked right. You may think the Irish are forthcoming, but it's a cover. They hide the important things.

So there I was one August day, up to my unmentionables in the Kells Blackwater. The Irish never wade that deep, perhaps on principle, but I maintain that it is a good thing for unmentionables to keep them cool—something I read in Margaret Mead. Besides, as will be revealed in chapter 4, wading is a good way to learn trout language.

This was a soft day, as they say in Ireland when it is about to rain buckets down your collar. A good day for hatches. And some thirty feet upstream, a trout was taking Blue-Winged Olive duns with a deep, resonant swirl that made my fingers fumble. I tied on a fly that had worked once during a daytime Blue-Winged Olive hatch on a different river. She had a sleek blue-gray wing and a green-olive body—much like the natural female dun, to my eyes, and beautiful.

The trout told me that she was not beautiful. Not even vaguely interesting. The real duns, even bedraggled ones in pajamas, kept disappearing with a ploop, which is strong language in troutese. My dun, all fancied up in a tight sweater, did not get a nod. Dumb trout.

So I tried a nymph, painstakingly copied from the monthly magazine that features Blue-Winged Olive nymphets. I greased my leader, except for the last few inches, and soaked the nymph in my mouth. It drifted down nicely, a few inches under water, on the first cast, and the second, and the third. Besides lacking in discernment, this trout was entirely defective in libido.

From Ned Maguire standing on the bank, I thought I got a smirk, although it can be hard to tell through all the cigarette smoke. He had a big stupid brown fly on his leader. All right, if I couldn't get a rise out of the trout, I'd get one out of ould Ned. I generously offered to let him try my fish, since I couldn't catch it and besides the disadvantage of his fly, he was in difficult casting position way up there on the bank.

From his awkward angle, he could not have got a long float, but he did not need one, because his fly lit a foot in front of the trout. Even from a distance, that fly was a real misfit, a tattooed weightlifter among the ballet dancers. Yet the trout rose on the first float, with exactly the same ploop accorded the naturals.

"Ahaah," said Ned. Now, Ned is not one of your playboys who chatters while into a fish. He does not bother even with the "Ahaah" unless he feels the hook set solidly in a substantial weight. In this case, the substantial weight plunged upstream, leaving a visible furrow in the water, and shot into a mass of weeds. There are some refined methods for working on a weeded trout. I used the one that best suits my temperament—hot pursuit. Dreadfully untraditional. Fortunately, Ned's leader was stout, and the fish was well hooked in the corner of the mouth. I netted a seventeen-inch brown out of an underwater garden.

The reader will please note the scenario. Your eager author is now up to his armpits in river, holding a dripping net. The net contains a large, disconsolate trout and about a pickle-barrel-full of weeds. On the bank is Ned, patched old hip-boots down around his knees and not quite the boy-o he used to be. And when he was the boy-o he used to be, he stood about five-seven and weighed a hundred and thirty in wet tweeds.

My indisputable conclusion was that I had possession. I couldn't exactly run off with the trout, because Ned was driving, and it was a long walk home in waders. But Ned's leader was not nearly strong enough to pull me out till I had a good look at the fly and interviewed the trout.

The fly, besides being too big for a Blue-Winged Olive, had neither blue nor olive nor wings about it. It had a drab brown body of pheasant-tail herl ribbed with gold, plus a shiny, sparse hackle of mahogany red. This was, in fact, a well-known fancy fly, the Pheasant Tail Red Spinner.

The interview went like this.

AUTHOR: The jig is up, fishface. If you'd played my game, you might have got off with a toothache. Instead you picked that smirking Irishman. Can you imagine him letting a fat, pink-fleshed trout swim away?

TROUT: (A visible shudder)

AUTHOR: Skip the dramatics. You have murdered mayflies by the score, to say nothing of sedges and shrimp. I want you to do the only decent thing in your life. In your last words, I want you to tell me why you, who must be intelligent to have lived so long, showed such bad taste in the end.

TROUT: Get yer t'umb outa me mout'.

AUTHOR: Sorry. I was looking at that fancy fly.

TROUT: You can keep yer sermons and yer Yankee accent and yer fancy flies. I never looked at a fancy fly since I was humiliated in me catechism. The fly that fought back just now looked like a hatching dun.

AUTHOR: Thanks, old man. Now here's Ned with the priest.

NED: Thunk!

A poignant exchange, you say, but not profound.

Consider, however, another quotation for which you do not have to take my word. In his excellent book entitled *Quill Gordon*, John McDonald says that "both fancy and imitation flies take trout, but the reconciliation of the theories behind them would be the most revolutionary event in the history of fly-fishing. It would be easier to reconcile Plato and Aristotle."

Ned's trout had just done the revolutionary reconciling. He cared nothing for theories, Plato, or Aristotle. But he had made clear that what we thought a fancy, he thought was food. And what I thought was an imitation, he thought was *not* food.

Now who do you want to believe, me or the trout? Even I point to the trout.

I am not claiming that every fly taken by a trout represents an imitation. That would be ridiculous. Trout eat salmon eggs, lures, Rat-Faced MacDougals, and some things I would hate to mention.

But when "educated" trout, proven to be selective, consistently take a given artificial fly with the same rise-form they use for naturals, that fly must be considered an imitation. One trout would not establish that the Pheasant Tail Red Spinner imitates a Blue-Winged Olive. I later learned, however, that Ned was not just taking a random chance. Trout feeding on hatching Blue-Winged Olives will often take a pheasant tail body (which presumably looks like a nymph) with almost any hackle. If you ask me, such a fly is an imitation.

This point is basic to the fly designs shown later. And it must be controversial, because such giants as Halford called flies imitative only when they looked good in *human* eyes. This is in fact the traditional approach. McDonald had reason to accept it. But it does not work very well.

Halford's final flies were described and illustrated in his *Modern Development of the Dry Fly*. I have some of the flies tied in his time after his patterns, and the odd thing is that they do not look like good imitations to me. They are the wrong shape (too heavily dressed) and often too big. Even the colors seem wrong, but that does not prove much, as colors of the naturals vary from river to river. The whole thing may simply demonstrate that different people in different ages see objects very differently. Anyone can satisfy himself on that score by walking through a museum and observing paintings from different periods and cultures.

Trout are not a bit interested in style—just survival. Food presumably looks the same to a trout today as to his ancestor centuries ago, though today's trout must look more carefully to be sure that the food is authentic. Drab old wet-fly patterns that were designed by experimentation to suit smart trout still work admirably. We still have the same old fish around to teach us humility and to puncture theories that have more to do with human culture than with mother nature.

Here we may need a parenthesis to explain the meaning of "fancy flies." The term is British, and Americans are often unaware that fancy does not mean gaudy. There is room for confusion, since some fancy flies also happen to be gaudy. Many others are sober creations that happen to be products of an *angler's* fancy. John Waller Hills says that a fancy fly may imitate insect life generally but cannot be "connected with any particular species or genus or group." By way of example, he gives Stewart's famous Black, Red, and Dun Spiders, which are small, drab, wet flies for upstream fishing.

Hills then distinguishes fancy flies from "general" flies, which "imitate a genus or group, but not an individual." The difference is a fine one. There is, however, a clear difference between fancy and general flies, on the one hand, and imitations of a specific insect, on the other. Or, to be more modest, we fishermen see a clear difference. Trout do not always agree.

Finally, to round out definitions, the British use the term "lure" if the creation is designed only as an attractor, or if the creature imitated is not an insect. We Americans have never used this British definition, but it has one recommendation: the *trout* use it. They react in a special way to lures moved quickly in relation to the current, whether those lures are made of feathers, hair, or metal. Their response is more deliberate to flies, natural or artificial—including the flies we call fancies. Insects, and artificial flies representing them, can usually move only very slowly in relation to the current (see chapter 4). Thus, by the trout's definition, streamers are certainly lures, and so are flies like the ancient Parmacheene Belle. Henry Wells designed her to imitate a trout fin, not a fly.

So, returning to John McDonald, fancy flies work for two reasons:

- They may not be fancies at all, but good imitations.
- Alternatively, *anything* would have worked, within reason.

The second alternative often applies, especially in America. The conditions for a selective rise may rarely be present in our fast streams, where you have to look harder for a hatch than for a trout.

There is no reason to apologize for using fancy flies. They are not like what the Victorians called fancy women. It is, however, futile to argue over the relative merits of, say, the Parmacheene Belle and the Scarlet Ibis. They reflect human whims, not those of trout, and human whims are erratic, as anyone can see from comparing the plates of fancy flies in old books of different periods. Many a famous angler has promoted an all-purpose killer fly which has enjoyed a brief surge of popularity and faded with its author.

Imitative flies vary within much tighter limits. The trout holds us to account. Aldam's Black Gnat, in his *Quaint Treatise,* looks as effective as ever a hundred years later, whereas many old fancy flies now seem merely quaint.

The term "imitation" is, of course, misleading to begin with. It expresses good intentions and reflects angling history, but the best of our materials do not approach the delicacy of a natural mayfly spinner. Even if they did, we would still have the problem of a hook, which distorts our efforts. Our designs must be modified to compensate for the crudeness of our medium. Careful fly-tyers often speak of a "representation" or "suggestion" of the natural, rather than an "imitation." In this book, I shall use the terms almost interchangeably, which seems the most honest of the alternatives, but I do not think there is any such thing as an *exact* imitation.

Anglers who think of their flies as representations are more likely to avoid the pitfalls in some patterns, such as the use of precisely three hackle fibers for tails, or the use of fragile, stiff wings. Probably the best approach is to suggest as many as possible of the natural's *prominent* features, even exaggerating some of them, while overlooking minor points.

I would hate to be read as suggesting that we should ignore the appearance of the natural insect and experiment by blind trial and error. On the contrary, experience teaches us that trout often seem to perceive insects much as we do, with some differences that we will discuss later. A fly tied to copy the natural insect frequently is better than one tied after someone else's pattern. When there is no experience to guide us, a fly that looks right in human eyes is the only logical starting point. With practice and an open mind, anglers can often tie an excellent imitation on the very first try.

It is expensive to buy flies, and time-consuming to make them. Either way, it is a waste to start with flies that are not even plausible. You might find that the following *rough* rules of thumb will help to eliminate some wasted motion. The rules derive from many conversations between this amateur fly-tyer and the trout. And I can claim that I have given the trout plenty to laugh at.

Flies That Appeal to Trout Are	*Flies That Appeal to Anglers Are*
• Simple and sparsely dressed, capturing only major points of the natural fly	• Complicated, striving for an imitation that is "exact" in human eyes
• Light, if the fly is intended to float	• Heavy, because too many materials or the wrong ones have been used

• Easy to cast, with only enough air-resistance to ensure a gentle landing	• Difficult to cast because of wings that twist the leader, or because of excess bulk generally
• Soft, so that all fibers yield easily in a trout's mouth and allow good hooking. Most hackles are soft enough for this purpose, even if they come from a gamecock	• Prickly, with stiff wings and tail or a hard extended body. Very large and thick hackles can also impede hooking
• Durable, so that the angler can cover fish rapidly without frequent fly changes	• Fragile, requiring a change just when a good fish starts rising
• Reliably balanced, so that they always land on the water in a position that looks natural. Winged flies must land upright, or cocked	• Top-heavy or otherwise out of balance, so that they cannot be counted on to land in a natural position
• Copied with the natural insect as a guide	• Copied from a book or other source of patterns
• Unconventional if necessary to imitate the natural, but otherwise orthodox	• Tied according to human conventions that have nothing to do with the natural insect (five winds of tinsel, and so forth)
• Tied in only one or two sizes. Natural insects of the same species vary in size, but usually within this range	• Available in the usual "wide range of sizes"
• Aimed at imitating the behavior of a natural fly first of all	• Aimed at imitating less important features of the natural—at the expense of behavior

2 ⚘ *More Talks with Trout*

⚘ ⚘ ⚘ This book is about the kinds of artificial flies that we humans design to imitate insects. And this chapter tries to get more specific about what the *trout* think is important in our designs. The first experience is with trout that have never seen anglers; the last is with some of the most educated trout in the world.

I lived in southern Brazil for three years of my checkered diplomatic career. The mountains there have streams that start deep inside and flow down through dreams years later.

Water runs clear, cool, and dark through a tunnel of tangled forest. Wading wet up a mile of stream, you can see a hundred kinds of nameless trees, each camouflaged with moss and vines. Mostly the forest is quiet. Occasionally a bird flashes across a brief opening in the middle of the stream. If you are lucky, a macuco —the largest and tastiest tinamou—calls timidly from somewhere, or everywhere. Occasionally a snake drops into the water from a limb in front of you.

But the water is what really gets you. It is perfect: riffles, gentle rapids, long pools, sheer banks, never a sign of erosion. On shore, vegetation everywhere. In the water, there are few plants—perhaps because the sun seldom penetrates. How could all this have existed without trout? But it did, for geological ages. Although Brazil has maybe half the species of freshwater fish in the world, practically none are adapted to cool water. The Rio Funil, above its falls, seems to have been fishless until the introduction of rainbows from the United States.

The native fauna of the river, as far as I could make out, consisted mainly of cased caddis larvae. Trout loved them, of course. When I was there, you could stand on a steep bank, look down a shaft of light between the trees, and watch great shapes materializing in patches as they drifted across the sun-rays. We caught trout to two pounds, and we saw far bigger.

Virgin jungle or not, the catching was difficult. I thought I knew what to do. My sedge larvae, cased and naked, would have been approved by Michelangelo. The trout were stuffed with the larvae, so my flies had to work.

There were three problems. First, I had to get a *long* cast up through that tangle of trees, with a bamboo clump waiting for every backcast. The cast had to be long and upstream because the trout heard or saw me at a great distance in that clear, slow water. I have still never seen anything like it elsewhere.

Second, I had to hook the trout when they took at the end of sixty feet of slack line.

Third, I had to get them to take. A couple of days of trying proved almost fruitless: just an average fish or two whose stomachs confirmed that I had the "right" fly. Only once did I see a rainbow taking mayflies. (Maybe the caddis larvae were eating most of the nymphs.) Two or three times I saw fish take an unidentified terrestrial. For the most part I just saw scenery. My only real luck was in the evening, with flashy wet flies or streamers. But these had to be fished downstream, and that was successful only in the half-hour before dark. I never saw a good hatch or fall of those sedges. Perhaps they were nocturnal.

Finally, in frustration, I decided to listen to the trout. The only tongue we had in common was a kind of hillbilly Portuguese, which translates as follows.

"We do not like your fly, boy," they said. "It looks like a caddis. But we never saw a caddis plop in the water and drift along. The ones we eat have to be pulled off rocks. There are so many that we do not mind. Most of the time we are stuffed. Sometimes we take your fly just for the hell of it. But frankly, you are beginning to bore us too."

I got the message. I never did find a fly that worked, except for those brief, special opportunities. Up till then, I had thought that fishing would not be fishing without my fly rod. Thanks to those voices from the water, it dawned on me that spinning was better than watching television. A six-and-one-half-foot bamboo rod would throw a one-sixteenth-ounce spinner sixty feet upstream. The trout would take it. They were, after all, innocent. The spinner was not food, but it provoked an aggressive reaction. I was far below, out of sight. Next thing the trout knew, he was talking to me face-to-face.

The rod was a sort of halfway step between one for fly-fishing and one for spinning (it later came to be known as a "fly-and-spin" model). It worked equally well with a fly line, to which I could switch for targets of opportunity. But I had to go to Argentina for any protracted fly-fishing.

I still do not have much taste for spinning on open streams. It is too easy and mechanical. Rather than working with nature, it provokes an unnatural response from the fish. Then too, for some reason, a lot of trout miss when they strike at upstream spinning lures, while the ones that do not miss tend to get hooked badly, so that many have to be killed. So this is no way to fish in civilized water where the trout should be released. But for what it is worth, any upstream fishing—even spinning—is for me more interesting than downstream fishing. I like fishing better when I can avoid lures of metal, feathers, or hair, but I will use any of them again if

the alternative is to stay home. Fishing, someone has said, is a little like sex. There is no bad fishing.

You can listen to any voices you like.

Since those jungle trout did not know much about flies, they could not tell me much. There was one clear lesson: the *behavior* of a fly is more important than the way it looks pinned on a piece of cardboard. Caddis behavior is to sit on rocks.

It is worth crawling out of a soft sleeping bag in time to see the Rapidan River with the first rays of sun. In April, the air is frosty at dawn, but that improves the coffee aroma. Smell of pine needles and sound of stream punctuate the pancakes. The water is cold through hip-boots and jeans. You must wade up the middle of the brook: the banks are steep and covered by old timber, for this has been a national park many years.

The water is clear after spring rains. It looks alive, but neither insects nor trout are visible. You start by casting upstream into the rocky pools with a weighted March Brown nymph at the end of your tippet and, eighteen inches higher, a weighted, white dropper "fly" with the entire bend of the hook cut off. (Two normal nymphs would be a little better, but a quirk in Virginia laws forbids the use of two hooks.) The dropper provides extra weight and visibility. Weight is needed both to get the flies down fast and to straighten out your short line and leader. Visibility is needed because you must strike at the flash of a fish near your nymph, or at any unnatural pause in the dropper. This is something like bait-fishing with a fly. The nymph must drift slowly, deeply, and naturally.

The trout take the nymph well but get rid of it in a second. You flip the flies as often as you cast normally, and sometimes you hang them in a hemlock behind you if you strike a little too slowly and miss the fish. When you get everything right, you may hook more than one fish in a pool. They flash like jewels, and they are: brook trout of ancient stock, eight to eleven inches long, colored in translucent greens and decorated with reds, whites, and blacks. As far as I know, they are the only char that behave like trout. For those of us in eastern America, they symbolize earlier days and wilderness. You admire them for a moment at the top of the water and release them carefully from a barbless hook, as the law requires. This is a "fish for fun" stream.

The sun rises over canyon walls and filters through breeze-turned leaves. Moving light strikes running water in an infinity of patterns. When you look up and to the east, you see bright columns of light slanting through dark branches. If you look at the rays more closely, you see points of light hit them, glow, and go out. These are flying insects, and if you can watch them more closely, you will see a variety: enormous March Browns, medium-sized Quill Gordons, and two or three smaller mayflies; big stoneflies, small yellow stoneflies, and small dark ones; a few sedges; and even the occasional fish fly—without counting midges or land-bred insects.

Unfortunately, even brook trout in such surroundings have a low sense of aesthetics. They would certainly prefer to feed on a single species of predictable habits and in large quantities, so that breakfast could be caught and eaten with less effort. Lacking this, the fish grab anything buggy that floats by in a natural way. Sometimes that includes your ungainly, dead-white dropper. You might continue to do well with the nymph. But a fisherman would be as rudimentary as his quarry if he thought only of numbers caught. When the day warms, you snip off the dropper, lengthen your tippet with a couple of feet of two-pound-test nylon, and knot on a floating fly: a size 14 *Epeorus* dun if it pleases you to use an imitation, a sparse Royal Coachman with white calftail wing if you need more visibility. The trout will not mind much, but they will reject your fly quickly if it floats unnaturally. The long, light tippet is to postpone drag after bad casts; you must get the fly out any way you can among the trees.

If a good trout rejects your fly, you may catch him after five or ten minutes. Use the interval to catch some elusive duns or watch the warblers. Then put on a smaller fly of different shape—say a size 16 hatching dun hackled from the wing of November's woodcock. With luck, you might get one of the rare twelve-inch brook trout. They are as big as the stream produces, and they are present only in good years. They will discuss your fly more carefully than young fish. If you hook them and fail to treat them with the respect due old men, they can even break your tippet.

By early afternoon, you will be a long way from your camp. The day will be warm. It will feel good to lean against a big tree by an especially good pool, idly watching it while you eat cheese and rye bread and sip cool water from a spring, letting your thoughts wander back to what the trout have said. They have been eager but wary: as a species, they have been exposed to many predators for millennia; as individuals, they may well have been caught and released by other fishermen. They can tell you something.

They say, first, that they would never have taken your fly if they had seen you. And you know how hard it is to hide when the trees require you to cast a short line.

Second, the fish say that—hungry though they usually are—they cannot afford to waste energy by staying in active feeding lies when there are no insects about. Even a sparse hatch or fall will

get attention quickly, but when there is no insect activity, the trout will be slow to converse even with a deep-sunk nymph. And there are days at the peak of the season when the flies refuse to hatch for puzzling reasons.

Third, and most important for you, the trout will tell you what they expect from your fly. It is easy for them to say, hard for you to do: *The fly must behave right.* If it is a dry fly, it must not drag appreciably. A deeply sunken fly can drag a little more. The level at which the fly floats may matter. All of this comes under the head of *behavior*.

Finally, the trout will tell you that they do not usually care much about the color or shape of your fly. They might complain about its size, but sometimes they will settle for a fly far larger than those they are used to eating. Their natural food is predominantly small, despite those big March Brown spinners dancing at the tail of the pools.

Of course, you do not need to listen to any of this. The needs of these trout are so simple that traditional angling usually works. You can just enjoy the bright fish, the smell of hemlocks, and the sound of fast water—without straining your ears.

Then again, suppose you are fishing one of the classic streams of eastern America during an evening hatch of sedges. It may be in the Catskills or Poconos, and the water will look like that in the Rapidan, but the stream will be forty feet wide instead of ten, and the pools will be correspondingly longer. Much of the time you could fish in the same carefree way, but there are some pronounced hatches.

Now the trout are taking the small sedges that emerge and struggle briefly against surface tension. You will hope to have an imitation of the right color, but you may not, for you have been away from the stream for a while. You do have a low-floating fly of the right size and with the right silhouette. You have a fair chance of taking fish even if the natural has a green body while you are using an imitation dubbed with fur from a gray squirrel.

The same sedge may (or may not) be accessible to the trout when the female flies return to lay their eggs. If they land occasionally, and if the trout get used to slashing for them, you are back to carefree fishing. You have a fly that is only a thin peacock-herl body on a size 16 hook, with a single, stiff grizzly hackle palmered over it. The fly looks nothing like the natural, but you dip it in a good flotant, let it dry well, and cast it in almost any direction. Your leader is long but not extremely light. The fly rides on the tips of its hackles. If you cast upstream, the trout will take your fly as it comes back to you on a drag-free float. You may do even better by casting cross-stream or even a bit downstream on a tight line, then skipping the fly back gently. Your fly suddenly looks like the real thing, to you as well as to the trout. The palmer fly is one of the most ancient devices for reducing trout to dinners. It works even for some hatching sedges, depending on the habits of the species.

These trout are giving you a more complicated message. If you do not listen, you will catch far less than you might.

The *behavior* of your fly, they say, is again of top importance. But the *size* has to be about right too. And if you imitate sedges that are floating quietly, the trout are critical of the imitation's *shape*. If you move your fly along the water, its shape is not easy to see.

Rarely does color matter. You may try to match the natural fly's color as a routine precaution. When you get back to your car, you will probably find that your fishing partner—who did not try to match color—had just as many successful interviews with the trout as you did.

Next, try the Liffey River a few miles above Dublin on an August evening. Early on, the trout may be rising only occasionally and for a variety of insects. These browns will not be easy to catch, but you might pick up one or two if you fish fine and far off with a Black Gnat. The evening is warm and dry, and you have a fair idea of what to expect later. The Blue-Winged Olives hatch from early June through September, and their Sherry Spinners have to re-turn to the water on fine evenings. The spinners usually migrate upstream (occasionally down) and lay their eggs in fast water. The female spinners are easily spotted in the air, for they bend their tails around under them to hold their large green egg-sack.

You have fished the Sherry Spinner in other limestone streams and have some proven imitations. Most are in a true size 14, but you have some 15s in case of a spinner fall during a bright after-noon, and there are a couple of underdressed 13s for big fish after dark. The hackles are pale ginger or dun and most are pulled into two flat bunches at the sides, but there are a few full-circle hackles for use in heavy weeds. The main variety is in the bodies, since this spinner varies greatly from stream to stream. One set of flies has a body of sherry-brown dubbing mixture on orange silk; it works in the Meath Blackwater. Another body is of pheasant-tail herl spun around orange silk, which usually works on the Rye Water. One of the best bodies is Skues' mixture of dubbings in colors from green through orange; this works almost anywhere. Finally, there are a few of Skues' traditional Orange Quills, which have only occasionally been good late in the evening.

The spinners fall on schedule and are taken by small fish in the riffle. Soon three or four good trout move up into the deeper water just below the current and start taking the flies with a small but excited rise. Sometimes you can see the little spinners come down the fast water with wings upright, then give a convulsive shudder and let one or both wings fall. With both wings down, the dying flies are hard for you to see, but the trout certainly manage. It is remarkable how eager a two-pound trout becomes at the opportunity to gulp a score or so of Sherry Spinners, which will make only a small bulk in his stomach.

Catching the trout, however, is something else. And they won't say a word to you. You can cover three without moving, and you try to land your fly three feet above the last natural rise. Many of your floats are good, and you are using four feet of two-pound-test, .005-inch tippet. But one fish after another refuses all of your flies without comment, sometimes taking a natural spinner a few inches away.

Eventually you catch a natural yourself and find that it is a remarkable, almost glowing, red-orange. You have nothing quite right, but you tie on a spinner that you had thought was too red. When the next wave of natural spinners falls, it is almost dark. Whether the light or the fly is responsible, you land two fish over the pound mark. At home, you put the stomach contents in a white dish. There are plenty of water lice, with occasional Blue-Winged Olive and other nymphs mixed in, but all of the surface feed is

Sherry Spinners, and almost all of them have that glowing red-orange body. You tie a couple of good imitations next morning before going to the office, using natural daylight to get the right shade of seal's fur. That evening, under similar conditions, you get rave reviews from five fish, the largest two pounds and a quarter —not counting two more heavy fish that straighten your hooks.

Trout are by no means always selective about the color of flies, or about their shape, or even about their size. If the fish were that selective, few standard flies would ever work, and the history of trout fishing would be very different. In England and Ireland, there are not many important natural flies, and imitations of them have been evolving for hundreds of years, yet anglers in every generation think they discover that the existing patterns are unrealistic. J. W. Dunne, in his *Sunshine and the Dry Fly,* gives a vivid description of this personal discovery. I must confess to the same experience, despite a disposition to respect tribal artifacts. When I arrived in Ireland, most of the imitations in use seemed to me larger than the naturals. (The Black Gnats and *Caenis* imitations, in particular, were Brobdingnagian.) Shapes were better, but only for the mayflies, which are well imitated by traditional designs. Colors were usually far off the mark. Yet the Irish are good fishermen, and they caught fish on those flies. I thought I could catch more on my own, but no doubt someone looking at mine in thirty years—or thirty days—might reject them.

One could conclude that all attempts at accurate representation are nonsense. Some fishermen do. I have seen them trying to catch good trout during sherry-spinner falls. They get the occasional fish

—perhaps one-sixth as many as they could with better flies. Once, Ned Maguire and I saw three disgusted fishermen leave the river in the middle of a spectacular rise.

One might equally go to the other extreme and conclude that every detail of the natural fly must be imitated with painstaking care. This would be the safer course, and I would accept it if I thought it were possible. But I think the option is illusory.

In practice, most of us probably wind up on the middle ground, but we may get there unintentionally and in a state of some frustration. We might do better to listen closely to what the trout say about the different features of the natural. In doing so, it will obviously be helpful if we can get the features in rank order, so that, if necessary, we can omit one or more in favor of those more important.

From talks with trout like those mentioned above, one can suggest four features of artificial flies that seem to be involved in adapting to the trout's point of view.

They are:

- Behavior
- Size
- Shape
- Color

The order of these four features can help in making rational decisions based on priorities. For example, if trout are rising for skittering sedges, and if no fly in the box is a really good match, it is better to pick a fly that will move like the natural rather than another that is the right color but which floats low in the surface film. Behavior takes precedence over color, say the trout. The example may seem extreme. Nevertheless, most fishermen picking an imitation look for color, which is easier to discern than behavior.

The rank-order of the features above will be worse than useless, however, if it is read to mean that the lower-priority features are unimportant. On the contrary, *all* of the four features may matter in difficult conditions, although frequently not otherwise.

There is another qualification. The rank-order of the features is only a helpful generality; it is no law and not even a rigid rule. In working over a real trout, we are dealing with relative values, not absolutes. Trout do not reason like humans, but they are still individual beings, with a capacity to learn. They do not have mechanical responses—not the wild ones I have talked to, anyhow. Sometimes trout in the same environment—the same bay of a lake, for example—have stomach contents that show striking individual preferences. One may have scuds and another a variety of surface food from midge pupae to grasshoppers. This is as great as the difference between the diets of a natural-food fan and a red-nosed consumer of beer and pretzels. (Speaking of gourmets, the scud-eating trout will be the best on the table, but the surface-feeder will be the most vulnerable to anglers.)

On rare occasions, the color of flies may be more important than their shape, even though my rank-order shows the opposite. Scotty Chapman, an artist highly conscious of color, tells me of an extreme case. He found Dolly Varden trout (char that behave like char) feeding on salmon eggs in Alaska. No fly would interest them till he tried an old squirrel-tail wet fly with a body close to the orange of an egg. In this case, color was more important than any other factor, with the possible exception of behavior. (I doubt that the fly would have worked on the surface.)

There is nothing necessarily wrong, the trout say, with exaggerating one or more of the four features. Behavior is frequently exaggerated, as in the dragging of a wet fly, while size is best understated (see chapter 6). Hackles wound in the usual fashion exaggerate the number of legs and wings on a natural fly (chapter 7). The color of artificial flies is commonly more gaudy than that of the natural model (chapter 8).

The exaggerations are usually accomplished by accident, but not always. Skues specifically recommended them, using hackles on nymphs as an example. Personally, I have little confidence in exaggerations of behavior and size, but I like to experiment with pronounced shapes and colors. Recently I saw a report of some research done by a Scottish scientist on hooded crows, which have the disagreeable custom of pecking the eyes out of young lambs in the spring. The scientist fitted some dead lambs with artificial eyes of extra-large size and found that they were attacked three times as often as normal dead lambs. Now, the hooded crow probably has at least as advanced a brain as the trout, and I see no reason to suppose that a trout dislikes a mayfly with extra-large wings—for one example.

But before exaggerating, it does seem like a good idea to assess the natural priorities as perceived by the trout. To take a human parallel, a good impressionist painting is an effective exaggeration of nature, but not a violation. As applied to trout and trout flies, I think nature can be summarized in terms of our list: behavior, size, shape, and color.

I claim no originality for this list, although as a matter of interest, I did in fact think out my ideas on my own. Then, having published them in a preliminary way in 1974, I found two good precedents. The earliest of the two also happens to be the best. It is in G. P. R. Pulman's little *Vade-Mecum of Fly-Fishing for Trout,* which is a remarkable book. My third edition, published in 1851, contains the first really complete instructions for dry-fly fishing. It also recommends imitating only the "general characteristics" of the natural fly, which are "size, form, and color." The author then adds that "action" is an even more important "part of imitation."

The details are not spelled out, but by changing two words slightly, Pulman's list of "characteristics" is the same as mine, in both rank-order and components. One of the changes is almost meaningless: Pulman speaks of "form," while I have used "shape." My term "behavior," however, is broader than Pulman's "action." The difference is significant. "Behavior" has the virtue of describing a fly whether it is sitting still or moving, whereas "action" suggests only movement. More important, "action" describes only something the angler does with the fly once it is on the water, whereas "behavior" also describes how it gets there. Behavior, in other words, includes not only the old concept of action but the newer one of presentation. This is especially important to Americans, who have evolved a whole school based on the idea that only presentation really counts. It does count. But is is only one part of imitation, as Pulman might say.

The term "behavior" also gets closer than any other to expressing the trout's view of an insect, which is probably more often influenced by the level at which the fly floats than by any movement or action.

For fishermen (as opposed to fish), it is convenient to look separately at behavior before and after the fly touches the water. The former is "presentation," which requires both good tactics and good tackle. Behavior *on* the water depends on the angler—as when movement is purposely imparted to a fly or avoided—but also on features built into the fly. The different problems of behavior take up all of Part II of this book (and there is much more that could be said). Size, shape, and color—the other features of an imitation—then get one chapter apiece in Part III.

PART II

Imitating Insect Behavior

3 ⚘ How Insects Behave

⚘ ⚘ ⚘ Falling Springs Creek in Pennsylvania still has some of the wild browns. You might get a heavy one on a Sulphur Spinner just about dark, but the good fish are outnumbered by anglers. A few years ago, before the fishery acquired progress and a hatchery, there were lots of the stream-bred browns left, plus an old strain of colorful rainbows. The ability of a small stream to support so much life seemed a mystery. They should have made it a national monument. Instead, it is becoming part of a housing development.

The browns were the best, and my favorite spot was in the shade of a drooping willow. I could sit and watch the trout feed in the sun, while they could not easily see me. And if the trout would not rise, I could look for the tiny underwater creatures clambering around the plants of that other world. The trout could almost be forgotten—until one made a good boil upstream.

One bright, late April day, a number of middle-sized fish fed busily in the heat of noon. There were no *Tricorythodes* mayflies yet, and only a few early Sulphur Duns were hatching. Their nymphs did not interest the trout. Ants were no better. It was also too early for the Japanese Beetle, but I tried a smaller, floating Black Beetle on the same lines—a derivative of the Marinaro Jassid. This brought real interest, but no solid rises. Finally I hooked a twelve-inch fish by a thread of skin. The beetle may have sunk a trifle on that cast.

The small end of my marrow spoon showed the fish packed with black beetles about three-sixteenths of an inch long. If the beetles were terrestrial, they would fall into the water only by mistake and should remain floating for a time on the placid currents of Falling Springs. But my floating imitation had not worked well. And when I searched through the meadow grass, I found no quantity of beetles.

The next logical guess was that the hero of my story was an aquatic beetle. I waded into the stream well below the trout and had a little hunting expedition with my insect net. Result: two kinds of *Ephemerella* nymphs, some scuds, and a few "cress-bugs." No beetles. So that was why the trout were concentrated in one spot; it must have been a beetle factory. Should I scare the trout and satisfy my curiosity about the source of the beetle, or should I be content with what the marrow spoon had told me?

You guessed it. I can't pass up a rising trout. Besides, I thought, there would be other times for chasing the beetle. But he has never appeared again for me, and other fishermen to whom I have talked have not met him. To the marrow spoon, then, I owe all I learned about that insect.

To tell you what the trout are actually eating, the spoon is more reliable than the insect net. Yet it can damage fish if misused. It should be employed only when needed, only on fair-sized fish, and with care.

In this case, the result was a fly that caught most of the rest of the trout in the beetle factory. (They were returned with a warning to be more careful.) That would have been ample reward, but the same fly has since turned out to be my most effective summer design on the Pennsylvania streams. How often have you checked the stomach of a trout at the end of a summer day and *not* found a beetle or two?

The right combination of features did not come in a sudden flash of insight. My flashes are not to be trusted; perspiration pays better. First, I tried variations on the theme of the flat-wing silhouette beetle. Most had a black wing made from crow feather, cemented and trimmed to shape. Bodies were of black dubbing, black ostrich herl, and natural peacock herl. The design, described in detail later, is good for floating flies. The trout told me that it did not look good underwater, though I did hear one or two fish comment favorably on the peacock body. That was another clue.

Back to the vise. The most peacocky imitative fly in existence is the traditional Coch-y-Bondhu. I had doubted its effectiveness, because I had not seen American fishermen using it. The models I saw in shops were big, with anemic bodies and bushy hackles. Nothing like a beetle.

My new flies were tied with the natural insects as a model. They had come from a trout's stomach, and they floated unhappily in a small white plastic box full of water. A Partridge hook in true size 16 would take a body of the right length, would be heavy enough to sink the fly when I wanted, and would still hook the fish well. (Note that this hook is almost equivalent to a size 20 Mustad. See chapter 5.)

The body was more difficult. Three peacock herls spun around a waxed black thread would be strong, but they were still not as thick as the natural beetle's body. A couple of attempts showed me how to pile them up so that they would stay put. The body was now as thick as it was long, and strong enough to pass on to my grandchildren—in case there are still any trout in Pennsylvania then.

My hackle was the traditional color: shiny, dark red, with a black center and tips. But I used only three turns, with the shiny outside of the hackle facing forward. The hackle was the smallest a coch-y-bondhu rooster has to offer—with a width hardly greater than the thickness of the peacock body.

My *pattern*, then, was as described in books for decades, but the *design* was like no fly I had actually seen. (For all I know, every angler in Wales has one.) It looked ridiculously small and plump, with an undernourished hackle—like a fat lady in a miniskirt. No wonder dealers sell no such flies. But when I put mine in the plate of water with the defunct beetles, the fat lady was also a fat beetle.

Evidently the trout agreed with me. One of life's nicest little miracles is the way in which a primitive, three-year-old, cold-blooded creature like a brown trout can detect a tiny difference in a fly. May you never change, Mr. Trout. Damn their pollution, concrete, dredges, and silt. Life without you would be a dull business.

Well, another nice thing is that not all humans pursue the same chimeras. Some like fancy flies; some even stay home and watch television.

I cannot, personally, be happy with a fly unless I can rediscover it—as I did with the beetle—relating it to the naturals and to such few wild trout as have escaped the notice of the Army Engineers. Lots of flies will catch *some* fish. The interesting thing is to learn why.

Of course, when you get close to an insect, the danger is that it may become as interesting as the fish. Why not? Bird-watchers get their thrills through binoculars, and insects let you get closer than birds. There is far more left to learn about insects. Even in Britain and Ireland, where there have been centuries in which to study a few insects, anglers will find gaps in the best books available. In America, with its vast number of insect species and short history, the gaps are chasms. This chapter cannot begin to fill them, but it will identify some.

It is worth dwelling for a while on the size of those gaps. From the nice new books on the market, and from the amount of Latin being thrown around by anglers, you might conclude that "the experts" have the problems of angling entomology all sorted out. Such a conclusion would be quite wrong. The full-time, professional entomologists are eager to admit the dimensions of what they do not know. Often they are reluctant to make positive identifications of individual species. They commonly lack solid information on behavior. The most complete *angling* entomology of mayflies as of this writing, by Caucci and Nastasi, also identifies gaps. For me, this adds greatly to credibility. Solomon and Leiser, in the first American angling entomology of caddis-flies, make clear that they are forced to leave even larger gaps.

Compare this to the situation in Britain and Ireland. They had a good angling entomology in 1836. Harris, in 1950, gave all the information needed to identify any significant mayfly by species, not just genus. Harris also has extensive information on insect behavior. His information on sedges is less complete, but is still far ahead of ours. There are fewer things to learn. To an entomologist, the British Isles are "impoverished" in insect species, even by comparison to continental Europe. For anglers, this kind of poverty is a blessing.

In Ireland, I always knew what mayfly was on the water. There might be some doubt between the Large Dark Olive and the Medium Olive, but Harris's book and a five-power magnifying glass would settle the question. (Incidentally, it always turned out to be the Large Dark Olive, even when the fly became light-colored and medium-sized late in the season.)

By way of contrast, consider a recent example from Pennsylvania, where there has been more work by angling entomologists than in any other state except New York.

From an angling viewpoint, the most impressive hatch of sedges I have seen anywhere in the world occurs on Penn's Creek in mid-to-late April. The flies are of fair size, and they hatch in massive quantities. I have seen tens of thousands of them packed in a single patch on a shady tree trunk. This behavior is not mentioned in any of the literature I have consulted. Even more interesting, both male and female flies frequently die *on the water* and come floating down. I do not know how to explain this either, but the trout ask no questions. The spent sedges are sometimes so thick that the trout can take only a small percentage. Fishing is superb all morning, and then again in the late afternoon.

Some local anglers call this sedge a "Grannom," but neither its behavior nor its near-black body resemble the real Grannom. Could it be a new species? I asked Dr. O. S. Flint of the Smith-

sonian Institution, who also helped Larry Solomon with his identifications.

The Penn's Creek sedge, Dr. Flint said, is *Brachycentrus
numerosus*. This is an important species in many eastern streams,
and is correctly identified as such by Solomon and Leiser. But now
the plot thickens:

- The Penn's Creek sedges show some morphological differences
  from Solomon's Beaverkill specimens. Eventually, entomologists may prefer to classify the two as different species.
- More important to the angler, the Penn's Creek flies are mostly
  taken *spent*, while Solomon refers to imitating hatching flies.
  This involves major differences in fly design and tactics.
- Most of the Penn's Creek flies have a near-black body well
  imitated by peacock herl, black dubbing, or crow herl (the
  closest of all). Solomon describes a body of dark grayish olive,
  which appears on only some of the Penn's Creek flies.
- Finally, the Penn's Creek fly hatches much earlier than the
  early-to-mid-May dates quoted by Solomon. This can be explained by the difference in latitude. But Solomon also noted
  that *B. numerosus* usually follows just after the Hendricksons,
  while during the three seasons that I have visited Penn's
  Creek, the caddis-fly twice started earlier.

Despite these differences, the Solomon and Leiser book comes
close enough to be of help. It gives an idea of what to expect in
size, color, and time of year, though not in tactics. We are fortunate to have this thoughtful, pioneering work on American caddis-
flies. The point is that angling entomologies in this country will
eventually have to be deep and narrow, covering single biological
zones: perhaps even single major rivers.

One of these days, we shall have Pennsylvania sorted out. But
it will not be tomorrow. Tools for the job will have to include
expensive dissecting microscopes, not just five-power lenses. The
help of professional entomologists will be essential. The new angling entomologies, of course, will be references, but so will the
scientific entomologies. Prices for these start at twenty dollars, and
many are long out of print. At present no single work gives all we

need to know, even about mayflies in the eastern United States, let alone about all kinds of flies in all regions. Just to keep track of major angling species in the important genus *Ephemerella,* scholars need scarce research papers in addition to books.

When it comes to my favorite Montana/Wyoming streams, there are few hatches that I understand thoroughly from both the entomologist's and the angler's viewpoint. Hatches are better than in the East, because the streams I fish are much as nature made them, and there are some fascinating flies. But I do not plan to write much about them until I can learn a lot more. I hope many good anglers beat me to it.

Fortunately, we need not wait for the gaps in our entomologic knowledge to be filled. Let us instead use them as excuses for more fishing. My description of the problem has two objectives: (1) to urge a modest, simple, regional approach to the study of the insects on which trout feed—an approach based on firsthand experience described with painful frankness, and (2) to explain what this particular chapter is about.

Good fly-tying starts with the ability to design flies that will behave like the observed naturals, not like something from a book.

Whatever the creature being imitated, two basic questions about behavior must be asked:

- At what level in the water is it?
- How is it moving?

The answers, of course, are not so simple. From the viewpoint of the trout, most aquatic flies go through about six stages. These are listed here. For illustration, I have matched common fishing methods to each, although these methods must be incomplete.

Stages in Life of Aquatic Insect	*Fishing Methods (Illustrative)*
• On stream-bed as nymph or larva. Often hidden from trout, but sometimes picked off rocks. Readily taken when dislodged by accident or high water	• Imitate dislodged insects by fishing as near to the bottom as possible, with minimum drag

• Moving toward surface. Free-swimming nymphs or pupae may be readily accessible to trout. Others crawl out and are less accessible	• Fish a sunken fly shallow or in mid-water—usually upstream but occasionally cross-stream for fast-swimming forms
• Hatching—usually in or close to surface film. Habits vary widely, but insects at this untidy stage are likely to be available to trout	• Fish in surface film with low-floating fly—usually upstream with dead drift, since insects caught in surface film cannot move well
• Freshly hatched adult	• Normal dry fly, fished without drag, except in the case of a few insects that can move along the water
• Egg-laying adult. Only a few species are important to trout in this stage	• One of several dry-fly variations, often with an oversize hackle. Usually fished dead-drift, but slight movement sometimes acceptable
• Spent adults, after laying eggs. Important to trout and fishermen in many species	• Fish upstream, dead-drift, usually with a low-floating dry fly, occasionally with a wet fly

Anyone can find exceptions to this list. It omits insects in the egg stage, which are of more interest to entomologists than to anglers. Nor is there any mention of adult insects that can be found underwater, blown onto the water, or drowned while hatching. In America, trout will sometimes jump clear out of the water for flies, but this can well be left as an exception.

This book is not an entomology and is not intended to replace the information available on individual insect species in a good regional entomology. Unfortunately, detailed bug-watchers' guides are still scarce in America, and it happens that those that are available are not concerned with a wide range of fly designs. The following sections give purposely generalized descriptions of the major kinds of anglers' insects, focusing on the behavior problems that will have to be met by the designs shown in Part IV of this book.

What Bug Is That?

The first step in imitating an insect is persuading it to pose. Here are some ways to get your model, starting with the most convenient.

Look at a Picture There are plenty of them in books and magazines. These are educational, stimulating, but emotionally unsatisfying, like girlie magazines. Besides, the technicalities of photography and printing are such that the picture will seldom be a reliable guide to the insect next door.

Catch a Trout Then kill it with a merciful knock on the head, remove the insides complete with gullet and gills, and make a careful slit all the way from the top of the gullet down to the bottom of the stomach. The insects in the mouth and throat are most useful to you, because they are what the trout has just eaten. But it is a short trip to the stomach, and some insects there will be in good shape. If you wish to preserve them for home study, put them in a small, tightly *plugged* glass container filled with rubbing alcohol. Threaded caps do not hold alcohol as reliably as plugs. Scientists use a better kind of alcohol, but the drugstore stuff will do for a while. Write identifying data in pencil on a small piece of paper and put the paper inside the container.

For immediate identification by streamside, put your recovered insects in plain water, using a white container. I carry three little plastic boxes in my vest. Each is shallow, with a white bottom for dead flies or nymphs, and a transparent top to hold live flies. Sears sells nuts and bolts in these boxes. Back home you might prefer the traditional white plate. With either box or plate, a good ten-power magnifying glass will help.

Another useful gadget is a small plastic tube holding a cheap magnifying glass and a container for insects. The container can be filled with water. These devices are sold commercially and are small enough to carry in a vest pocket.

Marrow spoons and stomach pumps will retrieve insects from trout that are not to be killed.

Surface Net The next-easiest method—maybe the easiest, if the trout are stubborn—is to take the flies from the surface of the water. This is essential for any real collection, since mayflies in particular suffer wear and tear from being swallowed. A live model is especially important for imitations of the belly color of floating flies.

If you have ever tried to pick a small insect from the surface of flowing water, you will have gained a healthy respect for the trout's task. You may also have ruined the insect's wings. Duns handled by finger will seldom turn into spinners.

A fine-mesh net makes it easy. I rig one on the throat of my landing net, but an easier way is to buy a little aquarium net at a pet shop. So armed, you can beat the trout to the draw.

Direct Observation With experience, you may be able to identify familiar floating insects with the naked eye. Small binoculars are about eight times better. At a minimum, they will tell you whether trout are taking mayflies or caddis-flies.

Some flying insects can be identified at a glance: for instance, the Sherry Spinner laboring upstream in columns with her distinctive egg-balls. J. R. Harris gives many other such tips for British and Irish spinners. There is not much in the American literature.

Air Net Insects dancing around in the air, prior to mating or ovipositing, can be caught—sometimes—with a butterfly-type net. And insects at this stage are the ones entomologists like best for identification. You will not want to go fishing with a six-foot net, but you can compromise on a net with a hoop about eight inches in diameter and a handle a foot long. This device will hang on the back of your vest where your landing net is supposed to be.

For a real chuckle, forget yourself some day and try to scoop up a sixteen-inch trout in one of these insect nets. The chuckle may take several days to stabilize and gain resonance.

Nymph Net The surest way to find out what a stream contains, and what is about to hatch, is with a nymph net. You can make a portable one by using two sticks a foot long and stretching two feet of fine mesh between them. This will roll up and tuck into the back pocket of your vest. The same net can be used to conduct a surface census if you find trout sipping something invisible.

For nymphing, hold the net downstream in front of you and shuffle the stream bottom with your feet as you move along. This should, at least, give you an assortment of mayflies and stoneflies. The wing cases will tell you if your victim was ready to hatch before he met you. You might want to keep him in a well-oxygenated aquarium and get a perfect adult.

For rearing methods and better ways to preserve insects—plus a number of scientific devices for catching them—see *The Mayflies of North and Central America* by Edmunds, Jensen, and Berner. This same work should help you identify your mayflies down to the genus level. With most other aquatic insects it will be difficult to get even that far.

Once, in Yellowstone, I hiked a couple of miles up a promising stream, carrying my little boy in a backpack. We failed to find any trout by fishing blind. A bit of seining showed that the sandy bottom contained virtually no insects except angleworms. This did not save the day, but it saved waiting around for the evening rise. Yellowstone is an odd place: that little stream flowed into one of the most fertile rivers in the country.

Mayflies (Ephemeroptera)

Different species of mayfly nymphs vary enormously in their activity. *Baetis* species are dominant in English and Irish fishing much of the year, and their nymphs are agile. Even so, anglers have accepted for decades that nymph imitations are usually best fished upstream, on a dead-drift or with only the slightest twitch.

(In practice, I suspect that many of our "dead-drifts" have a slight drag, since movement is hard to detect underwater and less objectionable to the trout.)

In America, most of our medium-to-large mayfly species do not swim as well as their English and Irish counterparts, although there are certainly exceptions. Our species of the *Baetis* genus are smaller than the British Olives, though otherwise similar in appearance and behavior. Our *Baetis vagans* looks very much like the Old World Large Dark Olive *(Baetis rhodani),* and both can be counted on for fishing on St. Patrick's Day. But *B. vagans* takes a true size 16 hook, while *B. rhodani* can carry a husky size 12.

When the early-spring *Baetis* duns are hatching, I have also caught trout well on an artificial nymph fished across-and-downstream on a tight line. This has been true in Ireland, Pennsylvania, New York, and Yellowstone. Downstream fishing has for me a smell of old grass wet with spring rains.

But I do not know whether the trout really take those fast-dragging artificial nymphs for the insects they were intended to represent. Fancy wet flies work as well. My guess is that when the river wakes up, the fish are simply too hungry to be careful, and the water may be so high that upstream fishing is difficult. A fly holding in the current is easier for a fish to catch, and who cares whether it is really a fly, minnow, or shrimp? So I doubt that downstream fishing is usually nymph-fishing in any strict sense of the term.

Nevertheless, on both sides of the Atlantic, there are a few occasions when a real fast-swimming nymph is needed. The Greendrakes *(Ephemera* species) are fast and large enough to move against a normal current almost like a minnow. In Ireland, when I found trout taking Greendrake nymphs, I had good fishing by casting an imitation cross-stream, above a rise, and stripping it back. It was easy fishing, duffers'-fortnight stuff, but I did not find enough of it to feel guilty. I have also enjoyed at least the illusion that I was fishing dragging *Isonychia* nymphs in Pine Creek, Pennsylvania, and Siphlonurids in the Yellowstone River. But these did not appear to be selective occasions. It still seems fair to start with the assumption that mayfly nymphs fished shallow require dead-drift imitations. Gentle movement can then be added when necessary (see chapter 4).

Big nymphs and wet flies fished deep in fast streams are a different proposition. This method does imitate the behavior of much trout food. In fact, deep fishing is the most dependable way to catch sizable trout in the heavy water of the western Americas, whether in Montana or Argentina. The method works elsewhere, too, though by no means all the time. In fishing deep, drag is hard to avoid. But trout on the bottom seem to feel secure enough to take risks. They also tend to be less selective. And since deep water is relatively slow, the drag on a deep-fished imitation may be less than the angler judges as he watches higher, faster currents tugging at his line. Readers with an interest in this specialized method of fishing should see Charles E. Brooks's discussion of tactics. He has caught the old tricks well, made some creative contributions, and designed his flies to match the tactics.

Whether the nymph swims or drifts, it will have to sink quickly if it is to fish well below the surface. Weight helps, but you cannot build enough of it into a really small nymph, so a streamlined shape is also necessary. Frank Sawyer uses no hackle at all, since hackle fibers delay sinking. I do not think that a *small* wrapped or beard hackle gets in the way on flies larger than, say, size 14. But someone else can have those loverly nymphs with lots of stiff legs and tails and eyes. They are ideal for hanging on the wall in a neat shadow-cabinet, to impress the yokels.

Hatching nymphs—or emerging duns, if you prefer—must cope with surface tension, which makes motion against the current very difficult for a small creature. Besides, the fly's full energy is likely to be needed in struggling out of its own husk. This is the easiest time for the trout to catch most mayflies, the stage that is most important to imitate carefully. Traditional dry flies may not work well here, while traditional nymphs are hard to keep in the surface film. But see the low-floating designs in Part IV. You need something to imitate the untidy wings of the new dun, together with either the nymph's body or that of a freshly hatched dun. The right combination may take some experimenting, but it is likely to be effective when you have it.

There is an interesting special case of insect behavior: at least one American *Epeorus* species (the Quill Gordon) is reported to hatch under the surface and swim to the top in adult plumage. Real wet-fly fishing, for once. But I cannot confirm it. Justin and Fannie Leonard also report that *Ephemerella* subimagos often emerge from their nymphal skin when six to ten inches below the surface.

Fully hatched duns are among the easiest of all trout-stream insects to notice—and the most often described in the classic literature. The fishing is correspondingly satisfying. As a rule, the most difficult point is to discover when trout are taking the fully hatched dun as opposed to the hatching dun/nymph. Sometimes bad weather can also cause strange behavior by blowing duns around or drowning them. Considering that duns have been imitated for centuries, it is amazing that an angler must sometimes do a good deal of experimenting before finding an effective pattern for difficult fish. See both the "normal" and "low" designs in Part IV.

Spinners win my nomination for the most beautiful of all insects: even more attractive, because more subtle, than the butterflies. Their fragile beauty is a result of mayflies' unusual final molt as adults, which leaves them with translucent colors. It also leaves them as good fliers—able to stay away from most of the birds that fed on them as clumsy duns. Since the spinners can escape many airborne enemies, they usually have elaborate, distinctive mating flights. They are easy to see glinting in the sun's rays like small falling stars. On the water, however, their translucency can make them hard to detect, especially after their wings have fallen flat on the surface, when the fly is fully "spent" and ready to die. Spinners that fall in clouds will hardly escape notice, but those that return to the water individually have made many an angler wonder what the trout were taking. Most elusive of all are the *Baetis* spinners, which somehow manage to crawl underwater and come back up. A creature less evidently adapted to the water would be hard to imagine, yet a rock in a good riffle may be covered with these flies.

Some spinners touch the water to lay eggs and then return to the air. In this case, a light Spider (American style) is worth trying; high-floating designs are shown in Part IV. Most of the time, however, the spent spinner is more important, and an artificial fly that rides flush with the surface imitates it. The bunched-wing spinner is an excellent old design for such a fly. A wet fly should work for *Baetis* spinners, and perhaps it does, but I have done better with a dry imitation.

The simplicity of a good artificial mayfly is, to say the least, deceptive. The classic mayfly hatches will always be exciting to fish, and this book, like most, is perhaps overfull of references to them.

The last frontier of mayfly fishing is representation of the very small species. (The special problems of small flies are considered in chapter 6.) There are a great many tiny mayflies in America, and at least three main types in the British Isles (the Small Dark Olive, the *Caenis* species, and some Iron Blues).

For me, I suppose, the Pennsylvania *Tricorythodes* provides the prime example of "fine-and-far-off" fishing. The countryside is green and lush, but hardly noteworthy for scenery. Similar country elsewhere has muddy catfish streams. But the hills here catch the rain and filter it through limestone. The little *Tricorythodes* mayflies must be the most numerous creatures in its streams that are visible to the naked eye. Great clouds of them hatch every summer morning, turning from duns to spinners in the air and completing their adult life before the sun has dried the dew off the meadow grass.

There have been occasional triumphs on such mornings. A fish of twelve inches can snap an .003-inch tippet in a flash; a stream-bred seventeen-incher is a rare conquest. To be honest, the *Tricorythodes* mornings are most memorable for their frustrations. This is the best and the worst of angling—depending on what you like.

Sedges (Caddis-Flies, Trichoptera)

Sedges have given me just about as much fishing as mayflies in recent years—perhaps fewer fish, but more of the big ones. It just happens that I have been spending a lot of time on streams with good hatches of both, which at least allows a fair comparison. On many eastern American streams, sedges now provide the most

important hatches. Penn's Creek (as mentioned earlier) has the heaviest hatch I have ever seen. On most other Pennsylvania spring creeks, mayflies and terrestrials are far more important than sedges. I have had some good fishing to sedges in the Yellowstone country. In British, Irish, and other European streams, both mayflies and sedges tend to be important, with wide variations.

Originally, the word "caddis" referred only to the cased larvae. Adults were called "sedges" or "rushflies" from their habit of landing on vegetation at the river bank.

Almost everywhere I have fished, from Brazil to Switzerland, caddis larvae have made up a part of the trout diet (judging from autopsies). Often, they have been a big part. And I have enjoyed catching the larvae and watching them build their ingenious cases. Young caddises must, for their size, be the best construction engineers in the animal kingdom. Most boys who grow up near trout streams also make the discovery that the caddis is a good bait. In American mythology, the porcupine is supposed to save wanderers from starvation, but if I had some small hooks and monofilament, I would still prefer to rely on the caddis to find me a trout.

Such an appealing creature as the caddis is bound to find imitators. We have all tied uncased larvae; latex rubber is the latest style (thanks to Raleigh Boaze), and extremely realistic to human eyes. The uncased caddis does take trout. I have not personally seen much selectivity, as measured by stomach contents.

A few cranks—like me—have even made cased caddis. I shall not explain how, since the trout were not much impressed. In chapter 2, I mentioned that Brazilian trout feeding on cased caddis larvae could hardly be caught on a fly. Sooner or later, almost anything can happen in America, but I am still waiting for caddis cases to behave in a way that I can imitate.

The caddis pupae are far more frustrating. Whereas trout should not take an artificial larva, but do, they *should* take an artificial pupa, but often do not. Pupae are available to trout in concentrated bursts, and are eaten avidly. My artificials are fairly traditional, and sometimes they succeed, but they are just as likely to fail. I have not been able to figure this out with any confidence. The failures occur in the middle of good rises. Some species may have an air bubble that the fuzzy thorax of the artificial cannot properly imitate. Still, on the good days, my fly evidently *looks* about right. I am inclined to guess that on the bad days the naturals behave in a way that I have not been able to imitate. The books I have consulted are as inadequate as my own observations; we simply do not know enough about the hatching behavior of different genera. Until someone completes the research, I recommend caution toward new subsurface pupa imitations. Back to the aquarium.

On the other hand, I feel fairly confident of taking trout that are rising to freshly hatched sedges *at the surface.* Low-riding imitations can be tied so that the body hangs below the surface while the wing stays in the surface film. This fly may be taken for the pupa just clearing its wings.

There is an old—and puzzling—bit of American lore to the effect that sedges provide no dry-fly fishing. For that matter, it used to be thought that even mayfly spinners were useless. I suppose anglers got used to duns—many of which are big and conspicuous in the United States—and did not look for anything else.

The behavior of hatched sedges varies widely. Some get off the water too fast to provide much fishing. Some float as quietly as a mayfly dun. Others twitch and flutter. These last are fun to imitate, and relatively easy, since a drag-free float is not needed. I suspect that this is how dry-fly fishing began. A high-riding design is needed.

A few of the really big sedges have the strength to swim long distances against surface tension. The Irish have a sedge called a Green Peter that lives in lakes and often swims to shore. This seems an invitation to predators. I cannot explain such behavior, but there it is. A big, bushy fly is needed to make a realistic wake. Most of us like to fish a floating fly on the dropper and a pupa at the tail. In this case, both the "dry" fly and the pupa may be taken well.

Some few species of sedges are taken when ovipositing. A light, extra-high-floating design is then needed. And some sedges —even males—die on the water, allowing a low-riding, spent imitation.

For me, "sedge" has a grand, sibilant, antique sound. And it always conjures up a soft Irish evening.

Bats have begun to flicker in the twilight. An otter climbs on a rock near where I am hidden and begins his dinner of eel, intending to leave only the anus behind as a souvenir. (If you do not believe me, read John Waller Hill's *River Keeper;* you should anyhow.) Since I would not fancy an eel's anus for breakfast, but would like most of the rest of the eel, I make a motion and the otter shoots off downstream. I mark the rock and make a note to collect my breakfast after the main business of the evening.

A sparse flight of spinners fails to interest any notable fish. There is just enough natural light left to allow a sedge to be knotted onto my shortened leader. Some fair trout intercept the first naturals to hatch, but the big fellow lets half a dozen by. Then a particularly awkward fly comes hopping over him, and he takes it in two heavy swirls—missing the first time, perhaps, through lack of practice. The imitation comes over him after he has taken two more naturals. It is ignored. After that, it comes over him only after he has taken one or two more naturals—at intervals of a few minutes. I avoid any motion in my fly, though a twitch might catch a smaller fish. I am using a proven imitation of a hatching sedge, but it still needs the help of darkness to do its job. On perhaps the sixth cast, when my floating line can only be seen against the reflection of the western sky, the fly is taken confidently. The fight is violent, but not long: this is no time for light tippets. Besides, the big trout cannot see his opponent in the dark. Soon the leader stops making an audible slice as it cuts the water. The trout has only some fifteen natural flies in his stomach; all the rest is "bottom feed," including plenty of scuds. Only fifteen chances to get the best fish of the season.

Sentimentality aside, such a trout should be removed from the river in the name of good management. But he should be poached in wine and served respectfully. No frivolous treatment. Besides, for breakfast, there is that eel, intact on the rock except for a neat bite in the head.

Allow me one more stranger-than-fiction tale about sedges, this one for bug-watchers. I saw a thing I have never read about, although I was fishing in Ireland, the ancient world capital of sedges, and I was watching the best known of them all: the Grey Flag (*Hydropsyche pellucidula* or a closely related species). I was standing in knee-deep, clear, gently flowing water on a warm May afternoon, and the sun was just right to illuminate the bottom in front of me. A Grey Flag flew off some reeds near my elbow and dived at the water, hitting it with an audible "splat." I could see the small form swim all the way to the bottom, presumably looking for a place to lay eggs. I was rooting for the brave little bug, but a small fish—not a trout—darted forward and took it on the bottom. There must be room for a wet Grey Flag—but I have to report no success on mine. Do other sedges lay their eggs this way? I suspect the Grey Flag has other methods as well.

Beginning anglers are often told to identify sedges by their resemblance to moths. This is a fair rule of thumb, but it should be noted that there are also aquatic moths. If anglers could identify them, we might find that they provide some unexpected fishing.

Stoneflies (Plecoptera)

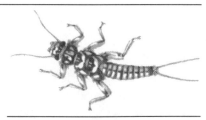

Stoneflies are at their most spectacular in the high country of the Rocky Mountain West. In Montana and Wyoming, they provide the only major hatch of the season in some streams. The hatch of giant Salmon Flies *(Pteronarcys californica)* migrates upstream with the wild flowers, following the season and the temperature. You have a chance of getting the best fish of the year in the big rivers down in the valleys—if the rivers clear of snow-melt by late June or early July.

My own favorite memories are of a smaller, friendly river in Yellowstone Park. This stream can be crossed in hip-boots in some places, yet looks impressive as it goes over its hundred-fifty-foot waterfall. I like to hike up toward the falls from the road below, following the river in its deep gorge. As the crow flies, the distance cannot exceed three miles. As the angler wades, it is too long for a day's fishing. The only competing fishermen are likely to be ospreys and water ouzels.

I began fishing the river as a boy, with a live stonefly cast upstream, the tips of the wings clipped off because the old-timers said this would avoid short takes. I could not help feeling sorry for the clumsy insect. The switch to a slightly more orthodox dry fly was easy, and it caught more fish because it could be cast farther. A Royal Coachman worked as well as a more careful imitation. On a bright summer's day, there was no great trick in catching (and releasing) a couple of dozen trout: browns in the less turbulent water, then rainbows in the fast bits. A cast where heavy waters turned glassy at the head of a massive boulder would usually bring a bright flash, a sudden violent play, and a half-pounder with the color and firmness of a silver dollar. There was no need to be a fanatic about drying the fly, because it worked just as well when sunk a few inches. There was one dream pool high up, where cliffs bottled the river on both sides. The water ran deep and still between yellow banks and green pines. The old man of the river had to live there, and long may he reign. He broke my leader on the first cast. I never saw the fish, so there is nothing to interfere with the dream.

So much for the glamorous side of the renowned Salmon Fly hatch. It can be fun, but I would not schedule a trip around it. This hatch has, in my experience, been as undependable as that of the Greendrake, another famous deceiver of giant trout. The drake is likely to last a short time or to hatch only sparsely. The stonefly always seems to arrive and to last for a while. And he does move fish, but most often (judging from stomach contents) to the nymph. When adults blunder into the water, they only occasionally do so in a way that causes a steady rise of trout. And when I *have* found the Salmon Flies out in numbers and the water clear, I have still spoiled the game by checking stomach contents.

In 1977, for example, water was low throughout the Rockies and conditions were perfect for the hatch. On the golden afternoon of July 9, the air above the Yellowstone was full of lumbering stone-flies. Using dry imitations, I got two fat cutthroats in minutes. The story sounds traditional, till I mention that neither fish had so much as one Salmon Fly inside. There were several sedges and some large mayfly *(Ephemerella doddsi)* nymphs, but the bulk of surface feeding had been on adult Net-Winged Midges. Ever hear of the famous Net-Winged Midge hatch? If so, you've read something I've missed.

On the average, I'll take August or September, when the water is almost always clear and there are hatches of mayflies that the trout actually eat. But note that seasons vary enormously with altitude. I am discussing the real high country of the headwaters. I have never followed the hatch up the Madison, nor have I spent much time on Henry's Fork.

From the angler's viewpoint, the big defect of stoneflies is that they crawl out on rocks to hatch. (Some are said to hatch in the stream, but I have not had the good luck to meet them.) On the other hand, the fast water dislodges some stonefly nymphs at any time of the year, and these are often present in a Yellowstone trout's stomach. It makes as much sense to fish a stonefly nymph as any other fly in these waters, although it would be stretching the point to expect much selectivity. The old-timers got along well with Black Woolly Worms. Fortunately, the trout seem to remember the adult flies all summer long—or in any case will take a big dry fly well in the same spot weeks after the hatch.

Stoneflies are also traditionally important in the English North Country and in parts of Scotland. I have not had the pleasure of meeting the big stonefly of the border districts (Stewart's "May-Fly"). In Ireland, the medium-sized stoneflies of May provide some interesting episodes. But they do not have the extroverted behavior of their cousins in the Rockies. Careful imitations are useful; my favorite is shown in chapter 11.

In eastern America, there are lots of stoneflies to be seen: fewer than in Montana but more than in Ireland. Some appear in fish stomachs, but these have not provided much surface fishing for me. Evidently they do not become available to the fish in quantities. On the Rapidan River in late February, there are hordes of tiny black stoneflies, but the trout are oblivious to them. Any Shenandoah Park trout caught in spring is, however, likely to have one or two large, dark stonefly nymphs inside. Perhaps that is why the fish are susceptible to big artificial nymphs fished deep: even one of the naturals is a fair meal for a nine-inch brook trout. Unfortunately, as a small-stream fishing method, this is not very exciting. Sometimes I fish a few pools with a deep, upstream nymph, partly to provide a comparison to other methods. I would feel like a meat-hunter if I kept it up all day.

On Penn's Creek in May, there are large stoneflies hatching and ovipositing, but only the nymphs work, and then only sometimes. The adults neither splash around like the Montana Salmon Flies nor float along quietly like the Irish species. The biggest *Pteronarcys* flies here are even larger than the Westerners, but trout evidently do not get many chances at them. And if trout cannot get stoneflies when they are oviposting, they may never get them.

Stoneflies have so little class that they crawl after their spouses rather than doing an aerial dance. What a waste! Think what you or I could do for mating behavior with two fine pairs of wings!

Diptera

The best of angling entomologies fail to give much help with this immense order of true flies. One problem is that there are about one hundred thousand species, and many are of only local importance. I have never caught a fish on a Down-looker or Gravel Bed, for example, even though both are classic flies that must still be important somewhere in the cradle

of fly-fishing. On American trout streams, I have never seen a Cow-dung fly—except in fly books.

Even the important dipteran species have not interested angling scholars as much as the prettier mayflies. The Black Gnats, for example, have been imitated by anglers since at least the time of Cotton, and they accounted for what is arguably the first description of dry-fly fishing, by Scotcher in the early 1800s. In my Irish experience, this fly usually provides the best fishing of the year. Yet some anglers still hate the hatch, and most do not know what insect is on the water when they speak of Black Gnats. If the authors of angling entomologies know, they are reluctant to say so.

The popular term "Black Gnat" appears to include at least three genera and far more species, some aquatic and some terrestrial. All are present in both America and Europe. But while they have been consistently sucessful in Ireland, they are only regionally useful in America. I have mentioned the Net-Winged Midge (family Blephariceridae). Charles Wetzel has illustrated the Pennsylvania Red-Legged March Fly, an American *Bibio,* and given a dressing. Either could be imitated with dressings based on the classic Black Gnat, which is supposed to be *Bibio johannis* and closely related species—terrestrials that often reach the water.

The larger species of *Simulium,* the Reed Smuts, resemble the *Bibio* species, are sometimes called by the same popular name, and are more important to the trout. The Reed Smut is a true aquatic insect, called the Black Fly (and worse) in the United States.

Finally, Ronalds and a few authors since him have mentioned Empid Flies as Black Gnats. A scientific publication of 1961 recorded 354 British species of this order, yet the author knew very little of the life of the immature flies. As near as I can make out, the great majority of Black Gnats in the Irish limestone streams are Empids of the genus *Hilara*. But much work needs to be done. Pending publication of better research, the least misleading approach may be to continue calling all three genera Black Gnats rather than applying names which suggest more knowledge than we have.

These insects are often available in great quantities, especially when they happen to be *Hilara* or Reed Smuts. Big trout will take them all day, lying right at the surface and sipping in flies until their intestines are packed like black sausages. Anglers may be ignored—and their flies too. These conditions make for great selectivity. I have probably tied as many designs for Black Gnats as for any other artificial, and several have been really necessary.

It must be seen to be believed, but trout will pass up single Black Gnats in favor of mating pairs. Sometimes a whole clump of mating flies is even better. (Black Gnats have orgies that would shame the Romans.) Again, the trout may be taking only small, single, spent flies. When conditions are demanding, the angler who cannot tie his own flies will soon see why the old-timers looked on these little insects as an "angler's curse." For the angler who likes to wade deep, fish fine, and tie flies, the Black Gnat can be a blessing.

Many other true flies blow into rivers everywhere, providing occasional good fishing. The rises to them are not usually heavy, but they produce some fishing on summer days that would otherwise be unproductive. Sizes vary from minute specks to the clumsy Hawthorn Fly, which is nothing but a giant Black Gnat. Most of these flies are terrestrials and might be best considered under that heading, since the trout do not care whether a chance dinner is of the order Diptera or not. It may be a coincidence, but true flies and beetles have provided my only fishing to terrestrials in Ireland. In America, the true flies (except for chironomids) have not been very important to me, but beetles and many other land-bred insects have. Other anglers have obviously had different experiences.

Almost every angler agrees that true midges—flies of the family

Chironomidae—are important. Most authors note that the chironomids should get far more attention than they do, but no one actually writes much about them. The problem is one of scale and diversity. Midges live in almost any water, including some that is too polluted for mayflies and sedges. Rivers have a share, but chironomids are more important in lakes, since there are many species that can live in deep water. Anglers think of midges as small, and many are, but there are also very sizable species— bigger than most common mayflies.

Anglers can usually recognize chironomids. They have a deceptively delicate appearance, with long legs, two short, flat wings, and an easy, graceful flight. The craneflies look much like them but are of a different family (Tipulidae), are usually larger, and reach the water accidentally.

Since only a few chironomid species are important to anglers in any given water, it may eventually be possible to do a good study for individual rivers. Pupae hanging or moving in the surface film are usually the most useful stage for fishermen. But the larvae are also important, especially in lakes. Fully hatched adults get off the water easily, but sometimes trout consider it worth the effort of catching them. One of the best designs (chapter 11) for me has been a fly that is apparently taken for both the adult and the pupa. To show how tough these fragile-looking pupae really are, put some of them in water after an hour or two in a trout's stomach. They may live and even hatch, giving you a chance to base two imitations on one fly.

In fishing pupa imitations, the important thing is to have the fly right in the surface film. If the position and size are right, there is at least a fair chance of catching a trout for an autopsy. The trouble is that, on your next visit to the stream, a quite different midge may be hatching.

Terrestrials

For fishing purposes, it is enough to define a terrestrial as an insect that reaches the water only by accident—as opposed to an aquatic insect, which has a reason for being there. The definition does not, however, take into account flies that spend their earlier life in or near the water, such as the Alders, craneflies, and Empids of the genus *Hilara.*

It is not possible to make many generalizations about terrestrials —except that they are seasonally important on most streams. Insect activity increases in hot weather, and terrestrials then fall or are blown into the water. This timing is highly fortunate: daytime hatches of aquatic insects are usually at their worst when terrestrials are most important. In streams that produce really good hatches of aquatic insects, trout may not pay much attention to the occasional terrestrial. Conversely, terrestrials give some of the best dry-fly fishing of the year on eastern American streams of both freestone and limestone types.

My most unusual experience with terrestrials involved cicadas, or seventeen-year locusts, in the summer of 1970. These enormous creatures really do emerge every seventeen years, and they last for only a short while in any given location. I caught them at their peak on a small Pennsylvania mountain stream, distinguished only by its scenery. One human life, obviously, provides very few experiences with this insect, which may account for two conflicting stories I had heard: first, that small trout will not tackle such vast bugs; and second, that trout quickly gorge on cicadas and will not then feed on anything additional. It did not take long to disprove both myths. I caught half a dozen trout quickly—not on an imitation, so please do not look in chapter 11. The best was an eleven-incher, which I killed and found stuffed with cicadas. The stomachs of the smaller fish also felt packed. The insects inside were the size of a shrew. The conclusion must be that hungry trout will quickly learn to take advantage of any food.

Ants are probably the most important terrestrials in eastern America. Crawling ants fall into streams regularly in hot weather, and imitations are accepted greedily. Flying ants are said to be eagerly taken in Britain and Ireland, but I carried imitations around for four seasons and never had occasion to knot one on. In some parts of Ireland, by the way, ants are still called Pismires. I thought this was a bit of murky Hibernian humor till the same term turned up in old British books.

In Britain and Ireland, beetles seem to be the most important terrestrials during hot summer weather. They are equally important in America, and some of the best designs are modern American ones. Traditional imitations look to me like almost anything, including beetles, and a fly like the Coch-y-Bondhu works well at any season. There is no profit in arguing with a trout about his diet, and if he will take a hackled fly when beetles are on the water, he shall have what he wants.

Grasshoppers are wildly unreliable (a careful choice of words). They are popular with anglers because, being big, hoppers interest big fish. Given a hot, windy, late-summer day on a Montana meadow stream, the fish always notice grasshoppers, often rise spectacularly, and sometimes get hooked. This is about the way Montana boys behave at the Saturday night dance. One surmises that the fish, like the boys, are simultaneously attracted and wary. As to the Saturday nights, I have no advice, but one way to handle grasshoppers is to fish them wet. You wouldn't expect to find a nice insect like the grasshopper two feet under water, but the trout don't seem to mind.

Hoppers also work in Pennsylvania meadow streams, but not as often. They are not common in the British and Irish streams I have fished; low temperature may again be the difference.

Possibly the best-known British terrestrial is the Alder—actually a semiaquatic fly. Charles Kingsley's essay "Chalk-Stream Studies" immortalized this "beloved member of the brute creation" in 1858. I have rarely seen Alders in quantity, but when I have, trout have taken them well. Once, on a difficult limestone stream in Ireland, an Alder cast on the water brought two or three trout racing for it. The effect was like throwing pellets on a hatchery pool, which is the last thing one would expect in such a stream. Unfortunately, I must record that the excitement was not equaled by the results. Most of the trout could not be hooked—reminding me of fish rising to grasshoppers in Montana. For what it is worth, however, a hair-wing Alder (like the sedge imitations in chapter 11) seems to work better than the traditional pattern, which was originally designed as a wet fly. There are reports of good hatches in eastern America, but I have not seen one personally. I have, however, found one Alder in an American trout's stomach, several on bushes, and many in angler's fly-boxes.

The Hawthorn Fly—the huge Black Gnat—is blown onto the water a little earlier than the Alder and is also taken well on its day. It can be tied exactly like the Black Gnat, but on a hook of size 12 or 14.

In America, imitations of the jassids (Cicadellidae) are important these days, but few anglers knew the creatures existed until Vincent Marinaro wrote about them. His artificial Jassid is not only an

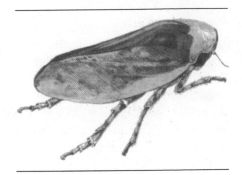

excellent pattern in itself, but also a design that works as well for many other small insects. As Marinaro points out, Ronalds' Wren Tail or Frog-Hopper appears to be the same insect, but Ronalds' tie bears no apparent resemblance to the natural.

Aphids, on the other hand, have been fairly well imitated at least as far back as 1916 by Edmonds and Lee. A modified jassid design seems better now. I never found trout rising to either jassids or aphids in Ireland, but A. Courtney Williams writes that both are of local importance in England.

The list could continue. Inchworms are well known (and easily imitated) in eastern America. So are crickets. American trout are enterprising creatures—perhaps because they are often hungry. English and Irish anglers will already be suspicious of my tales of grasshoppers and giant cicadas. What if I mention that American trout sometimes leap clear out of the water for butterflies and dragonflies? It is true. But this chapter has to end somewhere.

4 ❋ Tactics: Making an Artificial Fly Behave like the Real Thing

Plus a Much-Needed Clarification of What the Rhythm Method Is Good For

❋ ❋ ❋ Only the names are changed to protect innocent parties.

On second thought, Melvin is the only party requiring protection, and you might not consider him innocent. He had been telling stories nonstop for sixty miles. Some of the tales were on their third cycle. And his breath. You are what you eat, they say; Melvin was what he had been drinking for the last week. Must have been a case of Old Dog Wallow. Everything but his talk muscle was paralyzed.

You may infer that the fine points of fishing were foggy for Melvin.

Camp Robber Crick looked extra good as we fled from the car. It is always one of the prettiest meadow streams in Yellowstone Park. It flows too near the road—otherwise we could not have got Melvin there. So don't look for that name on the map.

Melvin opted for a nap while Scotty Chapman and I explored the fishing. No need to change Scotty's name: he is the best outdoorsman I have known at short range. Indoors, he is equally successful as an artist. You have to envy a man who has been fishing and painting the Yellowstone country for exactly fifty years, as of the summer of 1976, and who still looks as if he were forty-five. Wish someone would tell me what stopped the clock for Scotty. Let's hope it was the fishing.

This, unfortunately, was an August day on which miracles were needed more than skill. A brilliant high-altitude sun turned the thin water into a reflecting basin. There was no hatch and no prospect of one till evening. Here and there in the shade of a tree, small trout were taking terrestrials. Scotty wore down a few of the fry, using a little, sparse Quill Gordon with a near-black hackle. I did as badly with ants and tiny beetles on an .003-inch tippet. Neither of us saw a good fish moving, although a few were visible lying inert on the bottoms of deep pools.

We walked back for our lunch as Melvin came out of his nap and decided to build up a thirst. He wobbled down to the river only yards from the car. Breathing heavily, he stood on the bank and heaved out a big dry fly on a coarse leader. I did not bother to watch; the cheese sandwich was more interesting.

Next came a splash that might have been Melvin falling in. No, he was dancing on the bank, and his rod had the kind of bend only a stout leader could resist. On the end was a handsome fish—easily double the weight of any we had risen all morning. It never had a chance. Melvin hauled it to the bank and swatted it twenty feet back in the grass for safekeeping. Must have seen a bear movie. This was one of the good browns, maybe a pound and a quarter.

Now, this kind of thing simply does not happen in real life. Educated brown trout in thin water do not behave like that. But there it was. My tale is not fiction. A meteorite would have surprised me less.

When I realized that my eyes were not lying, the problem was to avoid laughter. Only a dry lump of Cheddar saved me from spoiling Melvin's big moment. Scotty had a more decisive escape mechanism: he stuffed his sandwich into both cheeks and headed downstream, looking like a chipmunk.

Melvin strutted up with his trout, both incredulous. "Well," he opined, "I move to the head of the class."

"Yurf," I agreed through the cheese.

Pause for deep thought. "Not that I wipe Scotty's eye often," Melvin modestly confessed. "Three times out of four, Scotty's the best in the business."

I needed another large bite.

"What's the limit?" Mel asked.

I held up two fingers.

"Might's well see about rounding 'er out." And he strolled back to the bank. His next cast was, if possible, more awkward than the first, but another insane trout rose splashily. Melvin did not hook it.

By now, however, it was clear that there was more to the performance than a once-in-a-million shot. When Mel retired for his next nap—which I hope produced the best dreams in a long time —I went to the scene of his triumph and had a good look.

Melvin had cast from the very pivot of a large curve. It was almost impossible to get a drag. And about forty feet away, at the far circumference of the curve, a deep channel lay against the opposite bank. Upstream for two hundred yards there was no respectable station for a feeding fish, so that every insect hitting several acres of water funneled down into the one little channel Mel had fished. The combination of feeding, holding, and drag-free water was uncanny.

I did not figure it out all at once. Before I believed it, a little tourist girl with a feather-duster cast by a spinning float had also risen a trout. The final irony was that the best piece of water in maybe twenty miles was right by a road jammed with traffic.

I told Scotty of my idea but did not want to test it while people were looking. Two days later I was there again at the end of dusk. I had walked a half-mile of river, and there had not even been an evening hatch—only a few ovipositing sedges with some small fish splashing at them. But in a few minutes, from the soft spot, I took a brown of seventeen inches and another of fourteen.

This being a proper fishing tale, I will pass out some clues for finding soft spots. They will hardly find you a place like Melvin's; I never expect to see its equal (but I know how to get back to it). Usually, you can figure that the best trout will have found precisely the spots where you will have the most trouble getting a good float.

Melvin's saga would be good for any number of morals in the hands of Ed Zern, but the best I can do is this old one: the first problem in dry-fly fishing is drag. If you can avoid drag, you have at least an outside chance of a fish, no matter what other errors you make.

So why write a book? Well, books on marriage surpass in number even those on fishing, yet the definitive advice to a Young Man Considering Marriage was given long ago, also in four letters: Don't.

In both cases, some action implications—as we say in the State Department—may be useful.

Let us refer back to the natural insects, since that is what the trout does. One old generality that works much of the time is this: floating insects are nearly helpless. They may struggle visibly, and attractively to the trout, but they do not move much in relation to the current—which means that the angler cannot easily mimic their actions by pulling the fly. There are a few exceptions, of which the most notable is the fluttering sedge. I knew a British gamekeeper on an Irish estate who timed his fishing by the sedge hatches. He could get away with a straight cross-stream cast and a simple palmer fly, lightly twitched. Leonard M. Wright, Jr., has written a good book on the moving dry fly. Throughout the year on most streams I know, these opportunities are fairly rare. If you take your dry-fly fishing as it comes, you will usually have to avoid drag.

The most efficient solution, speaking strictly of the mechanical problem of drag, is to cast *directly upstream.* This may not be possible for reasons given later. But it works fairly often if you bother to try. The current always has variations, of course; these can frequently be handled by a small move to one side or by a few slack curves in a long leader.

As a matter of personal opinion, the change to upstream fishing was—and still is for every beginner—the real dividing line in trout fishing, the revolutionary event to overshadow all others. With a drag-free float, the trout takes the fly confidently and often close to the angler. One can at least hope to fool the most wary, selective fish. Downstream fishing *with a tight line* brings a different reaction from the trout, something that is not as consistently a natural feeding response. (Downstream fishing with a slack line produces the same effect as upstream fishing, from the trout's point of view: a drag-free float. I am using "upstream fishing" here as a kind of shorthand to cover all drag-free presentations.)

Professor James Rennie, who earned fame of a sort by writing a "scientific" fishing book full of dogmatic errors, took pains in 1833 to dismiss upstream fishing as an "absurdity." In the days of long, limp rods and light lines, it must in fact have taken a skilled fisherman to work upstream, unless the wind helped.

With today's light, stiff rods and heavy lines, many anglers begin facing upstream in their first few days of fishing. The next step is to throw curves in the line and leader to postpone drag. There are several ways of doing this—as by stopping the cast in midair and pulling it back a few feet. The first few failures usually show the need of this.

My friend Ben Schley tells of guiding President Eisenhower on a stream stocked full of trout for the occasion. They failed to show due respect. Seems the President could cast a nice line—far too nice and straight to prevent drag. Possibly he had fished mainly in domesticated private streams where the trout were heedless. Ben could arrange a slack line only by a Machiavellian device: He interrupted the President with an urgent call in the middle of his cast, asking him to look at a bird on the bank. The line fell properly and the fly was duly taken by one of the rainbows that paved the bottom. Unfortunately, the angler had been so thoroughly distracted that he failed to strike, and Ben's plot came to nothing.

There is a price for the upstream cast: the leader comes down over the fish before the fly. So does the line, if the cast has been too long. The price is not excessive. It can be paid in three ways. First, the angler must often wade, which really bothers some fishermen. Second, the leader and the tip of the line should be light. Third, when conditions allow, it is best to move just a little to one side of the fish—something between ten and thirty degrees away from a position directly below him. At this angle, drag is still relatively simple to control, and a cast to the near eye of the trout will keep leader and line farther away from him than the fly.

The diagram shows the ideal dry-fly cast in its simplest form. It

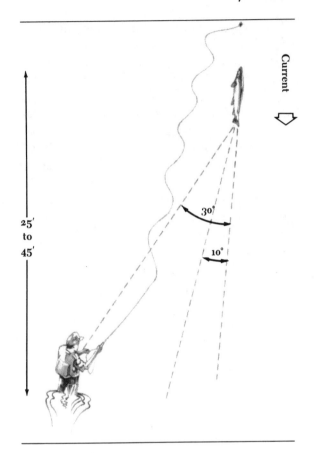

represents only one dimension, however: the angle of the fisherman below the fish, as seen from above. Two other dimensions
must be added to the diagram: the distance of the angler from
the fish, and the height of the angler above the water. From the
fisherman's point of view, these are very different dimensions, but
from the trout's point of view, they are so close to being the same
thing that they must be considered together.

The best distance is the shortest one at which an angler can
avoid frightening the fish. This in turn depends on how far he
sticks up above the water. For reasons not entirely clear to me,
what happens below the water usually frightens trout very little,

so long as the angler moves quietly and slowly. A week before this was written, while wading in water almost to my armpits, I caught two trout in a quiet pool with only my twelve-foot leader outside the rod guides. They were wild browns in a heavily fished public stream, too—the Liffey near Dublin. If conditions had permitted, I would actually have preferred to be a little farther away, so that there would have been some line in the air to help carry out the leader. The trout were obviously not worried. One, of almost two pounds, merely swam around my legs after being hooked, and I had the extraordinary experience of netting a strong, wild trout without even getting my leader splice out of the guides of the rod. Had I been on the bank, I could not have approached so close in plain view, though I might have done almost as well by lying down flat against a dark background.

Thus, while we fishermen find it convenient to think of both distance and height above the water, the trout probably perceives only one dimension: the angle between the surface of the water and the highest visible part of the angler. A nearby fisherman whose head is close to the water may appear less frightening to a trout than one standing on a high bank much farther away. A diagram that has been well known since the time of Ronalds shows this.

Even though the wading man in this diagram is close to the fish, he subtends a smaller angle than the man farther away on the

Fisherman on bank is visible to fish.
Note that he would be hidden
except for refraction

bank. In consequence, the wading fisherman is less visible. He is further helped by the fact that light entering the water at a low angle is largely reflected, so that much of it does not reach the eye of the fish. Although researchers have differed in other respects, they agree that objects near the edge of the trout's "window" of vision are blurred and compressed.

Colonel E. W. Harding, whom Skues considered the best angling mind of the century, gave a rough guide to fishing distances that is borne out in practice. Because of the angle of refraction, concludes Harding, a man whose head is six feet above water disappears from the view of a trout one foot under water at a distance of sixty-nine feet. If the angler's head is three feet above the water, he disappears at thirty-three feet.

Now, the difference between sixty-nine and thirty-three feet is the difference between a dry-fly cast of excessive length and one that is easy. This gives the wading angler a marked advantage. A fisherman confined to the bank must usually kneel or lie prone, or his head can easily be more than six feet above water. Yet experienced fishermen often cast from standing positions on an open bank. It is well to avoid following such fishermen in bright daylight, not because they will have caught all the fish but because they will have frightened them.

The refraction of light when it enters the water also affects the trout's view of insects, and this is discussed in chapter 8, on color.

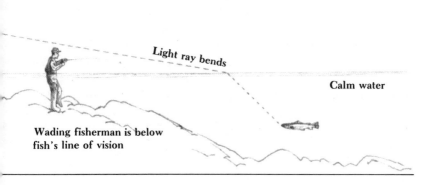

Light ray bends

Calm water

Wading fisherman is below
fish's line of vision

The bending of light rays does *not,* however, mean that the trout can see the angler while remaining hidden from him. This classic fishing myth is as scientific as Izaak Walton's gossip about the Sargus (a fish that amused itself by seducing "she-goats on the grassy shore"). The trout obeys the laws of optics, but he is small, well camouflaged by nature, and not in the habit of waving eight-foot rods.

The question of visibility cannot be entirely reduced to a computation of angles. Turbulent water, weak light, dark backgrounds, and dark clothes can help an angler get close to his trout. The fish cannot easily see a motionless angler against a blending background. On the other hand, light-colored, shiny clothes can frighten fish at long distances. So can rods waved against a light sky or against the moon. And I have never lost my suspicion of light-colored lines, though obviously they work well sometimes.

Still, we are left with an ideal fishing position that can often be attained in practice—unlike most ideals. This position is in the water, some twenty-five to forty-five feet below our rising trout (depending on conditions) and a little to one side of a straight line below the fish.

A warning again seems necessary. We humans need to form generalizations in order to learn, yet to generalize is to oversimplify. Actual stream tactics will call for a great many departures from my generalized ideal position.

Perhaps readers would find it more useful to think that every trout has a soft spot somewhere: a spot from which it is possible to present a fly naturally. This kind of thinking is dear to the American presentation school. Searching for the soft spot was, perhaps, Ray Bergman's basic tactic, though I do not recall that he used this term. Most often the spot is downstream from the trout, but it may be across from the fish or even above him. In a stream with a jumble of current, there may not even be a clear upstream. So the soft-spot concept is another useful generalization that does not always work.

I do not know how to give detailed guidelines for finding soft spots. Many books have contained pretty maps of pools with variations in tactics. They have not helped me much. One of the great charms of fishing (and the thing which makes a presentation school possible) is that pools are as individual as human beings. There are similarities, as between humans, but there are also infinite variations of water, weed, rock, and contour. The following problems are only to stimulate thinking.

Strong Downstream Wind It is difficult to cast light flies directly into a wind, so it is usually best to get across from the fish and cast sideways, letting the wind blow the fly around in a curve ahead of the line.

Trout Rising Directly Above a Rapid In this case, a cast from below the fish would at once be caught by the fast water, and there

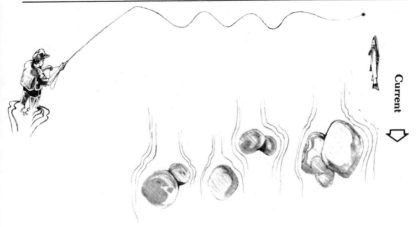

would be a prompt drag. Most of the pools in Shendandoah Park have this problem. Since the banks are wooded, my best tactic has been to sneak upstream while *crouching very low.* Then I count on a longish rod to keep the line out of the rapids. In a river with more casting room, it is usually better to cast cross-stream. But if there is no wind to blow a curve in the line, it is necessary to make a curve or "parachute" cast. The latter consists of nothing more than an exaggerated version of the usual slack-line cast, stopped very high in the air and allowed to fall limply.

An Obstacle Below the Trout If the obstacle is low enough, an effective cast can be made directly over it, keeping part of the line out of the water. Otherwise a cross-stream or even downstream cast may be needed.

Bad Direction of Sun or Moon I do not like to cast directly into the sun, because it blinds me and helps the trout see me. Sun or moon directly behind the rod casts a moving shadow.

Wading Not Advisable Sometimes the water is too deep, sometimes wading is prohibited, and sometimes the angler wants to cover a lot of trout quickly during the evening rise.

The Fly Needs to Be "Worked" That is, it must be moved against the current. This is best done from a position slightly above the fish, or at least not below it.

In Europe, there are a great many fishermen who keep to the bank, and who therefore do much of their fishing almost cross-stream, though they still aim for drag-free floats. Their tackle is different from that of wading fishermen, and the differences make sense. The bank angler must cast farther, both because he cannot wade close to the fish and because the fish sees him more easily. Long casts call for slightly heavier lines and stronger rods. With more line out, the strike must be more violent, so the leader is also stronger. Fortunately, the trout does not see the line and leader so clearly, because they fall to one side instead of almost overhead.

I have respect for good bank fishermen. They are excellent casters and stalkers, as they must be. The careful ones usually avoid being seen by fish. Even the best, however, do put down many fish with drag. The custom of bank fishing can be a great conservation measure, since it almost ensures that the fish will soon be educated.

American fishermen tend to be good waders, not because of superior virtue but because we often have no choice. Many of our tree-lined streams can be fished in no other way, except perhaps by bait from the bank. The best English and Irish streams, on the other hand, permit bank fishing and often encourage it, because of depth and soft bottoms.

Many anglers on both sides of the salt river have an unnecessary fear of deep wading. One Irish fisherman told me that he spent two whole nights stuck in a river (on different occasions) because his feet were deep in the mud of the bottom and he feared that he would drown if he tried to move. From experience in the same river, I suspect that his fear was unnecessary.

In *The Way of a Trout With a Fly,* Skues argues that the ability to use a nymph greatly widens the angler's chances of offering the trout a proper imitation of its food of the moment. The problem of drag is greatly reduced, and the fish can be genuinely deceived. On the other hand, he continues, "hammering" a nymph-feeding fish with a dry fly is inappropriate and ineffective. Change that to "hammering a fish with a dragging fly" and you have the case for wading.

There may, however, be one sound argument against wading. It must harm some of the stream-bottom creatures on which trout feed. In itself, this does not prove much. Well-managed angling often kills many trout, too, and yet natural reproduction can replace them with little effect on the population. The same is true of almost any other wild species, and presumably of trout-stream insects.

Research is needed to discover whether normal wading harms insect populations. The results would surely vary with different kinds of stream bottom. I know some rarely waded streams where hatches have fallen off because of ecological changes, and I know heavily waded streams where there are good hatches—apparently as good as ever. But I have not done stream-bed inventories. There may be cases in which wading does real harm to the insects in a stream, and where bank-fishing is feasible. This could be shown by objective research, and then we would all wish appropriate restrictions.

The kind of nymph-fishing that I personally enjoy most involves casting to a visible trout, or at least to a rise-form. This began— with G. E. M. Skues—as a variant of dry-fly fishing. The excitement and interest are almost the same. So are the drag-free tactics, at least as a starting point. But when they fail, a gentle movement of the fly close to the fish is more likely to work with a nymph than with a dry fly. Leisenring ("the lift") and later Oliver Kite ("the induced take") covered this more fully than is possible here.

Gordon Mackie suggests that Skues knew of the moving-nymph tactic but decided not to make his information public for ethical reasons. Once anglers began moving their nymphs even a little, they might begin "fishing the water" downstream and flogging away at non-feeding trout on the bottom. Skues' case against the dry-fly purists would, to say the least, be weakened.

What Skues feared has, reportedly, been happening even in England; and deep fishing with a dragging fly has long been popular in America. I should not wish to argue the ethical point with the next streamer-fisherman I meet on a spring creek. It is a plain fact, however, that downstream fishing with a non-imitative fly (lure, in the British sense) does not mix comfortably with upstream imitative fishing. When Falling Springs Creek was heavily stocked with hatchery rainbows, it was also heavily stocked with fishermen ambling down the banks and dragging a streamer in front of visible fish. The good wild fish were not visible: they were under the banks hiding.

When I grew up in the Yellowstone country, the most common tactic was to fish a single wet fly across and downstream. The man who helped me get started—Joe Joffe—had no other method. He would shuffle mechanically downstream, cast, and use what Ray Bergman called a "hand-twist" retrieve. The fly could only fish shallow and drag promptly. Joe had once caught many trout this way, but he had had little luck once competition increased after World War II. Old Joe, bless his soul, thought Montana was fished out. I figured that fly-fishing was an elegant hoax and went back to worms (an experience for which I am now grateful).

Eventually, with the assistance of books and some tips from Scotty Chapman, I turned upstream and tried dry-fly fishing. It was one of the revealing experiences of my young life—almost as much fun as looking through a knothole in the girls' shower room. The river next door had hidden treasures. It had, in fact, as many trout as ever. My first hundred yards with the dry fly must have produced a dozen of them, knifing up through tumbled currents after my Royal Coachman. A well-fished nymph would also have worked.

I leaped to the conclusion that any trout who would fall for the old mechanical, across-and-down method had to be pretty dumb. That opinion has not changed radically, but now I know that trout will take a shallow-dragging fly under handicaps other than innocence. They may do it in the middle of the night, for example, even in an Irish limestone stream. High water, spring hunger, even a strong wind may incline the fish to risks. More trout come to a fly slowly drifted through hotspots than to Joe Joffe's mechanical casting. And sinking the fly deeply changes everything. But for educated fish under conditions that protect them, turn around and cast upstream.

Not very many anglers seem to know how to fish a fly *upstream* and deep. Perhaps it's just as well. The method is not all that difficult: not the big deal that Hewitt and his disciples once made out. It takes concentration, of course, to see when there is a strike; but the tactics and casting are simpler than in dry-fly fishing, and the matter of flies rarely requires much thought. An efficient rig consists of two largish, weighted nymphs no more than two feet apart on a short leader. Since this combination is hard to cast, I just flip it—much like a worm, to be honest. The bow-and-arrow cast also works well. The conditions have to be right for fishing close, as in rocky pocket water. A bit of drag does not seem to matter much; the trout are often well hooked.

This method is probably much like Wheatley's fishing with artificial "grubs" back in 1849. And his flies were strikingly like some modern American nymphs. I hear that British anglers still use weighted flies for grayling, but they are not eager to admit to doing this for trout. There are streams and times when no other method works in America. I'll stay out of the argument about whether this technique is really fly-fishing. In terms of interest, it is for me ahead of most downstream fishing and spinning. And I have already opined that spinning is better than staying home with the television set.

There are, finally, two minor tactics worth mention: the first for catching easy fish, the second for catching difficult ones.

All of us joke about catching the stream's village idiot. Sometimes we really need him. Our efforts to match the hatch have failed and we need any old trout for a stomach check; or maybe the whole day has failed, and we need one fish for our ego. A tactic that sometimes works is to cover a lot of trout with a fly that can be presented quickly. Trout do vary greatly in experience, taste, and instincts. If you and I are on a stream with lots of fish in Montana, for instance, we will probably find a vulnerable one soon enough this way. This can even be the way in which to catch the most fish—under these conditions. Maybe this is how the idea started that trout get bored with their regular food and welcome a bit of variety. In my experience, though, individual educated trout show little interest in variety; only familiar food seems to create security. I suspect, then, that the tactic depends on variety in *trout*, not flies. Try it and see.

One of the nice things about my beloved Blackwater was that it had few tolerant fish. I can read back in my diary and find that I have forgotten days on some streams when fish could be caught by the dozens, but I can still smell those individual Blackwater trout in my net five years later.

Which leads to the second minor tactic—one for those difficult fish. They not only insist on the right fly, but also refuse to look at it unless they are in the mood. And the mood sometimes seems to come rhythmically. Thus, the trout will ignore many natural flies, then rise for two or three. I am not sure why this happens. It cannot be a question of economy of effort. Perhaps the trout is stuffed or perhaps he is getting most of his food from the bottom and simply takes a few floating insects to keep in practice. The rhythm problem does seem to occur most often with worthwhile trout. When it happens, the angler who can figure out the timing and get his fly over the fish at the right time is obviously improving his chances. Any attempt to figure out the rhythm is almost certain to be better than repetitive casting, which merely frightens wary trout, whatever La Branche may have found when he was "creating a hatch" for more innocent fish. Two or three good casts after every rise is plenty.

In Ireland, I played with the idea that the perfect evening rise would involve one cast and one carefully stalked two-pound brown trout. I never pulled it off.

When working on a trout that has a difficult rhythm or cruising pattern, I like to find a comfortable seat—on a midstream rock, for example—and keep my line coiled and ready to go. The ability to cover a trout quickly after it rises is a great advantage. Impatience, however, makes the whole thing hopeless.

It is handy to have a term to explain to fellow anglers why I am sitting on a rock with my fly in my fingers while peering intently at the water. Accordingly, I have called this the "rhythm method," partly because it requires a great deal of forbearance and may produce a big surprise.

PART III

Imitating Size, Shape, and Color

5 ⚶ *The Hook Problem*

⚶ ⚶ ⚶ Ned Maguire had warned me, shaking his head at the thin shank of my hooks. "But," I whined, "that's the strongest dry-fly hook in the catalog. It's only one-X fine."

"So long as you don't find a trout that's one-X stout," said Ned, closing the subject.

I was, however, using finer leaders than could be found in Ireland in the early 1970s: two- and sometimes three-pound test. They had come from Amerikay, and I assumed that they—and not my hooks—were the weak link. My first couple of dozen trout were what Ned called tiddlers (but was ready enough to eat): three-quarters of a pound to a pound and a quarter. They did break some leaders, and they opened some hooks. I put the hook failures down to hitting a bone.

Why are some trout so much stronger than others? Condition is part of it. Skinny fish are weak, and that is what is misleading about our American habit of measuring by length. American anglers will lovingly return "seventeen-inchers" that are really degenerating cannibals weighing a pound and a quarter. I do it myself, but I know they should be fed to the raccoons, or to someone I do not like very much.

Even some well-conditioned fish are stronger than others. Only rarely do I get a really mean trout in Pennsylvania. A few western streams produce them. The Meath Blackwater fish in Ireland are almost all violent. Itchen trout are beautiful but seldom so tough.

I credit the pike. The best Irish streams are full of them. I have watched them stalking trout for long minutes, and the trout are amazingly relaxed about it. They clearly know what is going on behind them, whatever you may read about their blind spot. The pike, stealth showing in every fin, hugging the bottom, sneaks up within six feet—and the trout just swims a wide circle downstream and resumes picking off duns below Mr. Pike. He looks as foolish as the cat chasing the canary in those animated cartoons. But he goes on trying; he has no choice. Every few days, every few hundred stalks, he must surprise a trout too intent on tipping up for the next mayfly. I have caught numerous Irish trout with toothmarks. This kind of thing would not be allowed in a proper British chalkstream. But it produces lovely trout.

What the Irish trout learn from pike is to dash instantly upstream, when startled, for preselected hides under weeds or banks. If you want the fish, there is no playing him for long, pipe-smoking minutes. You hold him in the few yards available before he can reach shelter. He is yours shortly, or he is gone. He is not drowned like a long-teased fish; you can release him in top shape after a minute's recuperation.

You wait so long, work so hard. Then persistence turns to violence for a few seconds. You get everything right, or you stand shaking and empty. Nowhere else since early adolescence have I been aware of trembling when it was over.

So now you know the secret of Irish fishing. They are not the world's biggest trout, and certainly not the most numerous. They are the best: the ones that burn through your layers to a hairy man heaving his spear at a mastodon, having to hit it deep on the first throw.

Enough of tiddlers. I would wait for the trout big enough to hide in the deep, still, pike-filled flats by day and run up to the edge of fast water for a feed at dusk. The island pool.

Later, at low water, I found a way to wade from the south bank to the island, through knee-deep muck and water at the top of chest-high waders. That first wet spring I had to settle for a long cast from the quaky shore, with only a foot or two of drag-free float and the ground trying to drift away underfoot.

Not a fish showed as the pink left the water, though I could hear smaller ones upstream mopping up the spent gnats—that silly term for the big spinners of the Greendrake.

When he came, at the edge of darkness, there was no mistake, no dainty pretense. A swirl eddied for seconds where a spinner had floated with one wing feebly cocked. Two more fast swirls. A blind man could have located the sucking noise. And I had a near-perfect fly: flat bunches of mottled hackle on each side of a dark thorax, with an abdomen of wound porcupine quill. The quill, unlike traditional dubbing or herl, catches the glossy white of the natural spinner and holds the color when wet.

The trout's erratic cruising pattern was aimed at filling a large stomach in minutes. When the rises were too close, I was afraid to cast. Too far, and I knew there would be drag. The middle of the cruising pattern was the only hope. But he did not always stop in the middle. As the trout rose far off, I began lazy false casts and waited. No more rises. Then suddenly a swirl almost too close. Had he seen my line against a half moon? Too late to worry. The fly dropped a yard above the swirl. And kept dropping through the surface as a second swirl opened. I tightened hard. He did not feel like a log; I never felt a trout that did. He felt like an angry alligator. I was glad he was swimming away from me.

The island was as far off as a fair shot at a mallard—say thirty-five yards. The trout went for the upstream tip, my line cutting water in a ruler-straight slash against a silver afterglow. With lots of room, I hooped the rod and felt confident. Ten yards, twenty yards, thirty, as fast as I write it. I let the fish pull the rod down so that I could increase the pressure to the leader's three-pound limit. It takes an awful fish to pull an honest three pounds under water, at the end of a run, with no jerks, against all of a spongy fly line and leader. I had no choice but to hold on; once around the island, the trout would snag the leader and break it with the first flip of his tail.

The last yard must have been pure line-stretch. But the leader held. I saw not even a swirl at the end, felt no pop of a tippet. The fly came back with its hook opened.

I had lost the best Irish trout I would ever hook. And I knew it was my fault.

Next day I got out my scales and began testing. Trout lost from weak hooks are trout that need not be lost.

In streams like most of those in eastern America, where the trout run smaller than we like to admit, hook strength is not the main problem. All a weak hook may do is lose the best fish of a season. Some philosophers can accept that. Day-in and day-out, the poor hooking ability of small hooks is more of a problem. Once a trout is well hooked on a tiny imitation, there is a good chance of landing the fish or breaking the leader. But many are never hooked; a confident rise often produces only a firm pull and a slack line.

One American angler, J. Edson Leonard, was delighted to quote a scientist who had opined that "the development of mankind can be measured by the improvements in his fish-hooks." If this is true, mankind has been on the way downhill since the 1930s. Many trout fishermen will already have arrived at this conclusion through less devious reasoning.

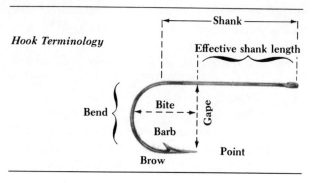

Hook Terminology

Neither of the leading hook problems—weakness or poor hooking ability—causes much trouble with wet-fly hooks. These solve the strength problem by using heavy wire. They also tend toward fairly long shanks, and this—as we shall see later—gives good hooking leverage in all but the worst of designs.

The hook problem, then, is almost reduced to a dry-fly problem. And it has three parts:

- First, the size of the hook, which we have to settle before we can measure anything else
- Second, the strength of the hook
- Finally, the hooking leverage, which is more difficult than the other measurements

The Problem of Size

What could be simpler than measuring a fishhook? Well, flying to the moon, for starters. We have done that, but we cannot agree on how big a trout hook is.

There have been numerous hook scales in our recorded history. Most of them, by the way, have been British, like the history of so much trout tackle. Jack Heddon, in his notes on Scotcher, has done more than anyone to sort the history out.

In the days of blind (eyeless) hooks, the makers apparently determined sizes by the *gape,* not the length of the hook. That made sense. Fly-tyers then often broke off the shanks to get the exact length they wanted. Only the gape remained constant.

My suspicion is that, for a long while, hook sizes were not held to tight standards. How could they have been? Until recently, hooks were made entirely by hand. Hooks bent around a peg by finger-power had to show variations. Today, with machine-formed hooks, there is less excuse. Makers have only the Alice-in-Wonderland logic that size 14 is anything they say it is.

In the late nineteenth century, there developed a standard scale that would eventually end the confusion—for a while. The point of its origin was Redditch, England, which dominated the hook-making trade. The scale was explicit and perfectly adapted to trout hooks. It still is. It measured length, not gape, and length is what we most need to know when selecting a hook to represent some insect. When using the Redditch Scale, the only way to make an error is to forget that it measures the length of the hook *less any eye.* That was logical in a scale meant for both blind and eyed hooks. The scale—adapted here from J. Edson Leonard—shows all you need to know.

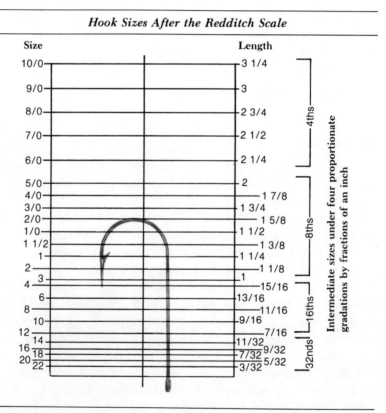

Hook Sizes After the Redditch Scale

The Redditch Scale of Hook Sizes American readers checking their hooks against the Redditch scale may find that they are using much longer sizes than they thought. The odds are that the hook being measured was made by the Mustad firm, which has dominated the market since World War II. This Norwegian company found a way to reduce production costs through new machinery. Prices are low. Shapes and strengths are adequate in the larger hooks, marginal in the small dry-fly models. Most important, the supply is enormous, so that dealers can catalog many sizes with confidence in keeping a stock. Except for fanatical fly-fishermen, most Americans these days are hardly aware of alternatives to Mustad hooks.

Mustad sizes, however, are peculiar. A recent book published by the firm shows no specific scale of sizes, and my inquiries have failed to produce one. My measurements of Mustad trout-hooks in model 94840 show that a size 10 is generally accurate on the Redditch Scale, but that a Mustad size 14 is actually a size 12. A size 20 is a true 17, and a size 28 is only a size 21. If you have been reading English books, or American ones a few years old, you may have been puzzled at what seemed to be the big hooks in use. Now you know they were not that big. But authors who have been repeating old patterns have been unintentionally confusing their readers.

I suppose two things happened: (1) Anglers love to think they are using fine leaders and small hooks. Manufacturers have cooperated by taking 2X nylon and labeling it 4X. What is not so widely known is that they have also been taking size 12 hooks and labeling them size 14. (2) Mustad hooks are (to some unspecified extent) sized by the ancient measurement of gape, rather than by length. Otherwise, a hook could not be described as "size 16, 4X long." It would have to be called a "size 12, 4X narrow gape."

The main problem of sizing by gape is that *there is no international scale* available to guide us. One could be worked out, but the measurements would be three times as difficult to take (because gapes average three times smaller than length). And when we knew the gape, we would still have to take a separate measurement of the length so that we would know which hook to pick for the March Brown beside our fly-tying vise.

There is more. A random sample of Mustad hooks in my fly-tying kit produces a "size 12, 4X long" hook that is much longer than a standard size 8. (They ought to have the same length.) The same "size 12, 4XL" is larger in all dimensions, including gape, than a standard size 12. (The gapes should be identical.)

It adds up to this: nowadays you cannot be sure what an author is recommending when he talks about a size 16 hook. We need a scale with *precise, stated measurements,* so we can know what we are buying without carrying a ruler. My preference would be to stay with the old Redditch Scale, which has both a comfortable patina and the information we need. This proposal will not be widely accepted; it is too radical or too fussily traditional (take your choice). Probably we shall have to describe hook length by millimeters, as we already do for natural insects. In that case, let's include the eye, making measurement by calipers easy. Manufacturers catering to us cranks will also be able to specify gape, though in this case millimeter steps may be too large. I don't like the sound of a "10 by 4 mm hook," but at least I'll know what I'm buying.

Hook Strength

Strength can be measured almost as easily in hooks as in leaders, and there is just as much need for a hook that is labeled for "pounds test." Hook-makers will, however, like this even less than my previous suggestion about hook sizes. For now, you will have to rely on my amateur tests or your own.

The important thing is that hook strength must be measured under the *worst normal* conditions, so that we really know the strength that can be counted on. Few hooks will yield, for example, if they penetrate fully in the fish's mouth. On the other

hand, leverage on the hook is much worse if it catches in a hard part of the mouth by the point only. In this case, failures are common.

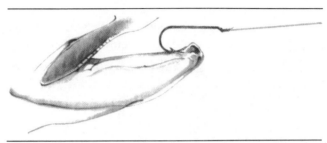

Hooks can be tested under moderately high-stress conditions by using a board that will let the hook catch but not penetrate beyond the barb. This closely approximates the hard parts of a trout's mouth. George Scotcher recommended a similar test in about 1809, though without precise weights or a scale. A hook must

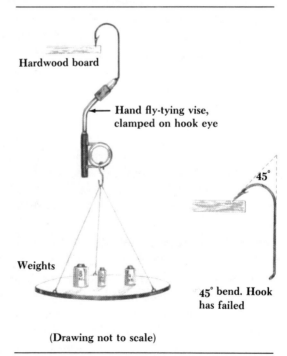

Hardwood board

Hand fly-tying vise, clamped on hook eye

45°

Weights

45° bend. Hook has failed

(Drawing not to scale)

be considered to have failed when it breaks or springs open far enough to allow a fish to escape. I have set this angle at 45 degrees, at which point it is easy to see how the hook could slide out of the fish's jaw.

Now, it hardly need be said that this hook-testing apparatus is primitive. A more accurate one could easily be worked out from, for example, a thread-testing machine. A major manufacturer might want to do this. My impression is that the margin of error in my simple gadget is acceptable, considering the even wider variations that often are found in the strengths of hooks from the same box. It would obviously be misleading to suggest double-digit accuracy.

The strengths of some of the hooks tested are shown in the table of "Dry-Fly Hook Strengths and Weights" (pp. 96-7). In comparing hook strengths, it is important to use the column that shows actual Redditch sizes, not labeled sizes. For example, the Mustad hooks labeled size 16 are actually size 14. They should be compared with the Partridge Code A in Redditch size 14. The "strength" and "weight" columns show that the Partridge is about half again heavier and three times stronger.

Some caution should be used in interpreting the results for any given hook. They were based on a sample of one box only, not on a statistically valid choice from numerous batches. Other batches might give different results.

Hooks with springy temper (mentioned in the last column of the table) might lose fish without showing any permanent deformation. All of us have lost heavy fish on the strike, after a good hard pull, and then found our fly and leader intact. I now prefer a hook that is tempered to break before bending far.

Other Comments on the Tests

- The strength of the hooks tested was not always proportionate to their size, as it should have been. Manufacturers naturally use finer wire for smaller hooks. On the other hand, a decrease in the size of the gape slightly strengthens the hook. Sometimes the two factors cancel out. Ideally, each size of hook should be a little weaker than the next larger size, since anglers are forc-

ed to use finer leaders for smaller flies. But I do not think that
any hook in size 14 should test less than two-and-a-half pounds.

- The English hooks tested did appear to use a stronger wire
than the Norwegian hooks. (The Partridge Company claims to
use a stronger steel.) Even so, the English hooks labeled "3X
Fine" or "4X Fine" were too weak for those strong trout. We
still have to look for a wise compromise between strength and
weight.

- The small dry-fly hooks now on the market are often the weakest link in our tackle, yielding even before our leaders.

Logically, there should be some relationship between hook
strength and leader strength. I was deceiving myself, for example,
when using a stout four- or five-pound-test tippet with a hook that
would open on a two-pound pull. In the end I usually settled for
a three-pound-test tippet and a standard-weight Partridge hook,
which in size 14 would take more than a three-pound pull. A
four-pound-test tippet still did not open the Partridge hooks, perhaps because they were strong enough to guarantee full penetration almost anywhere in a trout's mouth.

Leaders may need an extra margin of strength. The margin
depends on the type of fishing. Under prolonged casting, the vulnerable spot in a leader is just in front of the hook knot. A break
at this point shows that the problem is "hinging" under casting
stress. The effect is minor when casting a small fly deliberately
over a rising fish, as I was doing in Ireland. Hinging becomes
important when making repeated "blind" casts on a rapid stream
with a large hair-wing Royal Coachman. Under such conditions it
could make sense to use a three- or even a four-pound-test leader
with the usual Mustad size 14 hook (which is actually a size 12 and
is likely to open at less than two pounds of pull).

Hooking Leverage

Hooking qualities depend on two factors: gape and length of
shank. Using these factors, it is possible to calculate hooking leverage. In doing so, however, it must be noted that only the portion

Dry-Fly Hook Strengths and Weights

Identification	Size (Labeled)	Size (Actual)
Mustad #94840, down-eyed	12	11
Same	14 Extra Fine	12
Same	16 Extra Fine	14
Same	18 Extra Fine	16
Mustad #94842, up-eyed	20 Extra Fine	17
Mustad #94833, down-eyed	16, 3X Fine	14
Viellard-Migeon & Cie. (France)	16	18
Wright & McGill style 1225 "keel" hook	16	11
Partridge "keel" (upside down) hook	14	12
Partridge Code A "Wide-Gape Trout" 2X-Fine	14	14
	15	16
	16	18
Partridge Code L2A "Capt. Hamilton" 2X-Fine	14	14
Orvis (and Tiemco) Dry Fly Hook (Japanese)	14	12
	18	15
	20	16

Weight (grains)	Approximate Strength (ounces)	Comments
0.60	54	Fair shape for hooking in sizes larger
0.36	29	than 20. Point a little too long. Flat
		shank. Springy temper; most hooks
0.26	23	opened rather than breaking. Weak in
0.15	19	sizes 14 through 18
0.12	25	
0.18	15	
0.14	14	Soft wire in the batch tested
0.48	14	Very soft wire in the batch tested
0.42	45	Strong and well made
0.40	71	Sproat bend, not forged. Good shape,
0.26	40	temper, and finish. Heavier than
		most dry-fly hooks, but strength is
0.22	43	exceptional.
0.43	64	About the same weight and strength as the Code A, but with round bend. Flat-forged. Also available in lighter wire.
0.43	30	Similar in weight and strength to Mustad 94840, but with finer barb and short, sharp point. Springy
0.22	28	temper. Flat-forged.
0.17	25	

of the shank and eye *in front of the point of the hook* can exert any leverage. We might call this the "effective shank length." This is the only new term in the accompanying illustrations. For simplicity, that showing the gape/shank relationship shows a ring-eyed hook.

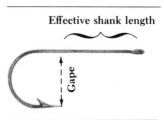

Effective shank length

Gape

Whether or not the hook point initially contacts the fish's mouth depends mainly on the absolute width of the gape. The wider the gape (within reason), the more likely the hook is to make contact. After initial contact, however, whether or not the hook penetrates depends on the *ratio* between gape and shank length. A wide gape is now a disadvantage, since it causes an indirect pull on the point. The angle of pull is best illustrated in the "parallelogram of forces" beloved of old angling writers and shown here.

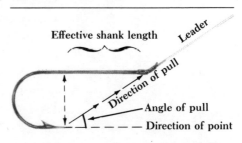

Effective shank length   Leader

Direction of pull

Angle of pull

Direction of point

It will be obvious that penetration improves as the pull on a hook gets more closely in line with the point (in other words, as the angle of pull decreases). Penetration can thus be improved by narrowing the gape or lengthening the shank. If the shank is infinitely long, the pull is direct and the penetration as good as possible. On the other hand, if the shank ends exactly above the point of the hook, there is zero penetrating power (by this measurement). Some very-short-shanked hooks on the market are almost this bad. With them, it is virtually impossible to hook a trout unless he obliges by pressing the hook down by the top of the bend —which may happen, but is hardly to be relied upon. Hooks with zero penetrating power may, however, be reliable for bait fishing, where the hook is swallowed. In this case, pressure on the top of the hook from the fish's gullet will ensure penetration. Even a thorn gorge from a bush will hook fish if swallowed. It does not trouble me to call this "zero penetrating power," but the reader should understand that penetration may occur in ideal circumstances.

If the effective shank length is exactly equal to the width of the gape, the hooking leverage is one to one (and the angle of pull 45 degrees). Hooking leverage is illustrated for three hooks.

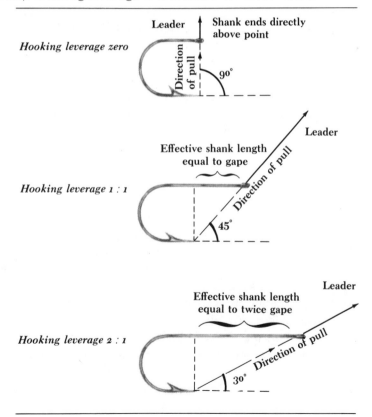

There is no way except experience to show exactly how much hooking leverage is enough. The hardness of a fish's mouth affects the outcome. But trout mouths do not vary enormously; probably the differences in hardness within the mouth of an individual are greater than the differences between the mouths of any two trout. (A hard-mouthed fish like the South American Dorado is something else entirely.) My own experience is that minimum leverage for adequate hooking power in trout is just about one-and-a-half to one. In other words, the effective shank length should be about half again greater than the gape. This is easy for an angler to measure roughly.

As already noted, the leverage of a hook can be improved by narrowing the gape. But this is only practical for relatively large hooks. Minimum gape must be determined by experience, and it depends on the average size and strength of the trout to be caught. For normal stream fishing, we might, for example, decide that there is no great advantage in a gape bigger than that of an average size 14 hook. If we are tying an imitation requiring a hook larger than size 14, we could then use a longer-shanked hook rather than one that is bigger in all dimensions. This is common practice, especially in America, although the reason usually cited for choosing long-shanked hooks is to increase the accuracy of the imitation rather than the hooking leverage.

In small hooks, absolute gape width is critical and should be kept as large as possible in relation to the shank (up to the limits of the one-and-a-half to one ratio). In other words, the proportions should vary with the hook size. This has been the practice with some good hookmakers.

There have been many attempts to improve hooking qualities without changing gape and shank length. For small fly-hooks, the most useful modification seems to be a slight shortening of the point, which increases the effective shank length. Short-point hooks also often use a Sproat bend, which has more bite than a round bend. Additionally, the barb can be reduced in size, which makes it more likely that the hook will penetrate to its full bite. The Sproat bend has the further advantage of decreasing the radius of curvature at the top of the bend, which is the weakest spot in a hook that has penetrated fully. The gain in strength is minor, but the hooking leverage is definitely better.

Average round bend, long point hook

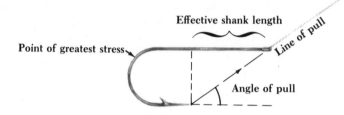

Sproat bend, short point, small barb hook

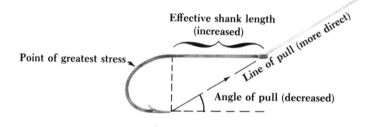

The disadvantage of the Sproat bend is that it exposes a lot of hook in relation to the size of the fly, perhaps making the imitation less effective. At the opposite extreme is the old square bend, which showed almost no hook behind the body of the fly. These were Skues' favorite nymph hooks, and if they were still available, they would still be excellent for this purpose. But a bend with a sharp angle at the top would demand strong wire.

Three shapes of a more radical nature are shown on the next page, not to scale. Many more unusual hooks could be presented. Such devices are favorites of inventors and have been appearing frequently since the mid-nineteenth century.

The "claw" hook with the in-turned point has its point bent almost directly into the line of pull, increasing the efficiency of penetration. Unfortunately, this has the effect of permitting the brow to mask the hook point—an effect well understood since at least the turn of the century. Old Limerick hooks and many other nineteenth-century hooks often had a moderately deep brow, but the point itself was not bent in sharply. The deep brow must not have been a fatal defect in a salmon hook, which had a wide gape to begin with. Even so, many anglers considered this design a disadvantage. Modern trout hooks with sharply in-turned points are generally considered suitable only for bait-fishing, where the hook is swallowed.

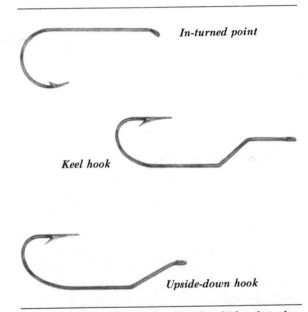

In-turned point

Keel hook

Upside-down hook

The accomplishment usually claimed for the "keel" hook is that it reduces snagging on obstacles. Dry flies, however, can be effectively "weed-proofed" by use of a hackle, and for them a more important function of the keel hook is to keep the point upright, out of the water and less visible to the fish. This is very useful when it can be done without reducing hooking power. The keel hook is therefore a thoughtful advance. While a very similar design was pictured by J. H. Keene before 1886, it has only recently been promoted by anyone aware of its possibilities. Unfortunately the design depends for gape on a length that is excessive for normal imitative flies. The smallest American keel hook now available is marked 16, but has the shank length of a normal size 11 and is of soft wire. Since I rarely use a fly this large, I have not given the design an adequate test.

A new Partridge hook on the market is aimed at helping even a small fly land upside down—or point-up. This hook is well made and has good hooking geometry in medium (but not very small) sizes. If wings are added, the fly will almost always land point-up, as intended. Some winged designs mentioned in chapter 10 will, in fact, make even a normal hook land point-up, and I have experimented with such flies. The drawback is that, in my experience, any kind of wings near the gape of a small hook create a fly that is likely to go fishless as well as weedless. But the new hook will sometimes land point-up even with hackle flies, especially if the tail is cocked well up (toward the point of the hook). In this case, the angler has improved his chances of rising a fish without in return giving up a good chance of hooking it.

Today, of course, virtually all hooks are eyed. This introduces some complications in hook design and in leader-to-hook knots. For a long time after eyed hooks became popular, most knots were tied directly on the shank of the hook, after the gut leader was first passed through the eye. Hook eyes were turned up or down to accommodate knots of this kind (like the Turle knot). But since the leader came almost directly from the shank, the effect on hook geometry was limited. The strongest convenient knots we now know attach to the eye itself rather than the shank. The geometry is then altered substantially (see illustration on the next page).

The turned-down eye actually narrows the angle of pull and improves the penetrating qualities of a hook. In our very first angling book, Dame Juliana advised tying the line to the bottom of the shank, though she did not explain why.

The turned-up eye is sometimes used to keep the eye from obstructing the gape of a hook. In very small hooks, this may be a consideration, but such small hooks also have (or should have) a slightly wide gape, so that their hooking leverage is precarious to begin with. A turned-up eye can make such hooks hopelessly inefficient. What is then needed is an eye that is *slightly* turned down and very small.

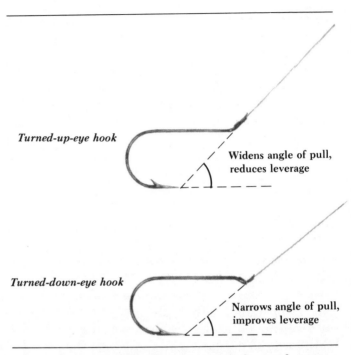

Readers may suspect that these are theoretical considerations, not very important in real fishing. So did I. For some time, I used short-shank, up-eyed, gilt-plated hooks for my dry Spiders, blaming my poor hooking average on the large hackles or the way in which trout took the fly.

Then came an invitation to go fishing with a wealthy lawyer who owned a private stream within commuting distance—by airplane —of our nation's capital. The host flew in a couple of dozen of us. Of that group, about a quarter preferred the stream to the Southern Comforts. I was among the moral minority.

The stream was lovely in the high water of April. Big pools— some artificially constructed—separated stretches of pocket water. The water must have come close to disappearing every August, because the only wild fish in it were brookies four or five inches long. When fishing for them palled, I caught some of the fresh-stocked rainbows in the pools. They were plentiful, puzzled, and hungry. A weighted nymph fished like a worm took more than I wanted in half an hour. I was unable to talk to them: they had not learned even pidgin troutese.

The only thing left was to sit on a high rock and eat my lunch. I idly flipped a few bits of sandwich to the trout milling below. They would take anything that sank: salami, cheese, or pellets of bread. Only lettuce or floating bread were ignored.

Then came the best idea of the day. I cut the hackle off one Spider, sunk it in a bit of sandwich, and drifted it to the fish. One twelve-inch rainbow took it instantly. My tug turned him sideways for a second, but the hook came free. In the next hour I had perhaps twenty visible takes, but only three resulted in hooked fish. I was trying to give the fish time to get the hook well into their mouths but not into their stomachs. The idea, of course, was to test hooking ability, not to fill a creel. (Those fish would have been scarcely worth cooking.) Having a problem to solve made all the fun.

The last step was to strip a normal down-eyed wet fly and impale my bits of salami on its size 12 hook. The trout took the new hook just as well, and my hooking average improved dramatically. It seemed to be in the vicinity of 80 or 90 percent. In my mind, at least, the experiment left little doubt; I have tied no flies on extra-short-shank hooks since.

In my experience, a hook-point bent to one side (kirbed or reversed) does not seem to catch more fish than a point in line with the shank, except perhaps in the smallest hooks. On the other hand, a minor offset of the point does no real harm. A pronounced offset is troublesome, twisting fine leaders in the air and making wet flies "swim" badly. Even at some risk of weakening the bend, I straighten such points in the vise before starting to tie the fly.

This account has omitted some factors in hook design and passed lightly over others. There has been no discussion of flat-forged shanks, which present a dubious advantage, or of fine points and barbs, which are of obvious importance. Conclusions are that a good dry-fly hook would have these characteristics:

- An honest three-pound-test strength, by worst-case test, preferably stated on the package, for a size 14 hook (less strength for smaller hooks)
- An effective shank length about half again greater than the gape in small hooks, and a still longer shank in the larger sizes
- The least weight possible consistent with adequate strength
- Very limited spring or softness in the wire
- Careful finish, with special attention to tempering, avoidance of weak spots in the bend, a neat barb, a closed eye, and a point that requires minimal touch-up sharpening
- An eye that is small and turned down slightly
- A short point with a small barb

These requirements should not be too tough if we anglers are willing to pay for quality. Prewar Hardy hooks were close to ideal, though a little heavy. Today's Partridge Code A hook is similar. To my taste the standard wire is a little too heavy, and the "4X Fine" is a little too light. A true size 14 hook of .25 grains would be about right.

It would be nice to see the old square-bends on the market again, although the wire and workmanship would have to be top-class.

The real breakthrough in hook design would require a stronger wire. The best of what we now have seems about what it was sixty years ago: not bad, but not the kind of thing engineers put in moon rockets. A true size 14 weighing .18 grains and testing three pounds would make more difference at the trout's end than any amount of miracle fibers in fly rods.

6 ✾ *Fly Size*

Including Weight and Buoyancy

✾ ✾ ✾ Slough Creek trout, being supernatural, do unearthly things. I have seen them disappear in August when the stream is low. As a boy, I could walk up a mile of it and not see a fish. In some miles there was nowhere to hide—just open gravelly runs and transparent pools. Then all of a sudden, when the sun left the water, there would be a boiling rise. I would waste the brief opportunity with the wrong flies. There is nothing very surprising in bad fishing by a fourteen-year-old, but at least I had good eyes and knew how to see fish. No wonder I suspected that I had levitated out of Yellowstone Park and was playing by different rules.

Today, with catch-and-release fishing, there are too many trout in Slough Creek for them to disappear totally. I think. But on the last visit, they had thought of something else surrealistic.

The little tent was back in the woods at the end of six miles of trail. Evening had started to cool the meadows, which looked exactly as they had in Jim Bridger's time. A family of coyotes yipped after a jackrabbit in the hills. A badger paused to stare at me in his stripy, nearsighted way, then waddled down a burrow. A minute later, on my way to the river, I stopped to watch a small weasel undulating around the base of an extinct hot-springs cone. Then we both saw a ground squirrel soaking up the last of the day's heat on top of a big boulder. The weasel slipped up on the rock and blocked the only easy escape route.

I waited for a wilderness drama, but it came out backwards. The ground squirrel bristled and moved toward the weasel, which turned and ran away. So much for that ruthlessly efficient, bloodthirsty predator.

There was, however, drama enough when I reached the river. Big craneflies were chasing each other across the water and grappling ecstatically on damp patches of shore and island. The larvae, I guessed, had hatched from that moist environment. A moderate breeze bowled the clumsy insects along the surface, and the trout made fools of themselves. Fine, glistening cutthroats slashed and leaped from the water. The water did not merely boil, it splashed out on the banks. Where else do these things happen?

Obviously the time for a Skater. In my haste, three knots came out wrong, but the rise—or commotion—went on. Easy fishing. I popped the fluffball out beyond a trout in midstream, pulling the fly back like a clumsy cranefly. Instant results—if you count excitement. I have never risen so many fish in such a short time. Finally hooked several and landed two. By way of consolation, I noticed that the fish were also missing most of the naturals.

Soon the evening cooled and the craneflies decided to get down to business with their mates, or at least to pursue them without the vulgar display. The fishing also settled down. Size 16 duns started to hatch. The rise was worth the hike: trout making neat bubbles up and down the river, and not another fisherman in sight. Every fish I covered rose, and every rise produced a throbbing weight. A perfect evening rise is in itself a pretty unreal experience.

The summer rise on the Pennsylvania limestone streams is a contrast, to say the least. It happens shortly after dawn. For years, most people did not bother with it. The word had not got around. The flies are almost too small to see in the air—Vince Marinaro has called them "The Hidden Hatch"—and for centuries they were beyond the cognizance of mere humans. But they were never hidden from the trout.

They are *Tricorythodes* mayflies: extremely abundant and correspondingly tiny. Fifty would not make up the bulk of one big cranefly. Since Marinaro wrote about them, they have sold a lot of hooks in sizes 22 through 28 (really 19 through 21 in Redditch sizes). The fishing is uniquely frustrating, which is also to say uniquely fun. You can cast feverishly over a rising trout for minutes without realizing that your half-pound-test tippet has broken on a bit of grass back in the meadow. In the heat of the summer, you have only an hour or so. In September the hatch may go all morning.

I suppose I have tied three flies for every trout I have caught on the *Tricorythodes.* Not all the flies were lost in the grass or in the fish; many simply did not work well. Some that rose fish were terrible hookers. One day just last summer, I rose five nice browns, tightened in good time, and felt only a brief tug. I was trying a new ring-eye hook. As the sun warmed, I changed to a hook with an eye that I had bent slightly down and a point that I had bent off to the side. It still did not hook really well, but it landed two fish before the rise ended. Then a much bigger nymph easily got two more, and they were the best of the day. With this hatch, it pays to look for a couple of still-hungry trout hoping for crippled nymphs at the end of the main action. Seems almost like cheating, but it can do wonders for wounded pride. The trout's selectivity diminishes when the fly gets a few inches under water.

Compare my Slough Creek Skaters or Pennsylvania *Tricory-thodes* to a box of traditional dry flies. Again we must turn to the mother islands for our example, because until the last few decades, it has been hard to find a history of imitative fly-fishing elsewhere.

A turn-of-the-century fly box usually had a few big Greendrakes and Greydrakes tucked into a corner. I never saw Greendrake fishing anything like as mad as that evening on Slough Creek, but perhaps such rises occurred elsewhere in more innocent times. Anglers complained that the trout were nervous about the big mayflies, and that there was a lot of splashing and missing. Certainly today the fish are slow to get interested in Greendrakes on either side of the Atlantic, and slower to take artificial flies solidly.

Old fly boxes had no really small flies at all. Admittedly, the British and Irish natural flies are uniform in size by comparison to the American variety, and the trout are less venturesome. (I never saw a dragonfly taken in Ireland except as a nymph.)

But the interesting point is that the traditional British imitations vary in size even less than their natural models. In their book of North Country wet flies, Edmonds and Lee show no patterns over one-fourth inch (six millimeters) in body length—not even the March Brown. Lures and other non-imitative flies (like most of the American patterns) have always been available in vast sizes, but the best imitative patterns have not. The North Country flies were fished in or near the surface film; trout "rose" to them rather than "striking" as in American books of the period. Today in America, flies like the old English wets are often called "emergers," which is more glamorous, like calling the game warden a "conservation officer." But by any name we can learn something about the problems of imitation from those sober old dressings on size 14 hooks.

Dry-fly history is shorter and thoroughly recorded. In his *Modern Development of the Dry Fly,* Halford showed only the Greendrakes and their spinners, plus a few sedges, on hooks larger than o on the "new scale." On the other hand, he gave no pattern smaller than size oo. Few authorities gave dressings below size ooo. The "new scale" is now obsolete (one hopes), but o is usually described as the equivalent of old size 15. New size ooo should be a conventional 17. It seems clear that, in the golden age of dry-fly fishing, Redditch sizes 14 to 17 did most of the work for most of the season.

There may be something to be learned from the fact that most early users of imitative flies settled on a narrow range of sizes. I suggest two tentative conclusions.

- First, at the large end of the scale, the trout's preferences seem to be the limiting factor. Selective, educated trout are more cautious about taking a big dry fly—say, anything over size 14 —than a small one. This applies to both naturals and artificials. Trout do accept big flies, but with more caution. In Ireland, I hate to see the fish switching from Black Gnats to Greendrakes in late May, even though a few more of the big, old fish may come up for the mayfly.

- My second suggestion is that, at the small end of the scale, the limiting factor has to do with human preferences rather than with those of the trout. Trout may prefer a size 16 dun to a size 24 midge, but they will take the midge readily when larger food is not available—and it very often is not. There is a great advantage in being able to fish with extra-small flies.

Since the problem of big flies is much the easier to work with, let us look at it first, and then at the small-fly problem.

In my experience, the designs that work well in small flies are not as good in very large ones. A bushy size 10 dry fly in the traditional style may work well for salmon, for wilderness trout, at night, or in lakes—but not for educated trout during daylight hours. Many unusual dressings have been tried for big flies. My own preference for big floating mayfly imitations is either a large variant or a bent-hackle fly, both of which are described in chapter 10. In both cases, there is a big sparse hackle and a relatively small hook, so that the fly rides lightly. For big down-winged flies like sedges, stoneflies, and grasshoppers, the hair-wing design described in chapter 11 seems hard to beat.

If the natural fly is medium-sized or a bit larger—say, a size 10 or 12—no special design is necessary, but you might try a hook on the small side. With mayflies, one can aim at imitating the smallest of hatching male duns rather than the larger females. A large dressing can also be put on a small hook. This disregards the classic proportion between hook and dressing. Commercial fly-tyers may observe this proportion to avoid frightening customers, but we anglers need worry about no such constraints when we are only concerned with impressing the fish.

For medium-small flies—say about size 16—the trout take standard-sized dressings well, and the hooks have good holding power. If the trout are particularly big and strong, there is the option of tying a small dressing on a large hook, which sacrifices some realism for better hooking power. If a bigger-than-usual hook is chosen, the standard dry-fly dressings with hackle at the front of the fly are not very good. Several of the designs shown in chapters 10 and 11 have the hackles (or hair) farther back toward the bend. Such designs do a better job of supporting the heavy bend of the hook.

With flies of a true (Redditch scale) size 18 and smaller, the real problems start. Traditionally, anglers almost ignored the small insects, calling them "smuts" and "curses." Where rises to them were fished at all, it was with a fly much too big and often fancy into the bargain.

I had thought that small flies were a problem only in America—until my weekend with the Small Dark Olive (*Baetis scambus*) on Ireland's river Suir. This was a very delicate little mayfly, as small as some of the *Tricorythodes*. A good imitation, on the Suir, required a size 20 or 22 Mustad hook, lightly dressed. The pattern I had tied from books on a size 18 Mustad was poor. I later found that traditional dressings for the *Caenis* mayflies and Black Gnats were also out of proportion.

There were few really small hooks available until the 1960s. This, in turn, probably had something to do with the fact that natural gut was seldom available in sizes that would suit a hook smaller than size 17. Even when extra-fine gut was available, it was likely to be weak. Leaders weaker than three-pound test—or two-pound, at the least—are hopeless when strong trout have access to weeds. (Much weaker tippets can be used where trout are weak or the water is weed-free.)

The best wet-fly fishermen used smaller flies than the dry-fly men. In the old fly-books I have seen, there were a few wet flies down to a size 18. A wet fly of this size can be tied directly to

.007-inch gut and still fish reasonably well, but a dry fly cannot. A wet fly can also be tied very sparsely, while a dry fly needs a minimum of material to make it float. Edmonds and Lee show a small Green Insect wet fly that occupies only half of a size 17 hook (000 in their description).

Technical developments have now made it possible to use much smaller flies. Synthetic leader material is quite satisfactory down to about .004 inches (.10 millimeters), testing at a fairly reliable one pound. This works with dry flies from Mustad sizes 18 through 22, depending on how lightly they are dressed. The true .003-inch (.075-millimeter) material available as this is written is inconsistent, but it does allow the use of fly sizes 22 through 28 (true 21). Small leader material will certainly continue to improve. Hook design has, in fact, almost become a worse problem.

Trout fishermen will continue pushing out the frontiers as rapidly as their materials allow. Anglers in eastern America have been especially innovative. They have to be: a lot of them are working on a few fish. During much of the season, those few fish are taking very small flies in low water under a bright sun. With few exceptions, the streams do not have as many weeds as the British and Irish limestone streams, so the trout are easier to play. It must also be admitted that a lot of the eastern American fish are puny specimens in both size and strength. Fine tackle has the advantage of introducing some suspense into the fight of even a ten-inch hatchery brown (or a skinny seventeen-inch kelt). More important, fine terminal tackle greatly increases the length of the fishing season and the challenge to the angler.

Many anglers profess the comforting belief that trout rising to small flies are not very selective. In defense of this idea, it has often been noted that midging trout will even hit leader knots.

It would save me a lot of trouble if I could be convinced of this theory, but the truth is that I have just as often found trout selective with small flies as with large ones. Leader knots are actually a pretty good imitation of the pupae of reed smuts, and perhaps of some other diptera. When those Pennsylvania browns are on the tiny *Tricorythodes,* fancy flies are just about hopeless except at the beginning of the hatch (or for nymphs). And I shall not soon forget standing in Colorado's South Platte River through several hatches of tiny mayflies—without getting one fish solidly. The right hatching nymph would probably have worked, but I did not have it, and the fish happily rejected size 24 dries on .003-inch tippets.

Unfortunately, even though fish may be selective to size 24 flies, fishermen cannot (as a practical proposition) tie complicated dressings in these sizes. Even the operation of tying in wings tends to make small flies pudgy. My own preference is to use simple hackle flies whenever possible in these tiny sizes. There is room to manipulate the hackle: it can, for example, be clipped on the bottom, placed back at the bend of the hook, or flattened into a bunch at each side of the hook. A soft, non-poultry hackle can be used to represent hatching flies. A hackle wound parachute-style, without wings, is also effective in small sizes. Apparently wings of small flies do not stand up high enough above the surface to be conspicuous to the trout.

Sparse Versus Thick Dressings

Flies tied with thick hackles, tails, and bodies are often called "heavily dressed." In terms of weight, however, they are only moderately heavy (feathers and even hair weigh little in proportion to hooks). I am using terms like "thick" and "bushy" to avoid confusion with real weight.

Traditional British wet flies, for stream-fishing, were usually small, as already mentioned, and also sparse. North Country wet flies are still remarkable for their simplicity and elegance. They are intended to sink, but only a little, and to represent frail insects. Exactly what stage they represent is still arguable. Drowned duns and spinners may sometimes be important, but emerging duns (and other insects) are more frequently of interest to the trout.

Early American wet flies were larger—of necessity—and also more thickly dressed. There are exceptions to this, but the generality seems fair. These sinking flies resembled the gaudy lake flies and sea-trout flies of the mother countries. My guess is that flies of the new country were usually fished downstream, as lures or attractors. (Those interested in more detailed history will not wish to pass up *The American Fly Fisher,* a periodical published by the Museum of American Fly Fishing in Manchester, Vermont.)

A strange design reversal came about when dry flies evolved on the chalkstreams. English floating flies became a bit plump and thickly dressed (always generalizing). They had to accommodate a lot of hackle on a small hook, and they had some other problems:

- There was no fly-flotant for a while, so the hackle had to do the job of flotation with little help.
- Mr. Halford wanted to break sharply with wet-fly precedents. He was not interested in what we call "emergers" today. The flies had to float high, no mistake.
- Hooks were moderately heavy, as they had to be for fat trout in the weeds.

Catskill dry flies were taken from British models and were almost identical in design terms. Theodore Gordon found excellent hatches; some Catskill streams still have them. He also found insects larger than most of those in the chalk waters. On a medium-large hook, the hackle and wings of Gordon's flies looked more sparse and left the fly with a more pronounced shape. But Gordon was also a man with a sense of line. This is clear from dressings of his that are still available.

The Catskill flies stayed elegantly sparse for a long time. See those tied in the 1930s by Reuben R. Cross and illustrated in his *Complete Fly Tier.*

But Americans soon became, and stayed for years, much more interested in "pounding up" fast-water fish than in imitation. La Branche and Bergman fixed the trend. Lee Wulff carried it about as far as it can go. Fast-water, blind fishing with the dry fly is very important in most of America, much more important than upstream wet-fly fishing. Thick dressings and fine hooks help to float flies cast repeatedly on a torrent.

The Catskill-type flies are still tied. They float reasonably well in fast water and are also effective on still pools. With care, in fact, the thin dressing can be put on a small hook, and this design works as well on the Itchen as on the Beaverkill. To take an extreme example: the famous Royal Coachman has always been my idea of a fancy fly, but when tied lightly, it gets so many fish that I wonder. Perhaps Preston Jennings was right in considering it imitative. For visibility, one can add to it a *thin* wing of white calftail without overloading the dressing.

The most telling criticism of sparse dressings is that they make the hook appear prominent. That is a hard problem to beat in assembling a small fly for a large trout. See, however, the reverse-tied fly described in chapter 10.

The thick dressings will also be used as long as there are trout to tease up in fast water. Oddly enough, most such flies are still tied like overstuffed mayfly imitations, complete with long tail. But mayflies are the only important naturals with a tail, and it is a light one. The long hair-tails often used on bushy dry flies must appear to the fish as body extensions. Possibly the bushy mayfly designs are fair representations of big sedges and stoneflies, but this was never intended, and there are better designs available for the occasions when it is necessary to imitate big down-winged flies (chapter 11). To say that a fly is overdressed is also to say that it uses a small hook, and such a hook is bound to be inefficient for strong trout, if there are any about.

Weight

The question of weight is obviously related to fly size, but it could as well have been examined under behavior. Weight is, in fact, one of the most important factors influencing behavior, since it has a lot to do with the level at which an artificial fly fishes.

Every now and then, I have a wave of suspicion that trout fishermen in general, and this one in particular, are really quite mad. One time when the feeling crept over me I was weighing a batch of duns. Has anyone else ever tried it? For the record, these were Large Dark Olives *(Baetis rhodani),* which are the main early-season flies in Ireland and remarkably similar in size and appearance to early-season American mayflies of entirely different genera. I weighed a number of olives in a light container, then evicted them and weighed the container separately. The duns averaged roughly .5 grains each. Winged imitations on extra-light-wire (3X-fine) size 16 Mustad hooks weighed 1.3 grains each, or about two-and-a-half times as much as the natural. One could tie a slightly lighter fly, but the hook on this one was already much too weak for the fish I was catching.

My conclusion was that even a sparse traditional imitation with a normal-sized hook in it must be much heavier than the natural. (Flies with extra-large hackles are proportionately lighter, but are not suitable for hatching duns or for small flies of any kind; see chapter 10.) Any way to reduce weight without increasing size or losing strength would be welcome. But there is not much hope. Hooks are the heaviest component of a fly, and even the 1X-fine Mustad hooks are not suitable for heavy, wild fish.

So we start the process of dry-fly design with a serious handicap —one that mocks any pretense of "exact imitation": natural aquatic flies are roughly the density of water; our imitations are three or four times as heavy. This must complicate efforts to imitate natural behavior.

Nature does, however, provide us with two assistants: surface tension and buoyancy. These assistants do not work well together. The design of flies to make use of surface tension is very different from the design of flies with naturally buoyant materials. This relationship is not widely understood—I have not seen it mentioned at all in the books consulted—so some explanation seems necessary.

Surface Tension

Since most of our flies are heavier than water but nevertheless float, surface tension is our most frequent ally. Most of us probably learned about it in a science class early in our school years. The teacher showed us that a needle, which is obviously much heavier than water, will be supported at the surface if placed on water carefully in a horizontal position. Once the needle breaks through the surface, of course, it sinks rapidly.

A dry fly that rides at a normal height (like the first design in chapter 10) is usually supported by surface tension on:

- The rear part of the body
- Most of the tail
- A few hackle fibers slightly below the side of the body (the ones entirely underneath the surface do not help the float)

Low-floating flies (also described in chapters 10 and 11) are usually supported by all of the body and tail, plus a few hackle fibers that protrude horizontally from the hook. Some low-floating flies are supported only by the hackle, with body and tail submerged. Wings can also be designed to float the rest of the fly.

A really high-riding fly must be very light in relation to its size. This means that hook and body will be small (as in American Spiders and Skaters, chapter 10), while the hackle and tail will be long. The fly can then be supported at its head by the surface tension of a few hackle fibers. The fibers at the very bottom of the fly will still penetrate the water, doing little work, but fibers a little further up will bend back at their points and be supported at the surface. The tail will also help substantially. But the fact remains that even such a fly is heavier than water. Like the needle, it will sink (slowly) when surface tension is broken.

This leaves us with a paradox: our highest-riding and lightest fly (in proportion to its size) is designed of materials that are much heavier than water when weighed individually. But they are small and light enough to work with surface tension. The important thing is not to interfere by bad design. Hackle points should not be clipped; when blunt and stiff they penetrate the surface more easily. Decorations that add unnecessary weight must be avoided.

Incidentally, I am not arguing here that high-floating flies are the best. That is a common belief, but it is not mine. On the contrary, I have found extra-high-floating flies to be useful less often than some others. But occasionally they are needed, and an understanding of their design is helpful for other flies too.

Buoyancy

There is an entirely different way to float flies: by using materials
that are individually buoyant, such as cork and hollow hair. Such
materials must float until waterlogged. Even if they are submerged, they will return to the surface. But the total weight of
these buoyant materials is much greater than that of a few turns
of hackle. Flies made with buoyant materials will therefore float
a long time *at* the surface, but are not easily supported *high above*
the surface by hackle points. Hackles do their work only before
they penetrate the surface, while buoyant materials work best
when almost submerged. This is a point that must be understood
thoroughly in designing flies. It is frequently written that deer's
hair, being hollow and light, is perfect for high-floating flies. This
is a basic error. Paradoxical as it may seem, *buoyant materials
make for low-floating flies.* Thus, while there is lots of nice deer
hair suitable for wings on low-floating flies, there is not much sense
in mixing it with hackle unless imitations of legs are needed. Occasionally we do need bushy, low-riding flies—as for imitations of
large swimming sedges.

Absorbency and Stiffness

Traditional wet flies, which drift just under the surface, depend
on soft, water-absorbing materials to sink, rather than on any especially heavy weight in the hook or elsewhere. Soft hackles from
birds other than roosters are normally used. It is possible to float
such flies for a few casts, and dry-fly fishing may have got started
in this way. Today, if a tail of hackle fibers is added, and if the
materials are waterproofed with fly-flotant, the traditional "wet
fly" stays right in the surface film. To my mind, this is an excellent
choice for imitations of flies at the level between "wet" and "dry."

As already noted, a fly can also be made to float low in the surface
film by omitting hackle entirely. Wings are then used to give the
right shape and (in the case of hollow hair) to provide some buoyancy. In the case of upright wings, stiffness again comes into ques-

tion: tall, stiff wings can make the fly a "bad hooker," simply because it does not get into the trout's mouth. A stiff tail or extended body is worse yet. Even long rooster hackles may occasionally get in the way. For the most part, however, the cock's hackle is something of a miracle fiber: water-resistant, weightless, soft enough to be sucked into a trout's mouth, and stiff enough to keep shape. Where materials stiffer than hackle are used, they should not be allowed to get very far from the shank. There is no problem in using stiff hair on flies that have short, flat wings, like sedges and stoneflies. There is a very real problem when stiff hair or feathers are used for high wings or for long tails on mayfly imitations.

Once I designed a female Red Spinner with long tails of stiff hackle-stem. She was a thing of beauty. Male spinners broke their hearts over her. So did I. One day she seemed to rise every trout in an Irish stream for me. She did not hook one of them until I cut her tails off. Then I quickly landed two fish—and the rise stopped.

If a sinking fly is given soft hackles, one caution is needed: they do their job well only on upstream casts. Fished downstream, soft hackles mat, cling to the body, and lose their life.

At one time, dry flies had to be made of very water-resistant materials. These still help, but they are no longer essential; modern fly-flotants will waterproof almost anything for a while. One quick method of waterproofing is to rub a bit of line dressing or other grease on the fly. This works surprisingly well and does not mat the fly as much as one would think. The best flotant of all, however, is seldom sold commercially, because it is so volatile that it evaporates on the shelf. It has two basic ingredients: a grease or wax for waterproofing and a solvent for cleaning the fly and dissolving the grease. The best solvent I have ever used is carbon tetrachloride. Americans may have trouble getting it, since it is dangerous in a closed space. Any light petroleum product is a substitute. Silicone line dressing makes a good fly grease, but paraffin wax and many other things also work pretty well. Enough of these should be added to the solvent liquid so that the solution is not quite cloudy at fishing temperatures.

Some aerosol sprays are fairly satisfactory, but heavy oils are to be avoided, since they never really dry out. I am not sure whether trout object to an oily ring on the water, and I cannot think of any pressing reason to find out.

Sinking Flies

So far, we have dealt with ways to float flies—a fairly complicated question, since most are heavier than water. To make a fly sink is easy: enough lead will sink anything. But it takes some care to make a fly sink through moving water to the right level at the right speed. Solving this problem is almost (not quite) the whole key to behavior. Other factors (size, shape, and color) are—usually—easy to control. Mind you, I am not writing here about fishing in still water or with fancy flies.

Behavior is mainly a question of *the relationship between weight, size, and the materials used.* I have never seen this explained fully, and it deserves analysis.

Weight starts with the hook, which in a deep-fished fly should be strong enough to hold any expected fish. Within reason, a heavy hook will penetrate almost as well as a light one if the point is equally fine. A hone will take care of that. A ridiculously heavy hook will, perhaps, diminish realism. After the hook, weight can be added with wire of any soft and non-rusting variety; lead and copper are the most common. If the fly is intended to have a flat body, the lead can be fastened on as two strips at the side of the hook. (Hewitt considered flat bodies important, but the trout I talk to are not much impressed.) If lead is used, plenty of lacquer or cement should also be used to prevent discoloration of the dressing. The amount of weight that can be added depends on:

Size of the fly. A large Rocky Mountain Stonefly nymph can handle many wraps of heavy lead fuse wire. The fly may be impossible to "cast" in the normal sense, but it will retain a slim, natural shape, and will fish well in the usual fast water. A small nymph will have to be weighted by lead on the leader or by no more than a few wraps of fine copper wire (like Sawyer's nymph). It will still not sink quickly, so you must also consider:

Material. A full-circle hackle gives the most attractive behavior but retards sinking. A stonefly on a size 2 long-shanked hook can be weighted heavily enough to cope with even a large cock's hackle. (I doubt that any stonefly nymph works much better than the old Woolly Worm, but I modify this by using a body of peacock or seal, then eliminate the hackle behind the thorax.) A smaller fly intended to sink fast should have no hackle at all. A beard hackle may be the best choice in a medium-sized deep-fished fly. Such a fly is shown in chapter 10. Any time I think I can get away with it, though, I omit the wing case and use a small, soft hackle propped up by a bulging thorax (Skues' design).

7 ⸙ *Shape*

With a Discussion of Wing Materials

⸙ ⸙ ⸙ By ranking behavior and size first among the characteristics of a good imitative fly, I have probably not caused the Pyra-
mids to crumble or the sun to alter its course. Both behavior and
size have been taken for granted, and thus neglected historically.
When they are identified, many anglers agree with their importance. Trout certainly do.

When it comes to the shape and color of a fly, the trout's opinion
is more difficult to establish. An angler's generalizations cannot be
rigorously scientific. If trout are not feeding selectively, shape and
color may perhaps be ignored. Any conclusions must, then, be
advanced with modesty (or a willingness to look foolish).

Until recently, shape was the most neglected aspect of imitation. There are many exceptions to this, probably beginning with
Mascall in 1614, who recommended copying both the shape and
color of natural flies. In practice, however, fly shape has usually
been a matter of custom rather than of logic. Most anglers have
learned to tie flies in a certain way and have then continued to do
so, with little regard to the shape of the natural. Flies from different regional schools can often be distinguished by shape before
any other factor.

A fixed shape was good enough for North Country wet flies,
which used soft hackles to imitate hatching flies or drowning
adults—both of which tend to be disheveled. With the invention

of dry flies, shape became important but was still treated as a matter of convention. Halford's books were almost blind on the subject of shape, as is evident from their beautiful plates. The ants were shaped like mayflies. Even Skues thought "form" unimportant by comparison to color and size. He did not like Mottram's "silhouette" designs for mayflies. This comment gave me a clue as to the blind spot of chalkstream anglers: their experience (even in Skues' case) was based largely on mayflies. Now, mayflies look elegant in photographs or perched on a leaf, but they are untidy when struggling out of their shuck and being blown down the stream in an April gust. As often as not, they have a wing or two caught in the surface film or crumpled. They may even be upside down and half drowned. No wonder that a hackle fly imitates them so effectively, even though it is not shaped like a perfect dun. On windy days, I have seen Irish trout rejecting perfect Large Dark Olive duns and taking fully hatched flies blown over into the surface film.

Most other important insects have a more distinct shape. Sedges look like a blur when buzzing along the surface, but when floating quietly, they have a sharp silhouette. (There are exceptions, especially when sedges are blown from the bank.) The smaller stoneflies are thin and neat. Beetles have a very hard, sharp outline. Ants have a distinctive hourglass shape that they could not alter if they wished. Most large dipterans have a distinct shape when floating down the river singly. So do jassids. In fact, if one looks beyond mayflies, only a few other insects come down the water in visible disarray. Craneflies and mating Black Gnats lead this list of formless creatures. There are, thus, two very different problems of shape:

- That typified by mayflies, which have three dimensions visible to the trout—height as well as length and breadth—but which are often so rumpled as to present no distinct shape of any kind
- That which applies to most stream insects *except* mayflies. These other insects are more compact, presenting two main dimensions to the fish—a silhouette—with these two dimensions being distinct and readily perceived

With respect to mayflies, Skues may have had a point in considering shape unimportant, if one ignores spent spinners. With respect to the down-winged silhouette flies, shape is very important. But it was not until after World War II that the best silhouette patterns were designed. This is one of the major American innovations in the art of tying imitative flies, although there are British antecedents. The development was logical, since mayflies are less important in the eastern United States than in England and Ireland.

The breakthrough seems to have been Vincent Marinaro's Jassid design with jungle cock feathers tied flat along the back. The important thing here is neither the pattern itself nor the idea of imitating a jassid, which goes back at least to Ronalds. This point must be understood very clearly. English anglers tend to focus automatically on fly patterns rather than on designs, and to record fly-tying history in terms of specific insects.

Marinaro's pattern was not the last word: we now know that many other feathers are about as good as jungle cock (and a lot more available). His attempt to copy a jassid was far from the first. But his use of a feather tied flat on a platform of flat hackle fibers opened many doors. The design is, for example, even more useful for sedges than for jassids.

As in all fishing developments, there were some earlier accomplishments to pave the way. C. E. Walker tried to get his contemporaries to put wings in their proper places in 1898. Mottram's silhouette mayflies have already been mentioned; his interest in duns was perhaps inevitable, but it seems to have led to a dead end. On the other hand, the Henderson Spinner described later seems impossible to beat.

Imitations of other insects lagged far behind. H. S. Hall's Pike-Scale Black Gnat looked more like a Marinaro Jassid than any earlier fly, but the Hall design differed in important respects. It could not readily have been extended to imitate sedges and beetles. The Pike-Scale wing was stiff and intractable, unlike Marinaro's jungle-cock feather. Most important, Hall did not use a platform of palmered hackle fibers clipped top and bottom to support the wing. Mottram's Black Gnats were better but still lacked an adequate support for the wing (see the section on Black Gnats in chapter 11).

To make a flat, silhouette wing that does not require jungle cock, choose a small feather with a straight quill in the center from any part of a bird. Color does not seem to matter very much, since the feather appears as a sharp, dark outline against the sky. Texture also matters little, since the feather is made narrow and dense by being pulled through glue-coated fingers.

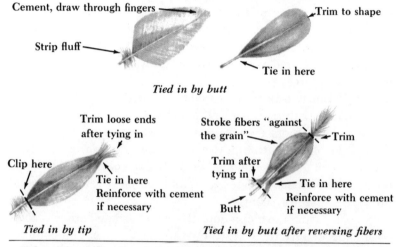

Cement, draw through fingers

Strip fluff

Trim to shape

Tie in here

Tied in by butt

Clip here

Trim loose ends after tying in

Tie in here
Reinforce with cement if necessary

Tied in by tip

Stroke fibers "against the grain"

Trim

Trim after tying in

Butt

Tie in here
Reinforce with cement if necessary

Tied in by butt after reversing fibers

When the wing has dried, it is tied to a body previously made of dubbing (or of plain tying silk in the smallest flies), which has been wrapped with a single palmer hackle. The hackle has been carefully trimmed top and bottom: its main function is to support the wing, although it also helps the fly float. Some care is needed to make a flat platform for the wing to rest on. Durability can be improved by gluing the wing lightly to the top of the body. The last step is to clip the wing to the shape of the natural. Three typical shapes are shown from a fish-eye view on the opposite page.

Like any other design, this one has its shortcomings. It is fragile at best: glue and feathers are not graceful partners. The design is too weak for flies bigger than size 14. Sizes 16 through 20 are best.

Sedge   Beetle   Jassid

Ernest Schwiebert, I believe, had a good deal to do with extending the jassid design to such other creatures as sedges. In any event, he showed the flat-wing sedge to me.

Large sedges (above size 14) are sturdy creatures, and I think they are better imitated by a bulky deer-hair wing. The same is true of big stoneflies, grasshoppers, Alders, and many other creatures. In the last few years, down-winged deer-hair flies seem to have evolved independently in many places. Sid Neff showed me the first good one (chapter 11). At first I used deer face hair, which

Hair-Wing Sedge

is straight and fine. Unlike deer body hair, it does not flare much, but it does not float as well as body hair.

Simple as the deer-hair sedge design is, it is very effective: more so, I think, than the traditional palmer sedge. The main advantage of the old hackled sedge design is that it can be made to skitter along the top of the water. But even the deer-hair sedge can be made to skitter if a few hairs are flared and pulled under the body. Most of the time, a low-floating hatching-sedge imitation works better, and I like one with a wing that goes exactly 180 degrees around the top of the hook, ending sharply at each side. The last hairs act as "outriggers" to keep the fly upright.

If fly-tying had begun in the United States, perhaps we would now be seeking rare shades of deer flank hair, and hackles would never have been discovered. For me, a life without hackles today would be as much fun as a monastery.

For down-winged flies, the body is usually easy to imitate. In a silhouette design, the body needs to be little more than a support for the wing. A body of dubbing or herl always seems to work, and most of the larger down-wing flies require no great delicacy in the tying.

Even in mayflies, body shape is easier to imitate than wing shape. The main thing is to keep the body thin; there are few mayflies with obese bodies, though some are stouter than others. It hardly seems possible to tie a small mayfly with a body that is too thin, since the hook is there to begin with. You can, of course, use a detached body, but that leads to unnecessary hooking problems (chapter 6). Just about three hundred years ago, Charles Cotton hung a fat London fly in his window to laugh at, and he would laugh no less at some of today's plump commercial creatures. A wisp of dubbing tightly spun on silk is as hard to beat now as it was then.

Mayfly wings are a more difficult and controversial problem. An argument seems to be based in large part on a misapprehension caused by the term "wingless." It is also possible to be confused by the old custom of referring to hackles as "legs." Trout are not at all confused by these things, since they do not read much fishing literature. Actually, most trout of my acquaintance cannot read without moving their lips. They find this embarrassing, so they just look at the pictures in the tabloid newspapers and pretend they are reading.

Strictly speaking, there is no such thing as a wingless adult mayfly imitation. Many flies omit the specific components known by fly-tyers as "wings," but these flies invariably have hackles, which in practice imitate mayfly wings well.

Roger Woolley was a convincing exponent of hackle-fiber wings. He apparently started with the spent-spinner design originated by John Henderson (chapter 10). For duns, however, Woolley pulled the wound hackle into one upright bunch at the top of the hook rather than two bunches at the sides. This makes an excellent wing—the best I know for small duns. See the Barb-Wing design in chapter 10.

Much of the time, a plain wound hackle is as good a wing as any for duns. There is an amusing passage on this in *Where the Bright Waters Meet,* by H. Plunket Greene. He confesses that hackle flies seem more efficient but rejects them as almost unsporting. Few anglers today would have this scruple, but I think I detect a feeling that "wingless" flies are too primitive to be effective. Human vogues truly run in cycles.

Trout, on the other hand, have no vogues at all.

Despite a personal admiration for good hackle flies, I think there are times when a darker, sharper wing outline works better for some mayflies, and especially for hatching duns. Naturals with big, dark wings are obvious candidates for this treatment.

When separate wings are used in imitations of mayfly duns, the correct position is, of course, upright or approximately so. This creates two problems almost absent in the down-winged flies discussed earlier.

The Airfoil Problem When upright wings are made of a stiff material with a sharply defined plane, the fly may act like a miniature propeller, twisting the leader. Feathers reinforced by glue are especially bad offenders; they should be used only for down-wing flies, where the airfoil problem scarcely exists.

The Hooking Problem A stiff upright wing—as of deer hair— can also prevent the fly from slipping into a trout's mouth easily. For down-wing flies, this problem only exists when the wing extends well behind the bend of the hook.

After cock's hackles, wound radially or bunched, the tips of cock's hackles tied in pairs are among the most practical mayfly wings. Rolled duck breast feathers are also excellent. American wood-duck breast feathers work remarkably well, even on flies where the color does not match perfectly at first glance. They are among those peculiar materials which, like stripped peacock quill for bodies, seem to imitate a wide range of insects. Neither is there much wrong with the old wings of starling, hen (European) blackbird, and other *light* quill feathers. The duck primaries sometimes used in America are too stiff and heavy for mayfly wings. Any quill wing is more dependable and durable if it is stripped, rolled, and tied on in a bunch, something like a duck breast feather. This was the old practice in America as well as in England. Neatly paired quill wings have always sold well, but they do not stay neat for long on the river. Hen hackles can be used for wings in a pinch but are inclined to become matted and bedraggled when they have soaked up some water. The same problem applies to most other fibers of soft feathers.

Upright wings do not have to be absolutely vertical in any plane. Natural mayfly wings are tipped well back, but the wings of the artificial are most durable if they are tied in pointing forward and

Wing Materials	
Material	*Good Points*
Cock's hackle fibers wound full circle	Durable, translucent, shiny, light, fairly flexible, good casting qualities
Cock's hackle fibers wound and bunched	Same as above, plus more distinct wing outline
Cock's hackle tips untrimmed	Same, but not quite as durable. Easily tied upright
Duck-breast feather fibers	Durable, flexible, good casting qualities. Available in good colors

then tipped back to a position that is approximately vertical. Dry-fly wings are often "divided" or opened into a *V*-shape. Roger Woolley points out that natural mayflies are likely to carry their wings together, so that a single upright wing is as realistic as anything else. While I fully agree with Woolley (and Theodore Gordon), I have noticed mayflies coming down the stream with wings in every possible position. Many duns have their wings slightly parted. I can thus see no reason to avoid parting the wings of the artificial when (and only when) it is helpful. It is helpful if the wing is large and the hackle is sparse (as in some of the duns described later). Such a wing can cause the fly to fall on its side. A pronounced *V* helps to avoid this problem by aerodynamics, turning the fly upright as it floats down. A slightly raised tail has the same effect.

In choosing a wing, then, the mechanical factors to look for are durability, flexibility (for good hooking), and good casting qualities (absence of an airfoil).

It may be helpful to summarize common wing materials in chart form for easy selection, since most of the problem of shape boils down to winging.

	Weak Points	*Application*
	Absence of distinct wing outline	Mayfly wings. High-riding and moving flies of all kinds. Fair for sedges and other down-wings
	Too simple to appeal to fishermen.	Ideal for spent mayfly wings and, if bunched upright, for small duns.
	Not translucent enough for many spinner wings	Excellent for mayfly duns
	Too dark for most spinner wings. Wood-duck feathers are expensive	Excellent for duns

Wing Materials (continued)	
Material	**Good Points**
Stripped and rolled segment of wing quill (snipe, starling, etc.)	Easily tied, cheap, moderately durable. Available in good colors
Matched quill segments	Attractive to humans
Bunched fibers from body feathers of turkeys, other soft-feathered birds	Easy to tie and cheap
Soft-feathers wound hackle-wise	Flexible, good color, fairly easy to tie
Trimmed hackles and similar feathers	Sharp wing outline. Good colors
Trimmed feathers reinforced by cement	Same as above, and stronger
Deer hair	Durable, cheap, easy to tie, contributes positive buoyancy (chapter 6). Good casting qualities
Fine hair	Durable, cheap, easy to tie, may contribute some buoyancy. Good casting qualities. Available in good colors
Synthetic materials (polypropylene yarn, etc.)	Cheap, easy to tie, can be chosen for high visibility

Weak Points	Application
Not very translucent or shiny. A bit heavy	Still fair for floating duns, but not as good as duck-breast feather fibers. Fair for sedges as well. Good for wet flies
Same as above, plus difficult to tie. May twist the leader	Not bad for duns, but previous materials are better.
Mat easily, opaque, little sheen	Some such fibers do a fair job for commercial flies, but amateurs can do better with materials listed above.
Fragile and sometimes hard to obtain. Suitable only for dense wings	Good for nymphs and for hatching flies. Can be treated to float moderately well
Stiff, fragile, may twist the leader if tied upright	Realistic, but fussy for duns and many other flies
Same as above, but even more likely to twist the leader	Good for down-winged flies
Stiff, heavy, coarse, little sheen or translucency, poor availability of colors	Good for down-winged flies. Fair for larger duns where a low float is needed
Still somewhat heavy and coarse by comparison to hackle	Widely useful, especially for heavier flies. Highly visible in white
Limp and coarse by comparison to cock's hackle. Colors not very good. Often lack durability and translucency	Makes an acceptable spinner wing if price is important

8 ❦ *Color*

In Folklore and Fishing, Including
Translucency, Sheen, and Light Patterns

❦ ❦ ❦ Color permeates our culture. You can do big things
with it: paint landscapes, photograph your girl on a mossy rock,
write a poem to the sunset, or discriminate against your neighbor.
Even make a trout fly. It would be difficult to overstate the
importance of color to humans.

There lies the problem. In no other aspect of fishing does the
human cultural overlay make it so difficult to hear the trout.
We demand that he agree with us. Most of this book is science,
in the broad sense that I try to discover results instead of fab-
ricating them. To discover is science; to fabricate is art. In discussing the trout's view of color, I do not know where to locate
the boundary between science and art, and the only honest
course is to confess. My suspicion is that color in trout flies is
mostly art. It is important, but mainly for building confidence
in humans.

Vince Marinaro doubted that the subject of color and the
trout should be pursued at all in the light of present knowledge. Anglers do insist on dealing with color constantly, however. Vince himself—on one of our last trips together—was
delighted by a cape he had just bought with silver-colored
hackles. (Not pale blue: silver.) He wasn't arguing that the
trout cared, though I didn't hear him ruling that out, either.
He just knew that he liked the hackles. Let us discuss color
with equal detachment.

Trout do take some flies and refuse others, which is selectivity. I have proved (at least to my own satisfaction) that they are often selective to the behavior and size of a fly; sometimes to its shape. I have also proved that trout are often nonselective or only very slightly selective. I am not sure I have ever proved—in the same strict sense—that they are selective to color. I have the *impression* that they are, occasionally. The examples that seem clearest are those with bright colors: red-bodied spinners (chapter 2), green free-swimming caddis larvae (cited by Gary LaFontaine), salmon eggs. It is easy to see how a trout could use such colors for identification.

Examples of selectivity to drab colors also seem to occur, and I have cited a few. For some reason, my examples have a way of coming from Ireland. I don't think it's magic. In discussing revisions to this second edition with a friend, though, I mentioned that I was growing more and more unsure about color and the trout. I couldn't think of a clear case of color selectivity in five years. He couldn't think of one either, and he fishes in many difficult waters.

Of course, we seldom try to prove selectivity. Catching trout is too much fun. We put on a fly of some color close to that of the naturals, and it works. We could say: he eats, therefore he is selective. (If you are not familiar with that kind of fractured Cartesian reasoning, pull some fishing books and magazines off your shelf and look at them more carefully.) But selectivity is choice. A trout has not made a choice unless he has rejected one kind of fly consistently while accepting another. We must look to rejection, not acceptance, to prove selectivity; and rejection is not fun.

There are, however, some things we do know. Scientists have shown that trout can perceive color. This suggests that color vision has had some evolutionary value for them. What we do not know is how trout use this vision, if indeed they do. Does it help them to avoid predators? Does it help them to tell good food from bad? If so, what do they look for? If they want some specific color, why do they ignore the big bronze hook that protrudes below the fly? The answers we have to these questions usually amount to little more than folklore.

There is plenty of that. Our oldest fishing book, the *Treatise of Fishing with an Angle*, describes imitative flies and explains their colors. We can make a guess at how the flies were intended to be fished (their behavior), but their sizes and shapes are not known. Some of the materials used, and the manner in which they were tied to the hook, have puzzled scholars. Only color is clear.

And color has remained important in imitative flies throughout the centuries. There have been a few—but only a few—who have scoffed at the need for imitating color. There have been a number of thoughtful writers who have assigned a low priority to it. The majority have described flies by color above all. When dry flies developed, Halford put color above other considerations, and his model is still with us. You can find serious recent books showing quantities of flies distinguished from each other mainly by color. But remember that books are bought by fishermen, not fish.

Writers who have thought that they were rejecting "imitation" have, in fact, often rejected nothing but the excessive emphasis on color. Stewart thought he was avoiding imitative flies, yet he stressed the importance of behavior, shape, and size, and he paid some attention to color. His flies (fished upstream) must have been far more realistic than those of most contemporaries.

Popular names of flies have long emphasized color: Blue Dun, Iron Blue, Olive, Blue-Winged Olive, Little Sky-Blue, and so on. It happens that colors, like numbers, are easy to describe in our language. It is convenient to say that a fly has three tails, a blue wing, and a green-olive body. Most fishermen would describe a female Blue-Winged Olive in this way. We know enough about successful artificial Blue-Winged Olives, however, to make a guess at the way a trout sees the natural. None of the above characteristics matter much. An articulate trout might describe the Blue-Winged Olive as "a fat food-creature of average length that does a lot of swimming around on summer evenings. It is difficult to catch at these times, though not impossible. It becomes easy to catch for a short while when it swims to the top of the world and tries to disappear. It cannot then move fast. It grows in size at this time but has no clear shape. Its body is a darkish brown (the nymphal shuck), and the confused mass (of legs) at one end is a speckled brown."

The trout's description is much longer than the human's, but the trout has the disadvantage of being translated into a foreign language. If there were such a thing as trout language, it would doubtless have very terse descriptions for hatching nymphs. Every culture has a good vocabulary for objects important to it.

By suggesting that color is less important to trout than to ourselves, I do not mean to say that we can always ignore color. It seldom matters, but if trout care about it at all, we will want to pay some attention. Suppose you are dealing with an individual, difficult fish: either you hook him or you do not. If color gives him a feeble excuse to refuse the fly, there is no consolation in believing that he may have found the imitation *almost* good enough. On an average day, a trout in a rich stream may be able to choose from several hundred food items, each of them insignificant in itself. It is easy to reject any that arouse suspicions.

Consider another far-fetched parallel between trout and humans. In a jar containing ninety-nine perfect cookies and one that is burnt, the burnt cookie is likely to be left lying at the bottom when the rest are gone. On the other hand, a burnt cookie will be eaten eagerly by a hungry human who has no option. An off-color fly will also be taken readily by a hungry, non-selective trout. This is just as well. Very few artificial flies are anything close to the correct color of the natural. Fly-fishing might never have had a beginning if close color imitation had been necessary.

Color and Related Qualities

Color can be objectively defined and measured in terms of the wavelengths of light. To the eye, however, color is perceived subjectively, under the influence of several psychological and physiological factors. Two examples may help to explain the difference between objective and subjective color. Objectively, black and white are not colors; subjectively, they are perceived as colors.

Objectively, a white tablecloth under candlelight becomes orange; subjectively, our eye tells us that the tablecloth is still white. (We have psychologically compensated for the orange quality of the light.)

Where we can get into trouble is in attempting to attribute our own subjective perceptions to the trout. The possibility must be left open that he *sometimes* uses a different set of subjective "filters" than we do. But it is a cheap evasion to shrug and say that there is no use in guessing how a trout sees. Objective color is the same for him as for us. We also know that he has the physical equipment to see much as we do. It is not sheer arrogance, thus, to suggest that we can begin by assuming some parallels between trout and human vision.

What we normally think of as color has three qualities: hue, value, and intensity. A general understanding of these qualities is as helpful in mixing dubbing for fly bodies as in mixing oil colors for painting.

Hue is what we think of as color itself: blue, red, and yellow (the primaries); and also green-olive, brown, orange, and any number of more useful fishing colors. Black, white, and grays are not technically colors, even though (as noted above) we may perceive them as such.

Value describes the amount of white and black mixed into a color. I can detect this quality when the light is too dim to see hue or intensity, and the trout may also be able to do so. This would make color value important late in the evening. An orange fur that is not of the right value can be changed by mixing it with white fur. This raises its value, since white reflects the greatest possible quantity of light and a mixture of orange and white reflects more light than the orange color we started with. We can also lower the value of the orange by mixing it with black, which reflects the least possible amount of light. In practice, it is difficult to mix orange and black fur thoroughly, so we might choose to mix the orange with a gray that is darker (lower in value). This will lower the value of the orange, but it will also lower the intensity, as described in the following paragraph. Scotty Chapman believes that value is generally more important then hue, and he knows more about color than any other fly-tyer of my acquaintance.

Intensity (also known as saturation, purity, and chroma) is quite distinct from value. The distinction is not quickly grasped by us laymen, accustomed as we are to using the same adjectives to describe both qualities. Intensity describes the color strength of a hue as compared to that of a colorless gray. We can, for example, change the intensity of our orange fur by mixing it with a gray that has the same value (is neither lighter nor darker). As more gray is added, the orange becomes dull (less intense), but its value does not change.

These qualities may seem unduly technical. In practice, however, most fly-tyers really do make decisions on both value and intensity. It is easy to get fur in white, black, and many values of gray. Scotty Chapman recommends getting the intensity about right—perhaps by mixing hues—and then correcting for value.

Two other qualities have to be mentioned. They are not color properly speaking, but they must be taken into account along with color in choosing fly-tying materials.

Translucency is partial transparency, and a great many parts of natural insects have this quality. The wings of mayfly spinners are often virtually transparent; mayfly bodies are translucent; the bodies of black ants, on the contrary, are opaque (meaning that they let no light pass through). In artificial flies, translucency can be achieved or simulated by methods discussed later in this chapter.

Sheen, for our purposes, is the same as luster or sparkle. Mr. Webster defines sparkle as "quick, brief, innumerable small flashes." This is a good description of light reflections from many natural insects, with spinner wings the outstanding example. In the bodies of flies, sheen can come from some dubbings (especially seal's fur), from tinsel, and from materials such as stripped and varnished peacock quill. Sheen is not color and must not be confused with value or intensity. Technically, sheen results from the reflection of light, while translucency comes from the transmission of light through a material. The two qualities are thus almost opposites. In practice, many good fly-tyers have thought that sheen creates an illusion of translucency—or at least distracts fish from the absence of translucency.

I have used an analogy to paints because most of us know something about them. But I do not want to be read as suggesting that color is as important to trout flies as to oil paintings. We fishermen have a small canvas and a primitive audience. But it is easy to mix dubbing carefully if we want to—just about as easy to get it right as wrong. Dye is a much more awkward tool.

Color and the Trout

We will have to look at three main variables in the trout's perception of color:

- The light (its amount and direction)
- The behavior of the fly (a function of its design)
- The optics of the water surface

The Light All of us are used to it, and if we are photographers we have worked with it, measuring its *direction* and *amount*.

The photographer knows, for example, that his picture will not show the color of his girlfriend's jeans clearly if she is "backlighted" (light coming from behind her and shining into the camera lens). If the back-lighting is extreme, she may be only a silhouette. This does not mean that the picture is bad. If she has my favorite kind of silhouette, backlighting makes a photo with impact. Similarly, the trout may feed on backlighted insects, but he is then going to see the *shape* of our imitation much better than its *color*.

When it comes to the amount of light, the trout also seems to cope about as we do. He probably has a little more trouble in bright sun, because he cannot squint, let alone wear sunglasses. He is also going to spend more time than we do with his prey backlighted, which—as noted above—multiplies the problems of bright sun. Trout, especially big ones, may refuse to feed at all if the sun is bright. When they do feed, you and I can catch them more easily than we can in conditions of moderate light. Their vision seems especially good early in the morning or evening. If fish ever drive you mad, it will be at the beginning of the evening rise.

Trout vision under low light—late in the evening rise, for example—gets more complicated. As far as I know, the first layman's book to cover this subject accurately was Eugene V. Connett's *My Friend the Trout,* published in 1961. It cited the experiments of von Frisch, conducted in 1925. These had shown that in daylight, a trout perceives color through cone-shaped cells in the retina. In darkness, the cones are withdrawn and rod-shaped cells come into operation. The rods are more sensitive to low light but cannot detect color. Accordingly, a trout cannot perceive color in very dim light. (And here Connett caught Colonel Harding in one of his rare errors.)

In a 1973 book entitled *Through the Fish's Eye,* Sosin and Clark report experiments showing that the change from cones to rods takes place slowly for some species of fish. As a practical matter, however, and speaking only of trout, I think the ability to perceive color ends quite abruptly. Trout seem able to perceive color a bit later into the evening than I can. When the trout "switch off" color, however, they do so all at once. This behavior could perhaps be explained by factors other than the loss of color perception, but this is the most likely explanation, since the silhouette of a dry fly and leader should remain almost equally visible as light fades.

Recently, for example, an Irish fisherman and I were trying to catch very good trout (some over three pounds) taking hatching sedges in a limestone stream. I tried both pupa and adult representations that I thought I had tied with great care from naturals caught the previous evening. But the trout ignored my flies as completely as the other angler's. Then suddenly, as it was nearly dark, I hooked a heavy fish on a dry fly. As I was playing it, the other angler got into one almost as big. By the time I netted my trout, the rise was over. Neither the other angler nor I had changed flies for half an hour. This kind of experience explains why I always try to stay till the bitter end of the rise.

As already mentioned, however, trout appear to be able to see the brightness (color value) of a fly well after they lose the ability to see its basic hue. This may explain why some night-fishermen do well with white or black flies.

The Behavior of the Fly The most important part of a fly's behavior is usually the level at which it floats, and we can control that level through design. Part IV shows flies designed to float at all levels.

Any components of a fly that are above the surface will be visible to trout only under conditions described in the next section, on optics. Upright wings should be well above the surface. High-floating flies are supposed to have their bodies above water, too. Dry-fly anglers generally like to think they are using a high-floating fly, so that is what they see on the water. In reality, most dry flies very soon come to float with their bodies in the surface and easily visible to the trout.

A fly that is just below the surface—such as a hatching nymph or small North Country-type wet fly—is easily seen by the fish. Anglers have always fussed over the color of such flies. The fish seem to support the anglers' judgment.

In deep-sinking flies, color has seldom seemed to me to be

Mirror

Concentration of light rays form
prism at the edge of window

important. Perhaps that is because trout do not see deep flies mirrored against the brilliant surface. And that leads us to the next variable.

The Optics of the Surface The literature of fly-fishing has some brilliant writing on surface optics, but only a little of it. My main sources are Harding, Marinaro (1976), an article by Butler and McCammon in *Trout* magazine, and the cricked neck I got in experiments at home.

Anglers who have read about their sport usually know that the trout can see upwards through the surface only in an area directly above him. This has long been known as the "window," even though, unlike most windows, it floats around directly above the fish's eye wherever he goes. It is also circular and variable in size, growing larger with every bit the fish descends. The window will follow you around too if you watch it from under water in your swimming pool.

Light rays are refracted, or deflected from a straight line, when they enter the water at an angle. In chapter 4 we considered the

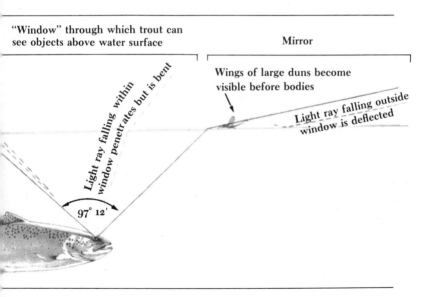

"Window" through which trout can see objects above water surface

Mirror

Wings of large duns become visible before bodies

Light ray falling within window penetrates but is bent

Light ray falling outside window is deflected

97° 12'

effect of refraction on the fish's view of the angler. Refraction also produces the window and its surrounding mirror.

If the angle of the light ray is low, only a small portion of it penetrates the water, and that at a sharp angle. The rest is reflected. The fact that low rays are reflected means that most of the surface is, from the trout's point of view, a vast mirror. He presumably takes the mirror for granted, but we humans find it puzzling. Perhaps this homology will help. The glass mirror on your wall at home reflects because of two things: first, an opaque back; and second, a source of light in front. The light is easy to understand: there is almost always a little, even at night, and even down there where the fish is. The difficult thing to grasp is that clear water and bright sky can form a background impenetrable to certain light rays. Perhaps a look upwards from the depths of a swimming pool will be more convincing than any number of words.

The trout cannot see through the mirror to detect the color or shape of anything above the surface, like your fly's wings. But rays that fall on the water from a higher angle do penetrate, forming the window through which vision is possible. So now our trout is swimming around under a window that is not only overhead, circular, movable, and variable in size, but also a window that is set in a mirror rather than cut through a wall.

All of this, of course, assumes that the surface is flat. Sometimes it is—in a chalkstream, a spring creek, a lake on a calm day, or the center of a pool. But even the impact of a fly disturbs the surface, distorting vision through it. If the water is further disturbed by a breeze or current, there is no clear window at all. Splash your hand in your pool and see: now the surface is a thousand changing reflections—tiny mirrors—with maybe a few tiny windows through the sides of the waves. Under these circumstances, what the trout sees must be highly variable. And we all know that we can now get away with rougher flies.

Even under good conditions, it is not possible in practice for the angler to know the diameter of the window, since its size depends on the fish's distance from the surface, and the trout is unlikely to sit still for measurements. As a matter of curiosity, a fish can see through the surface at an angle up to 48 degrees, 36 minutes from vertical. The window can thus be pictured as a cone originating at the trout's eye and subtending an angle of 97 degrees, 12 minutes (twice 48 degrees, 36 minutes). If you try to make a rough guess at the size of the window, remember that the trout is deeper than he looks.

The intention of this chapter is only to consider the effect of optics on the color perceptions of the trout. For that purpose, picture a dry fly as it lands upstream from the trout, then floats closer.

If the trout is lying high in the water, his window will be small and the fly will almost certainly land outside it. What does the trout then see?

- First, a light pattern of tiny depressions is made in the surface by the hackle points, body, and hook of the fly. The difference between a mirror of water and of glass is that the watery version has surface tension for the hackle-tips to play with. The resulting pattern can be very brilliant and noticeable.

- Second, parts of the fly will very probably penetrate the surface tension and protrude down in the water. *The color of any such parts will be easily visible.* It is not true that flies in the mirror create *only* a light pattern. That is part of the myth that proper anglers have only high-floating flies. In my home experiments, I can even see the color of one strand of seal's fur sticking down from a fly in the mirror. But what I see most clearly of all is often (depending on the light) a reflection of the hook point back against the mirror. This can be very conspicuous, and I suppose it accounts for many of the trout's refusals of artificial flies.

Now, as the fly floats downstream, it does not just slide from the mirror into the window, like a pedestrian walking by the window of your house. Two interesting things happen.

- The trout begins to see the wings of the fly appearing, in a funny, detached way, high above the light pattern in the surface. If you experiment at home, you will find this effect striking. Harding described it, and the ghostly prominence of the wing helped lead Marinaro to his Thorax Dun design (chapter 10). Refraction is still the cause. Light rays pick up the top of the wing, and are then bent downward as they touch the water, making the wing appear much taller than it is. You can see this in the drawing, but the three sources cited above have more detailed diagrams. This phenomenon seems important for flies with high, dark wings, like the large early-season duns in eastern America. Under these conditions, I reach for a design with a pronounced wing when an educated trout refuses a hackle fly. I like a hackle-tip wing better than Marinaro's clipped version, but the optical principle is the same.

- Then, at the very edge of the mirror, the concentrated light rays form a spectrum of the colors, just as in a rainbow or a glass prism. Harding wrote that the artificial fly looks "very brilliant as it comes into view there. It seems to be a collection of sparkling points of light, in comparison with which its color seems quite a secondary characteristic." In my home experiments, this phenomenon has also been easy to duplicate in a spectacular way. The "sparkling points of light" come mainly in the light pattern, where the fly plays with surface tension. The actual color of the fly is subdued by comparison, but it now becomes sporadically visible—and the trout may have learned to look for it. When the light is low, of course, the prism is more subdued. The trout sees the rainbow effect many times a day, and anyhow he is unromantic. My guess is that we will be hearing about the prism for many a year before we have it thoroughly figured out. It is the most variable of all these optical factors.

At this point the fly floats into the window. Maybe. Marinaro, who has spent more time photographing rising trout than any other writer, says that the trout rises in a way "that places the fly always at the edge of the window for all purposes: viewing, inspecting, and taking. He does not use the clear central area of the window."

No one can offer a second opinion without repeating Vince's experiments. Still, in some of his own photographs, the fly looks to me as if it is in the window (bearing in mind that the fish is deeper than it seems to be). So let us just suppose that fish lets the fly slip into the window occasionally, if only by mistake. What then?

With the fly in the window proper, most of the mystery disappears. The horrible double image of the hook disappears too, thank goodness. The fly is seen much as you and I see it when we pick it from the fly box and hold it up, but with one added factor —the distortion of a poor lens, the water surface.

There is another "if" that we examined in the preceding section on the behavior of the fly: if the fly is backlighted—and it often is —it remains a silhouette, window or no window. In my home experiments, however, I have not had much trouble in getting the fly front-lighted or side-lighted in such a way that its color is visible. A trout rising in the middle of the stream and looking toward the shade should detect the color easily.

Admittedly, the variables in all of this are far too numerous to resolve in any one presentation. So what? If our fly is right on all counts, it should look right to the trout anyhow. If the fly is rejected, we change it. And for myself, I like to make a change that will help me figure out *why* the first fly was wrong.

Partly because of the variables affecting the trout's color perception, some good writers have speculated that translucency and sheen are more important than basic color. In 1929, Skues opined that "the argument in favor of translucency has already been worked pretty nigh to death." But he accepted the desirability of translucency (or the illusion of it) in fly-tying materials. Leonard West, another fly-tyer of the period, designed some interesting "prismatic" flies to suggest the effect of sun passing through and over natural flies.

In summary, we can attach low priority to color under the following conditions:

- Very little light, as late in the evening
- Fly backlighted by bright sun
- Fly component held above the surface, outside the window
- Fly component so sparse as to seem almost transparent, like wound hackle

Conversely, we should expect color to be visible under these conditions:
- Moderate light, including that during the early-evening rise
- Fly front-lighted by the sun
- Fly component in' or just below the surface
- Fly in the window
- Fly component dense (the body or some bunched wings)

If the foregoing points still leave the issue too complicated, we can boil it down further by saying that the trout can see the color of some components of your fly sometimes. Now, which components?

Fly Wings The color of wet-fly wings is visible to trout. Fishermen of the Nore have traditionally used land-rail wings for wet sedges, and these anglers are unanimous in their opinion that dyed starling (the common substitute) is not nearly as good. Ned Maguire has experimented with three flies (on the same leader) which were identical except for the wings, and he says that trout will commonly pick out the only "genuine," no matter where it is placed. The trouts' preference may be hard to explain, but I have no reason to doubt their ability to discern between the real and the dyed. Human eyes can see the same difference.

Dry-fly wings are more difficult to understand. We all know of cases in which the right hackle did wonders, but its mechanical properties may have been the important ones. Stiff cock's hackle also has sparkle and translucency, and these may overwhelm the basic hue, especially in the lighter colors. When imitating spinners, it does not seem to matter much whether the color is pale ginger or pale blue. A perfectly clear hackle might be better than either.

At the other extreme, the wings of hatching duns tend to be damp and relatively dense, with less sparkle and more conspicuous color. Some of the best imitations of a fly in this stage come from the feathers of small birds wound hackle-wise, with hen hackles in second place. British North Country fishermen are very careful to get exactly the right feather. The Irish may well be right in believing that no other feather imitates a hatching Blue-Winged Olive so well as a wren's tail. Such a feather is dense, colorful, soft, and shapeless: almost the opposite of a cock's hackle.

Fully hatched duns have wings with some shine but a definite color as well. In my experience, dyed cocks' hackles usually lose the sparkle that makes them attractive for this application. A few dedicated amateurs have succeeded in dyeing hackle so that its good natural qualities have remained. J. R. Harris showed me some so realistic that they could be (and had been) passed off as "natural olive." Until recently, however, I had not seen a good commercially dyed hackle except in black, which is evidently easy to produce. Now there is a new photo-dyeing process (described by Eric Leiser) that has produced good commercial duns in the darker shades. The dyeing takes place in a cold bath. Color and sheen are added to the existing color of the feathers. So long as there is no bleaching, the stiffness of the feathers remains. But since bleaching harms any hackle, we have no substitute for the lightest natural duns—except possibly the lightest natural ginger. Fortunately, natural dun hackles are once again on the market, after a period of great scarcity. In all colors, superb quality is available (at a price). American breeders have developed strains of roosters surpassing anything our ancestors had—at least for the majority of fly-tyers who want short, stiff barbs.

Dry-fly wings imitated by separate, upright bits of feather or hair, rather than by hackles alone, are meant to be held above the water. In this case trout may not see the color clearly. But since flies can also land on their sides or sink, it makes sense to use a reasonable approximation of natural wing color. When whole feathers or thick strips of them are used, it is easy to judge the color before the wing is tied in. If thin fibers are bunched, however, the wing becomes more dense and the color deepens. For example, a "lemon" wood-duck breast feather does not look like a mayfly wing in the hand, but when it is bunched and tied in, the result bears an uncanny resemblance to the wings of many natural duns. Perhaps it does not matter, but British perfectionists should try such a wing for the Large Dark Olive of spring *(Baetis rhodani)*.

The wings on most floating insects other than mayflies are tied in low, and must sometimes be clearly visible to the trout. Skues, like Ned Maguire, thought that land-rail substitutes were poor for such wings—and Skues was writing about a dry sedge.

Fly Bodies For the bodies of dry flies, the color seems to be visible—but only when the body floats low enough. A few good anglers, like Marinaro, are unconcerned about body color, but then Marinaro advocates a hackle arrangement aimed at holding the body above water. With such designs, it seems unwise to burden the fly with a heavy body for the sake of color. Where approximately the right color can be obtained in a light-weight body, however, there is no disadvantage in using it. My high-floating flies often have the bad manners to sink.

There are at least four approaches to body colors, generally aiming at translucency or reflection:

- J.W. Dunne's system, which involved the use of oiled, translucent, colored silk floss over a white-painted hook
- The use (advocated by Skues) of transparent or translucent material such as gut
- The use of shiny materials to reflect light and perhaps give the illusion of translucency
- The use of a fuzzy body outline, perhaps combined with shiny dubbing

I have a number of Dunne's old flies but have not given them a fair trial. They are fragile in use and difficult to reproduce today.

The use of transparent material over a colored underbody is easier, and the result is more durable. Skues used gut; some plastics are probably even better. Latex rubber looks good but deteriorates fast. The underbody can be a white hook or any material that holds its color when wet. Shiny tinsel gives a nice effect. Skues also used a bare shank under floss silk for translucency with delicate color.

The third and easiest approach to translucency is to choose a simple material that is close to the natural in appearance and reflective, such as stripped-and-varnished peacock quill or horsehair. Minor defects in color may well be made up by reflections from the water surface or river-bed.

Some sort of shiny quill makes about the best of all bodies for very light-colored flies. A porcupine quill, for example, gives a dead white that stays the same color even when wet. Hackle quill or a strip peeled from a large white wing quill also works well. Stiff quills should be wound wet so that they do not crack, and I like to reinforce them with shiny wire, then varnish or lacquer the whole body.

Plain tying silk is rarely used for a body in America, but it makes a good one in dark colors, especially if waxed and ribbed with wire. The famous Greenwell's Glory calls for a body of yellow silk discolored by dark cobbler's wax and usually ribbed with fine gold wire. With minor variations, such a body will imitate that of many flies. But silk will darken greatly when wet or oiled, and so should be checked for color in one of these states. The Spanish achieve bright colors by using many coats of clear lacquer over a floss body.

The fourth and final approach suggests translucency by a soft, fuzzy outline of the body. The soft-edged body can be made either of feather fibers (herl) or fur (dubbing).

Peacock, pheasant tail, crow, and heron (natural or stained olive in picric acid) all provide excellent herls. So, undoubtedly, do many other dark feathers. In my view, herls are a bad choice for pale bodies, since they discolor more than dubbing, let alone quill. Swan herl is sometimes used for white-bodied flies, but they are white only in the angler's fly-box.

For durability, all herl should be spun around a heavy, waxed thread of either complementary or contrasting color, depending on the effect wanted.

Dubbing Much the easiest way to obtain closely matched color is with dubbing spun on a carefully chosen thread. Even Halford admired the effect provided by dubbing, although he gave it up for materials that would hold their color better. He also found dubbing too absorbent in the days before flotant was discovered. Today dubbing works well for all but the palest flies. Tiny flies can be dubbed if the fur is spun thinly and counterwound with wire or another thread.

You will read praises for the easy-to-use qualities of rabbit fur, spun angora fur, wool yarn, and a number of modern synthetic dubbings. If you are a commercial fly-tyer or have some other reason to seek maximum speed, then by all means use this kind of thing. Often fish take it well. But consider this: such dubbing is easy to use to the extent that its fibers are long, thin, soft, and regular. These are *exactly* the opposite qualities from those that produce sheen and a translucent (fuzzy) effect. The latter effect is achieved with fibers that are short, irregular, and somewhat stiff. Spinning such fibers requires a bit of practice. No amount of twisting will get rid of untidy ends. (I often use a fine wire rib—gold or silver—and pick out the fiber ends even further.) In my experience, the hairs that produce the best effect when spun are guard-hairs—not fine undercoat hairs.

Does this seem like too much emphasis on a simple problem? My motives might be of interest to those who follow the history of angling ideas: I have never seen a logical explanation of the qualities of dubbing. Many writers, especially in England, have noted the desirability of a fuzzy, translucent effect in a fly body; and they have also noted that this is achieved with a particular fur or furs, like seal or pig. I have not seen the mechanical properties of dubbing explained in a way that applies to all furs. Someone will probably call my attention to an oversight. The concept is simple and—as far as it goes—unexceptionable. It is based on physics, not on opinion.

Stiff dubbing does, however, have one objectionable property besides difficulty of use: it does not easily produce a clear shape. Where a sharp outline is desired on a small fly, you will want to use something finer than seal's fur, or at least to mix seal fur with something finer. Some fine, reasonably shiny guard-hairs are available and are listed later. If the fly does not require a clear shape, then seal's fur can be used on small hooks. I have used it unmixed on Yellow Mays and small Sulphur Duns, for example, to get the most brilliant effect possible. One Black Gnat design in chapter 11 depends on fuzzy seal's fur, and the fuzzy fur from a hare's ear is deservedly famous for duns and nymphs. Hare's ear (and mask) fur is finer and easier to use than seal's fur.

Several writers have recommended the use of fur from aquatic animals for dubbing, on the theory that it has special oils or sheen. But some of the most successful imitative flies use fur from land animals like the hare and mole. The throat of a summer marten provides the best pale dubbing I have ever tried. And most feathers used on flies are from land birds. For now, then, I cannot find much evidence to support the superiority of aquatic origin. This idea is another that would have been easier to understand before anglers developed good flotants for waterproofing flies.

There is an area, however, in which we lack adequate knowledge. This has to do with the special reflecting powers of some materials (feathers as well as fur) under light that cannot be seen by humans. Trout probably are sensitive to wavelengths that escape human vision; some materials may therefore look different to trout. Ned Maguire thinks that land-rail, pheasant tail, and wren tail have special "killing" qualities. Marinaro is impressed by European jay feathers and by the pale feathers on the "elbow" of a pheasant's wing. I cannot prove anything, but I am not laughing. Fishing needs its sacred mysteries. (I don't really believe that, but it's the traditional excuse for ignorance.)

If any fur has special qualities, they would presumably be diminished by dyeing, so it is nice to use undyed dubbing where possible. Unfortunately, there are not many orange, yellow, or olive animals in my part of the world; and dyed fur seems to work well in the absence of cooperation from Mother Nature. Fur can—of course—be mixed for color as well as texture. I mix because it's easier than dyeing. Skues considered mixtures better than solid colors, and this makes me feel better.

Thanks to an article in *Fly Fisherman* by Dave Engerbretson in 1973, almost every fly-tyer knows by now that the easy way to blend fur is in a dry household blender (liquidizer). It mixes thoroughly and quickly in large quantities, allowing fine corrections. Not so many know how to check the blended dubbing against the natural insect's body. The fur must be spun on thread of the intended color and wound on a hook. Then it must be wet thoroughly in water or the normal flotant. This often changes the color of the fur markedly. For a dry fly, compare the natural and artificial bodies low against the sky, which is the angle at which a trout is first likely to see the fly, and at which color is clearly visible.

Just for curiosity, buy a commercially tyed Blue-Winged Olive in America and get it wet. You may find that it's a Gray-Winged Gray. Many commercial tyers are now using fine polypropylene dubbing that comes in dozens of buggy hues—until it gets water on it. Then all the colors are about the shade of your hook shank. Polypropylene is supposed to resist absorption of water, so I am just reporting a fact, not generalizing. There is no reason why heavier synthetic fibers should not hold their colors well. I have not experimented much with them. Silly as it may sound, fly-fishing is for me most satisfying when most natural. That is an emotional bias.

There appear to be two reasons for color changes:

- Pale fibers, in particular, may darken when wet.
- Some fibers become translucent, letting the dark hook show through.

The table will help to summarize fiber differences, but note that it does not consider individual fibers, only generalized extremes.

With many flies, and especially mayflies, there can be an important difference in the color of males and females. There is no point in imitating a male spinner that seldom reaches the water. The answer, of course, is to check the naturals.

It is perhaps unnecessary to add that the *underside* of a floating fly's body is the part a trout usually sees. The imitation should match it, even though the artificial will then look unlike the natural on casual observation. For nymphs, the color of the back may be more conspicuous.

A special trick of mine is to tie hatching duns with bodies color-matched to the live nymph rather than to the adult fly. For this purpose, I use a new plastic gadget that holds the live nymph in a small compartment, to which water may be added. The whole thing is backlighted through translucent plastic and magnified by a cheap lens. The artificial is put right in with the live nymph, and

	Fiber Differences	
	Dubbing of Coarse, Natural Guard-Hairs	*Dubbing of Fine, Long, Regular, Soft Fiber*
Ease of use	Requires skill	Easy and quick
Shape of body	Difficult to produce a neat outline on small flies	Good, even on tiny flies
Color when wet	Tends to maintain color, except in palest shades	Tends to darken
Translucency	Good	Poor
Sheen	Good, especially with shiny rib	Poor

both are viewed wet with light coming through them. Flies tied this way have taken brown trout that refused normal dressings.

In America especially, there is an odd custom of using black thread for the standard patterns of flies. Nothing could be less appropriate. Black thread should be confined to black flies. Any dark color will show through wet, pale dubbing if it is spun sparsely, as it should be for mayfly bodies. White silk thread, on the other hand, is translucent when wet, and hence widely useful; a thread of appropriate color is even better. Silk changes color when wet, while synthetic threads absorb less moisture and may undergo less of a change, but the color change can be an advantage. Real fanatics will want to experiment with white hook shanks for pale spent-spinners.

Legs and Tails In natural flies, legs are not so conspicuous as wings, but they may have a distinct and visible color. Sometimes this is suggested by winding on a second hackle of different color from the first. Even then, I am inclined to think that the blended hackle remains largely a wing imitation, at least on mayflies. From underneath, the most prominent effect of insect legs on the surface of the water is the light pattern mentioned earlier. Hackles wound in the normal manner make a pattern that has worked for a long time but is not, to my eye, especially realistic on large flies. A sparse hackle flattened on the bottom looks better.

Harding regards the light pattern as "the primary stimulus to the fish to rise." He would probably have agreed with me that another function of hackles can be to disguise the hook point, since he speculates that the chief characteristic of an educated trout is a learned ability to notice the hook of the fly. Some of the designs in chapter 10 hide the hook point or provide realistic light patterns, or both.

Most insects we imitate have no tails, but mayflies are a big exception. There is much variation in the strength and use of tails among mayfly species, but when their tails touch the water, these also leave a light pattern. In the artificial mayflies, tails help so much to float the fly that they are almost always used. Sometimes they are made of such heavy deer hair that they seem to be merely an extension of the body of the artificial fly. This makes the fly, as seen by the fish, several sizes larger than intended. A few long, widespread fibers of stiff hackle, however, make a light pattern that is plausible and which greatly aids behavior. Color seems inconsequential, though I often imitate it roughly as a sheer conceit.

In connection with tails, it is worth repeating the warning that nothing much stiffer than hackle fibers should be allowed to extend beyond the bend of the hook. A really stiff tail greatly reduces hooking power; a nice extended body on a short-shanked hook is one of the great conservation measures.

There is at least one remaining color puzzle: Why do some colors work better on one stream than another? The Blue-Winged Olive, again, is a case in point. Natural insects do vary in color from season to season and stream to stream, but this does not seem to be the entire explanation.

There is an insight by Romilly Fedden in his *Golden Days From the Fishing Log of a Painter in Brittany.* Fedden happened to have an artist's knowledge of color, and he found it necessary to dress all of his flies in colors darker and warmer than the naturals. He thought that this was because the beds of his Breton rivers were dark. "This color tone would naturally react on any floating object above, so it must follow that the natural fly, being very receptive to color refraction (that is, less dull and more reflectant in surface than the most lifelike imitation), would assimilate an undue proportion of the surrounding color."

I am not sure that a natural mayfly's body is much better as a reflector than stripped peacock quill ribbed with sparkling wire and given a coat of shiny varnish. If the mysteries of color seem too oppressive, it is not sheer superstition to cross the fingers and fall back on some such ancient expedient. It will not always work, but it will be more fun than mowing the lawn.

Hackle Fly
(size 12 hook)

Traditional Winged
Fly
(size 12 hook)

Thorax Dun
(size 12 hook)

Reverse-Tied Fly
(size 13 hook)

Big-Hackle Fly
(size 14 hook)

Fore-and-Aft Fly
(size 13 hook)

Bent-Hackle Fly
(size 11 hook)

Shaped-Hackle Fly
(size 13 hook)

Soft-Hackle Fly
(size 14 hook)

Parachute Fly
(size 14 hook)

Perfect Dun (side)
(size 14 hook)

Perfect Dun (front)

**Dun Without Hackle—
Quill Wing**
(size 16 hook)

**Dun Without Hackle—
Hair Wing**
(size 16 hook)

Barb-Wing Dun
(size 16 hook)

Invisible-Hackle Fly
(size 15 hook)

**Palmer Sedge—
No Wing**
(size 13 hook)

Deep-Sinking Nymph
(size 8 hook)

**Palmer Sedge—
Winged**
(size 13 hook)

Flat-Wing Sedge
(size 14 hook)

Hair-Wing Sedge
(size 13 hook)

Sedge Pupa
(size 14 hook)

Sedge Larva
(size 14 hook)

Small Stonefly
(size 13 hook)

Large Stonefly
(size 8 long hook)

Hard-to-Believe
Stonefly
(size 10 long hook)

Midge Pupa
(size 17 hook)

Low-Riding Adult
Midge
(size 16 hook)

Ant
(size 16 hook)

**Jassid—Jungle Cock
Wing
(size 18 hook)**

**Jassid—Hackle-Tip
Wing, with
reversed fibers
(size 18 hook)**

**Coch-y-Bondu Beetle
(size 15 hook)**

**Flat-Wing Beetle
(side)
(size 15 hook)**

**Flat-Wing Beetle
(top)**

**Grasshopper
(size 10 hook)**

**Black Gnat—Single
(size 15 hook)**

**Black Gnat—Knotted
(size 15 hook)**

**Black Gnat—
Clumped
(size 15 hook)**

PART IV

Fly Designs
for Important Insects

9 ⚜ *What Makes a "Design"*

And When to Change Designs
Instead of Patterns

⚜ ⚜ ⚜ Angling books traditionally emphasize fly patterns. That is one reason why this one does the opposite and focuses on fly designs. Patterns are fascinating and useful, but we have a lot already. When it comes to fancy flies, we have too many.

The difference between pattern and design is important but not obvious. Most listings of patterns describe the materials that go into a fly, with emphasis on their color, and with design taken almost for granted. Not much has been written conciously on design.

Let us now define design as *the way materials are chosen and assembled in order to achieve a desired structural task.* That task is to control *behavior* above all; but size, shape, and color are also involved.

Architects will have no trouble with this concept. Fly-fishermen are used to thinking in different terms, so the idea may be unsettling. That is why the definition of fly design was not promulgated to a startled world in chapter 1. Most of us have been reading trout-fly patterns for a long time, which means we have been reading things like:

WINGS: Light starling
BODY: Peacock quill undyed
HACKLE AND WHISK: Pale blue dun
HOOK: 0, 00, or 000

This dry-fly pattern—Halford's description of a Blue Quill—is better than most. It tells us most of what we need to know about color. It gives sizes, which many patterns omit. But the shape and behavior can be known only from the context. The same pattern could, for example, describe a sparse wet fly or a high-floating, thickly dressed variant.

The designs in the next two chapters will describe flies in almost the opposite way. They will be classified not by color but by behavior: mainly the level at which they are designed to be fished, and sometimes their ability to be moved. The description will then focus on their shape. Size and color—Halford's two features—will be mentioned only when necessary. I am breaking this all to you gently because some of my dear old friends will by now be into their third Scotch and melting the ice cubes with their snorts. Have patience; if the trout can cope with this, most trout-fishermen should be able to get used to it. Pour another one.

The trout really do take to designs better than patterns. That is to say, they look at how a fly is behaving before they consider its color. The concept of design makes sense when you hear what the trout say, and therefore the title of this book.

Put it another way: the difference between design and pattern is the difference between geometry and painting. A geometric figure may be colored and a painting may be geometric, but they start from different directions.

Design factors are especially neglected in fancy American flies and in Halfordian dry flies. As Halford got older, he even discarded the Gold-Ribbed Hare's Ear, which (lacking a feather hackle) had been his only design suitable for hatching duns. Ray Bergman's books had plate after plate of flies with scarcely any design variation, though the artist may have failed to catch differences that were significant in the originals. Donald Du Bois, in his impressive *Fisherman's Handbook of Trout Flies,* did anglers the service of listing almost six thousand patterns. This is probably the apex of pattern books, both for sheer number and because design factors are almost entirely omitted. Even size is not mentioned.

Even where American flies were not fancies, they were designed to meet a situation or imitate a natural fly that the originator did not describe, so that the resulting pattern meant little to anyone else. Recent American patterns, on the other hand, are often both meaningful and imaginative. But American conditions vary so much that even the best imitative patterns are meaningful only in a specified area.

Designs, on the contrary, are universally relevant, and American dry-fly designs have always been good.

I have no intention of disparaging patterns. Tackle and fly patterns are the first things I look for when I get an old angling book, even though these things are not always relevant to my own fishing. Many of the old writers on the eastern side of the Atlantic made their patterns so explicit that the design also emerged clearly, though unconciously. North Country wet flies are the outstanding example. Stewart's Spiders could hardly be tied wrong from his description. He then spent most of his book on the flies' behavior.

A writer like Halford who dwells on the color of his hackles is usually talking about pattern, while anglers like Baigent or John Henderson (both discussed in the next chapter) are evidently interested in design, since they vary the size or shape of their hackles. Most of Marinaro's flies have innovative designs.

Few fly-tyers (excepting Marinaro) explain their structural principles, much less offer alternative designs to meet changed situations. Patterns are studied consciously; designs are absorbed unconsciously and defended irrationally. Cotton, as I have noted, laughed at a London fly hung in his window. Ever since, anglers have exchanged "sour censures" on the merits of wings versus hackle, stiff hackles versus soft ones, dry flies versus sunken ones, general flies versus imitations, and so on. Yet the arguments usually disappear (and the sour censures with them) when the principles of each design are related to fishing conditions. No major fishing school has worked out fly designs that are stupid for local insects and waters. On the other hand, no single fishing school has worked out all the designs that are useful, even on local waters.

The blind spot with regard to design is especially puzzling because design is usually more important than pattern. Put a man who understands design down on any insect-rich river and he will, after a period of study, do fairly well. Move a man who knows only patterns and he will be lost. This was about what happened when North America was settled.

Nowadays an American angler may consent to talk about designs when pushed, and conditions often push him. British and Irish anglers can afford to be more comfortable with the old patterns and more suspicious of new concepts. Sometimes when I was talking to my Irish friends about designs, they looked at me as if I were carrying on about the *Kama Sutra* in a convent. Nevertheless, Skues and Mottram were notable fly-designers.

The lack of interest in fly design makes it difficult to trace the origins of the major styles. John Waller Hills, an excellent historian, traced twelve flies through the centuries with almost no questions on design. He did not even look deeply into the origin of wound hackles. If the present book manages to arouse any interest in fly designs, my sparse findings on origins will rapidly be amplified by other anglers. Fortunately, it is not necessary to know much history to figure out which designs are now most useful. My own comments on origins rarely go back more than a century, both because I lack many early editions and because many of the designs that follow are of dry flies, which share few mechanical principles with wets.

In the last twenty-odd years, a number of new designs—or rejuvenated old ones—have been well described, though not in any single book. The effect has been to give anglers a choice they did not have before.

It is no coincidence that fly designs have proliferated as traditional materials grew scarce. Some new designs are simply excuses for avoiding the use of no-longer-inexpensive top-quality hackles. Modern science has perfected a chicken with hackles like cotton wool (and flesh that tastes about the same way). When we cannot afford good hackles in the scarce colors, we might as well make a virtue of necessity and try some designs that are really different.

The Reasons for Trying Different Designs

Shortage of materials is only one reason for trying different fly designs. The best reason of all is that most insects are available to trout at several stages of development, in each of which the insect has a characteristic behavior. Any big change in behavior usually requires a different fly design. A trout that refuses a "normal" mayfly should, for example, be tried with a low-floating imitation of a hatching dun, or with a high-floating design that keeps the hook out of the water.

Many good anglers cannot be bothered to tie complicated flies. Simple designs that work well are available, and a number of them are described in the following pages. It is a curious thing that rough flies tied from a portable kit, with trimmings falling off in the morning coffee, have a way of catching more fish than the complicated products of my winter's evenings.

Fly designs are also related to personal angling styles. Writers are not always aware of this, but the point leaps out of a comparison of almost any two fishing books. In choosing a floating design, for example, it helps to know whether the angler casts upstream or cross-stream, uses fine leaders or stout, takes time to dry and and re-grease his fly, casts often or seldom, has good visibility or bad, fishes to rises or blind, and so on. No wonder different anglers swear by different flies. And no wonder anglers come to rely on old reliables that work for their personal styles.

My normal stream tactics require the use of long leader tippets. This in turn means that I do best with flies that naturally land upright, with no assistance from me. Some winged patterns have a tendency to land on their sides when cast on a loose leader. If I use such patterns, I must also switch to heavier leaders so that I can give the fly a slight pull as it lands, helping it to cock.

There is yet another reason for varying fly designs: trout that have been educated may accept a new design just because it does not arouse old suspicions. In this case it may make sense to try a really novel design, such as one that keeps the hook out of the water, or one with extra-large wings. This is what makes fly-fishing interesting. In America, I have a whole fly-box devoted to the little *Tricorythodes*. In Ireland, I have a box for the Large Dark Olive, a box for the Blue-Winged Olive, and a box for the Grey Flag sedge

(Hydropsyche pellucidula). On the other hand, I do not smoke tobacco, dye my hair, or consult a guru. Anyone who thinks I am daft is probably right and is certainly welcome to follow his own kinks.

Which Designs?

At the risk of returning to a tired theme, I should make clear my own personal assumption that the purpose of trout flies is to catch trout. This may not be quite as obvious as it appears. Chapter 1 has already suggested that many flies are bought to impress human beings. To aim flies at humans is to make fly-tying an art, or at least a very clever craft. I have no philosophical objection to this. Certainly trout flies are decorative, and Salmon Flies more so. To make a fly well requires skill. With all these attributes, it is inevitable that flies should be tied for reasons other than fishing. It is inevitable that there should be exhibits and human competitions in which flies are rated for aesthetic values, which is to say values not directly related to trout.

The comparison between fly-tying and the arts does not seem as far-fetched today as it might have been in the days before soup cans were a legitimate subject for painters. There is (in my opinion) no such thing as a fly that imitates nature as closely as a Goya, although imitative flies have often been compared to impressionist paintings. Since no fly I have seen made anything like the emotional impact of a Van Gogh, I am inclined to think that fly-tying is a very simple art, if it is an art at all. Still, any good fly means something to me, and if I know of an insect it represents, the meaning is greater. Fancy flies are on the border between the representational and the abstract, and they mean less to me, though not necessarily to the fisherman just downstream.

But none of this is really my game. For me, fishing is a friendly contest with nature, with the rules written to give nature a maximum of chances. Art is a human game. When I see an artful, impractical fly, I cannot help a slight feeling of relief that another human being has gone off on a sidetrack and left the trout to me. I try not even to be distracted by fly-tying as a craft, except as the craft is related at every step to the trout's taste. Give me sunsets, birdsongs, and even trout in the net for aesthetic pleasure, but not flies that are purposely artful. The fun is in really working with nature, trying to know what I am doing, and then seeing if the smartest trout I can find agrees with me. One of the things I like about trout is that they cannot be influenced by wealth, station, human emotion, or even art. But they are impressed by functional flies.

All of which may be a complicated way of saying that I have not intentionally put anything that is merely clever in the following chapters on fly designs. In most cases, the simplest design that will fulfill a given (and specified) function gets pride of place. A few designs that I rarely use are mentioned because they are very widely used by others (like the traditional winged fly) or historically important (like the original Thorax Dun), or both. All of the designs discussed are related to insects, and the relationship has been made clear in this and previous chapters. Many designs (possibly good) are omitted because they overlap with others or because I have not been able to test them to my satisfaction. All of the designs shown do work for the stated purposes, and their disadvantages are noted.

10 ❧ Mayfly Designs

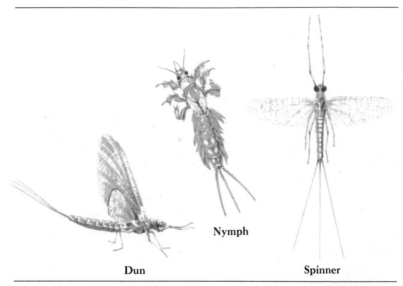

Nymph

Dun

Spinner

❧ ❧ ❧ Imitations of the mayflies are especially numerous, perhaps because they got off to a head start historically. Imitations of floating mayflies also require the angler to worry about three dimensions (chapter 7), whereas imitations of sedges and other down-winged flies can often be two-dimensional. I would not want to leave the impression that mayflies are more important than the other flies, but they may be a little more difficult to imitate.

Designs That Float at a Normal Height

"Normal" simply means that most conventional patterns of dry flies float at this height. Unless the dressing is very bushy, the point of the hook soon breaks through the surface film, leaving the fly supported by some few of the horizontal hackle fibers and by the

tail. The body, however, is often partly above the water. Fully hatched mayfly duns may float at this height, so it is a logical starting point. Spinners tend to float either higher or lower, although plain hackle flies are fair spinner imitations. Hatching duns typically float lower.

<u>Hackle Fly</u> As used here, the term "hackle fly" describes a dry fly with a cock's hackle forming a full circle behind the eye of the hook. The hackle suggests especially the wings but also the legs of the natural. Two hackles are often used, in which case those of mixed colors may be most effective. The hackle fly also has a body and a tail. The tail is important in floating the fly but should be sparse, like that of the natural. The fly floats best if the tail is widely spread, but this is a departure from tradition.

Origin The origin of this fly is lost in the mists of time, at least where wet flies are concerned—and the dry version evolved gradually from the wet. Winding a feather hackle-wise seems to me an ingenious invention, and far from an obvious one. Wound hackles were not clearly described in Dame Juliana's *Treatise* (1496),

Hackle Fly

though they may have been in use. John McDonald, the outstanding American angling historian, finds the first clear reference to wound hackles in the 1651 edition of Barker. By that time, however, they must have been evolving for many decades or centuries.

Since the present book is concerned with design, we must note that dry flies ask more of hackles than wet flies do—so much more that we are really dealing with different problems. Hackles had, of course, long been in use when dry flies evolved, and must have floated at least some of the first ones, but certainly not all of them. Over the last century, hackles have sometimes been assumed to be essential for floating flies, though they are not. There is an ancient controversy as to the merits of hackle versus winged designs (chapter 7). Sometimes only winged designs have been considered real flies, while designs omitting wings have been called mere "hackles." Although the controversy is still not dead, it is an example of human whimsy. In the eyes of trout, hackles are clearly an imitation of wings.

Tying Notes For an imitative fly, the hackle should normally be sparse. Start with one of the long new "genetic" hackles and not more than two of the short kind. Traditionally, the hackle barbs (fibers) should also be short—not longer than about one-and-three-quarters times the size of the gape. My own preference is to use a slightly bigger hackle to lighten the float and make the hook less prominent. Hackles with fibers double the size of the gape seem about right.

Some anglers maintain that trout do not object to trimmed hackles, but I suspect this to be true only when soft, non-poultry hackles are used. Cocks' hackles, when trimmed, have stiff, blunt ends that break through the surface film. The most durable flies are made with hackles reversed—tied in with the dull, concave side forward. Hackles tied in bright-side-forward bend back along the shank when cast, but they have better color and sheen, and their bent points may help to hide the hook.

Advantages
- Simple and quick to tie
- Extremely durable

- Floats well (with good materials)
- Equally effective in whatever position it lands on the water (a very important tactical advantage)

Disadvantages

- Depends on good-quality hackles.
- Does not present a sharp wing outline
- Only partially hides the hook

Conclusions The advantage of hackle flies are impressive. They are a logical first try for mayfly duns. Where this design fails, however, one that floats differently or has a sharper wing outline should be quickly tried. Because this design is so widely used, I have taken it as a basis of comparison for the other mayfly designs discussed below.

Traditional Winged Fly

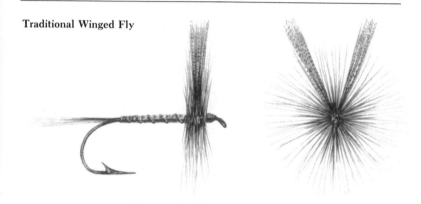

Traditional Winged Fly The traditional winged fly is the same as the hackle fly except for the addition of wings, which are placed in the middle of the hackle near the head of the fly. Despite the historical controversy about winged and wingless flies, there is little to choose between the two designs as traditionally tied.

Origin Flies with both hackle and wings are also very old. Since they apparently evolved through the addition of hackle to winged flies, rather than vice versa, the comments already made on the origin of hackle flies apply.

By the time dry flies began purposeful evolution in the last half of the nineteenth century, the fly with wings and hackles was the dominant dressing. In this sense, it grew up with the dry fly rather than having a clear-cut origin.

The double-divided-wing fly has a special historical place, since it was the design worked out by the first conscious pioneers of dry-fly fishing on the English chalkstreams. Skues describes its origin in his *Side-Lines, Side-Lights, and Reflections.* He attributes the invention to H. S. Hall. G. S. Marryat and Halford also had much to do with the development of this fly. Skues considers the double-divided-wing design a great advance on its predecessors, mainly because the wings are still visible after a lot of use. Personally, I have used such wings only briefly, since they take longer to tie than the older bunched-wing style and may twist fine tippets. Bunched wings cock a fly equally well if they are split to create more air resistance as the fly falls to the water.

American flies rarely used double-divided wings unless an English pattern was being consciously copied. Theodore Gordon seems to have set a lasting precedent when he used rolled wood-duck breast feathers, a light and excellent material. The famous Quill Gordon is as attractive a fly as ever was tied, for both humans and trout. I do not mean to detract from the fly when I say that it is the old Blue Quill, with the addition of wood-duck wings. Although the name Quill Gordon has in recent years been applied by extension to a specific mayfly, the artificial fly of the same name can be modified to imitate a vast number of duns and spinners. Most American fishermen (including Gordon) have used the pattern as a sort of general fly, much as British anglers use the Greenwell's Glory.

Tying Notes The wing is usually the first component tied to the fly after the tying thread has been attached. For neatness, the points of the wing should be tied facing forward over the eye of the hook. The wing is then raised, secured in an upright position by a few additional turns of thread, and finally reinforced by tight winds of hackle on both sides of it. So tied, a rolled wing is strong and realistic. A divided wing cocks the fly better and is advisable if the wing is large. (Any single rolled wing can be divided by a figure-eight wrap of the tying silk.)

Advantages
- Wing more dense than that of hackle fly
- Easier for angler to see than hackle fly (sometimes important)

Disadvantages
- May fail to cock or land with wings upright (sometimes a real disadvantage)
- Heavier than hackle fly, so not as good a floater
- May twist the leader if stiff wings are used

Conclusions The choice between the winged fly and the plain hackle fly is a matter of personal preference. I lean toward the hackle fly for most conditions and the winged fly where the hackle pattern is hard to see on the water. Where a high, dense wing is needed, a design such as the following may be more effective.

Thorax Dun

Thorax Dun This term is now often applied to any fly with the wing near the middle of the body, but there is a precise origin. The designer of this fly intended to create a better floating platform for a broad, flat wing. He considered the wing and the light pattern to be the important features of natural duns.

Origin The Thorax Dun was designed by Vincent Marinaro and described in his *Modern Dry-Fly Code,* first published in 1950. The book has been reprinted and should be on every fly-fisherman's bookshelf. Since the fly has a number of original features, it is best tied from Marinaro's own lengthy directions, although the notes given below will serve. If you change Marinaro's method, you have either a Thorax Dun that works badly or a fly—possibly good in its own right—that does not behave as Marinaro intended. *There is only one Thorax Dun. Its wing silhouette and light pattern are unique.* But you have to follow the recipe. Having discussed the fly with Marinaro and watched him tie it, I am persuaded that a number of flies I have fondly called Thorax Duns over the years should not have been given this title.

Tying Notes Extra-fine thread is essential. Marinaro is not fussy about the color. (Color addicts can ease withdrawal symptoms by muttering repeatedly, "This fly is for light pattern and wing silhouette, not color.") Wind a short bed of thread near the middle of the shank and tie on your wing just forward of the middle.

The wing is the most demanding operation. Marinaro believes that a special cutter is essential for the efficient making of well-balanced wings in his style. I agree. Scissors or nail-cutters will get the job done, but slowly, and you risk mismatched wings that will spin the fly.

If you do use cut wings, Marinaro recommends that you prepare them from the middle of the hackle, just where the stalk is beginning to thin down rapidly. The base of your wing will then be thick enough for strength, and the tip will be fine enough for flexibility. Strip the base, and tie each wing in *individually* with an X pattern of thread around the base. Align the wing carefully by twisting the *bare stalk* of the hackle, below the hook, with your fingers. This is important to ensure that the relatively stiff cut wing does not create any out-of-line airfoil that will spin your fly. Now bend the stalk back along the shank, tie the stalk down, and cut it off. Repeat the entire procedure for the other wing. When the fly is finished, you will *bend both wings back along the shank and press them down hard with your thumb.* This breaks the stalk, as Marinaro says, in the correct line.

Tied in this way, the cut wing really works, though I plead guilty to using uncut hackle-tip wings occasionally.

Now wind back and make the tail.

Marinaro was the first writer to bring out the importance of a wide-spread tail. I find his reasoning impossible to fault. His method of tying in the tail is exactly like his method of tying wings, except that the tails stick out *horizontally* instead of vertically. A number of wraps are required, so you have to use a very fine thread (my favorite, Pearsall's Gossamer, is a little too heavy, so for other designs I use a different way of making the tail, described in chapter 12). Vince uses only two or three hackle fibers for each half of the tail. He ties each half in separately, laying it at a *full right angle* to the hook shank and fastening it with wraps of thread in an *X* pattern. He then bends the butts forward, ties off the tail, and trims it. This should be repeated for the other half. The tail will now stick directly out from the hook until the fly is cast, when the fibers pull back at an angle. What could be more functional?

Marinaro uses no body in the conventional sense; he simply winds the thread forward to the wings again and ties in a piece of spun fur. Vince pays little attention to color here either, but he stays close to the natural. He winds a *tight* ball of fur around the base of the wings only. This is merely an aid in tying the hackle, which is—again—unconventional.

I believe that the hackle is the most original feature of all in the Thorax Dun design. Some fly-tyers prefer to wind two hackles around the wing in normal fashion, and then to clip the bottom fibers. A fly made in this way is neater and easier to tie. But Marinaro considers this variation a mistake; it gives a much lower float and an entirely different light pattern. Such flies do work well, but they constitute a different design.

Marinaro's hackle is made of two cock's hackles of different sizes tied in by the butt and wound in a unique criss-cross fashion, so that the hackle looks like an *X* when seen from the side. The larger hackle is tipped so that the fibers on top of the shank go in front of the wing, while the fibers below the shank go behind the wing. The smaller hackle's top fibers go behind the wing, and the bottom fibers are well in front of the wing. The fly is thus supported in a slightly nose-down position. The ball of fur helps to get the hackles in the correct, broad *X* configuration. Instructions for the ball of fur are in Marinaro's second book.

Advantages
- Very realistic for medium-to-large duns requiring large, dark wings
- Hackle well positioned to support the wing
- Body rides level, like that of most natural flies

Disadvantages
- Tricky to tie in proper balance
- Time consuming, especially if a wing-cutter is not available
- Fragile wings
- Sometimes fails to land upright, despite the careful provisions for balance
- May twist the leader

Conclusions The Thorax Dun has been unavailable so far to any but a good amateur fly-tyer. Professionals have not widely sold it (to my knowledge) *in the original version,* and many amateurs cannot tie it. But I do not want to leave the impression that Marinaro's design is purposely complicated. In some ways it is simple. Its difficulties flow from its accomplishments. Every component is new, ingenious, and functional.

Reverse-Tied Fly

Reverse-Tied Fly This is simply the old hackle fly tied back-to-front, with the hackle at the bend of the hook. I started using this design on a very weedy stream, so that I could cast onto a mat of weeds and pull the fly off without snagging. Trout took the fly so well that I began using it on other streams, where it was sometimes more successful than normal patterns. The reverse-tied fly is, in fact, one of those rare designs that can be tried with hope when "nothing else works." I eventually realized that trout accept it for a high-riding sedge or spinner as well as for the duns I was trying to represent. The design's success is probably explained by the fact that it is *the only fly of normal size and shape in which the hook usually stays out of the water.* This is quite an accomplishment: the fly has many of the advantages of the high-riding designs described in the next section without their exaggerated size and shape.

The reverse-tied fly goes even farther than the Thorax Dun in moving the hackle back to where it can support the heaviest part of the hook. Some anglers have suspected this design of poor hooking qualities, but I have not found it worse than any other fly with full-circle cock's hackles.

Origin C. F. Walker has commented that every beginner invents the reverse-tied fly and then drops it. When the design was recently discussed in *Trout and Salmon* magazine, one correspondent reported that the "back-to-front" fly had been described as far back as 1806 by Alexander Mackintosh. A reversed "fluttering fly" was patented in America in 1886. These, of course, were wet flies, and I cannot imagine their function. I am not aware that anyone has advocated reversed dry flies, although some have been used.

Tying Notes I often add tails to the reverse-tied fly as a matter of convention, but the fly seems to fish about as well without them: the leader does the same job. A strict imitationist could even argue that this is the only design in which the leader is camouflaged as a tail. Wings can, of course, be added, but I think they put too much load on a hackle that already has the bend of the hook to support. One advantage of the reverse-tied design is lightness and simplicity, and these qualities should not be diminished in the tying. Put the tail on first at the eye; wind the thread back to the bend; tie on and wind the hackles dull-side-forward (preferably two, of mixed colors); then tie on the body and wind it forward to the tail, finishing off with a whip finish at the tail. Take care to have a good, neat hackle, or the fly is worthless.

Advantages

- Usually keeps the hook out of the water, while retaining the small size and sparse shape necessary for good imitation

- Slightly more awkward to tie than the ordinary hackle fly, but still simple and quick; may be tied at streamside
- Floats especially well
- Equally effective in whatever position it lands on the water
- Almost weedless

Disadvantages

- Depends on good-quality hackles carefully tied
- Looks unattractive to anglers accustomed to traditional flies

Conclusions Anglers who have not tried this one are missing a bet. The advantages are marked. The problem of the visible hookpoint almost disappears. My own practice is to save this fly for difficult conditions, using the conventional hackle fly normally, simply because it is a little easier to tie. The reverse-tied fly could, however, be used routinely.

Preen-Gland Fly Jest, if you must, at this fragile beauty. Then hasten to assault a duck for the necessary hackles. You will find them atop the uropygium, which is the bulge we call "the parson's nose" at the stern of the bird. They are curious, specialized feathers, having to do—I surmise—with the transfer of oil from the gland. They are long-fibered, short-shafted, sparse, soft, and webby: everything that classic dry-fly hackles are not.

And they catch trout that refuse classic dry flies.

Those, in fact, are the only trout for which the preen-gland feather is worth using. It floats better than you would guess, thanks to natural oils, but once wet is difficult to dry. The flotant that does the job best is based on carbon tetrachloride, a dry-cleaning solvent that, unfortunately, turns out to be carcinogenic. Better just tie several of the flies. Don't bother with them in fast water or for easy trout. Do bother when cautious fish are rising to duns in flat water. The gauzy, supple, misty-gray barbs have the delicacy of a real mayfly.

The name of the fly in French is *Cul de Canard*, which is imprecise. The modest translation is "Duck's Rump" in the English-language version of Jean-Paul Pequegnot's book (*French Fishing Flies*, 1987). I have rejected Parson's Nose and D.A., neither of which are names deserving of immortality. "Preen-Gland Fly" is accurate and does not inhibit flirtation with birds other than ducks. Woodcock and pheasant preen-gland feathers look good too, though I have not given them an adequate test.

Preen-Gland Fly

Origin Dr. Pequegnot reports that the fly originated in Vallorbe, in the Swiss section of the Jura. It is also widely used just across the border in France. I have not seen the name of the genius—probably rural—who first gazed on this feather and didn't know enough to discard it.

I was introduced to the fly by Rudi van Alberda, a Dutch angler. Judging from the feathers he sent me, and from the French flies I have seen, domestic ducks are the original (or at least usual) source. Not mine, though. Wild ducks fly my way, frequently, and stay to be plucked, occasionally. I like their hackles even better.

Tying Notes First catch your duck. The hackles you seek form a sparse circle around the preen gland. To find them, be guided by the sculptor who made a marble statue by chipping away everything that didn't look like Venus. In the case of the hackles, larger tail and rump feathers almost hide what you are looking for.

This is a dry fly, despite its appearance, and it will float longer if you use a wide-spread tail of cock's-hackle fibers. The body should be light in weight (dubbing or tying silk, for example—not deer hair). The hackle is easy to wind in the normal way. My own preference is to use only one feather. Tied thus, the fly is as gauzy as a natural mayfly and slips into the trout's mouth with scarcely more resistance. French fly-tyer Aime Devaux, however, tied preen-gland flies with wings and a stiff little hackle behind the duck's feather, to reinforce it. I have not tried these and don't see a need for wings on this design, but would wind a reinforcing hackle if I needed a longer float. (The Bent-Hackle Fly uses that design.)

If you use domestic-duck hackles, they will be too long of fiber. The easy way to shorten them is to wind the hackle and then pull all the barbs forward over the eye of the hook. One snip will then clip all to the same length.

Advantages
- Easy and cheap, once you have subdued your duck.
- Light and air-resistant, but still supple. Falls gently and hooks deeply.
- Fools difficult fish.

Disadvantages
- Fragile and difficult to keep afloat.
- A catch-it-if-you-can proposition. The feathers are not in any catalog I have seen at this writing.

High-Floating Flies

A heavily hackled, high-floating fly can be used as a general pattern for "pounding up" trout in fast water. Where an imitative fly is needed, however, the dressing should be sparse. High-floating flies are not, in my experience, miracle-workers. Authors who have so described them can perhaps be excused, for the high-riding fly is likely to produce spectacular results when it works at all. Sizable trout may come clear out of the water after a teasing

Spider. This is also one of the few designs that can be moved on the water. In Ireland, I have found high-floating flies useful only when they imitated the behavior of the natural fly: a big dun being blown around, a spinner returning to lay its eggs (but not yet spent), or an egg-laying sedge. Such conditions are not very common. In America, however, trout must see more high-riding insects, because imitations of them work more frequently. I have included in this category all but one of the important designs that float with the hook-point out of the water. (The single exception is the reverse-tied fly, which has already been described. While it usually rides with the hook-point out of the water, the reverse-tied fly is of normal size and does not float extremely high.)

Big-Hackle Fly

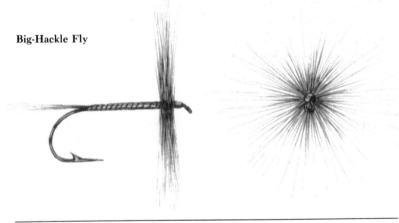

Big-Hackle Fly This category could be subdivided into at least three designs with different hackle sizes. The differences in behavior are substantial. Historically, however, these differences have been blurred, and so has the nomenclature. In all of these designs, hackle quality is a controlling factor, and patterns can be almost meaningless unless actual hackles are provided. For this reason, anglers must usually work out their own imitations from scratch, basing them on the behavior of the natural and the materials at hand.

Three terms in wide current use are as follows:

Variants, in the United States, are usually flies with hackles only a little larger than normal, and without wings. A dressing of this kind is very useful. In Britain, where the term originated, it is likely to describe a larger hackle and a sparser dressing, often with a small wing.

Spiders, in the United States, are usually dry flies with very wide, sparse hackles, little or no body, and no wings. Except for the absence of wings, they look much like British variants. In Britain, where the term "Spider" originated, it has normally been used to describe a hackled wet fly. A dry Spider in Britain is likely to be an imitation of a natural spider rather than a special fly design.

The Skater is an American fly with no British counterpart. It has an extremely wide hackle and no body, tail, or wings. The right hackles for this design are scarce. Such flies were designed to be fished with some movement; they were actually invented as butterfly imitations, incredible as it must seem to British anglers. Since then, the Skaters have been used during hatches of Greendrakes and other large flies.

In practice, the three labels described above seem to mean something different to everyone. Ray Bergman suggested that anglers simply specify hackle size when big hackles are wanted. Instead of saying "variant," the angler might then say "size 14 hackle on a size 16 hook." But hackle sizes are not standardized either, so it would be easier to specify hackle diameter in inches or millimeters.

Origin Although big-hackle flies are now most widely used in America, they seem clearly to have originated in England and to have been used there for a long time before crossing the Atlantic. First advocacy of the big-hackled dry fly—though not of the term "variant"—is almost always credited to Dr. William Baigent. His daughter has shed some light on the evolution of the design in two articles for the *Flyfisher's Journal*; she believes that Dr. Baigent began using wet flies with big hackles in 1875, intending them as imitations of the Gravel Fly. I have never seen this natural insect, but it is described by Williams as a close relative of craneflies, locally important to anglers. It is also known as the Gravel Bed or Gravel Spider, presumably from its long legs. A dry fly would seem to be a much more suitable representation of this insect than a wet fly, and Dr. Baigent's daughter believes that he began floating his imitations by 1890. He evidently did not claim to be the inventor: she quotes him as saying, "It is difficult to know who was the first to invent or use almost anything." Amen.

These days, unfortunately, few know how to reproduce Dr. Baigent's patterns (or to find the hackles for them). But the big-hackle design has endured, with many variations on the variants. The manner in which a dry fly evolved from a wet fly with very different mechanical requirements is interesting. Many other early dry-fly fishermen must have made similar experiments: it is almost impossible not to do so.

The Skater, on the other hand, can be attributed with certainty to Edward R. Hewitt, who describes it in *A Trout and Salmon Fisherman for Seventy-Five Years.* He first wrote about the Skater in 1937. Since it is tied and fished differently from the variant, Hewitt deserves mention here for it.

Tying Notes With variants and American Spiders, the important thing is to use wide, stiff, shiny cocks' hackles, and not much of anything else. To withstand repeated casting, the hackles should be tied with the concave (dull) side forward. Small bodies are often added but can scarcely be apparent to the trout if the fly rides as it should. The Skater uses the widest possible stiff hackles, and they are often tied in a special way. The rear hackle has the concave side forward. The front hackle has the shiny, convex side forward. Both are tied on with unwaxed nylon thread. After winding, the bases of the hackles are pushed into position with a fingernail, so that the tips of the two hackles meet and the bases are some distance apart. Hewitt does not describe this tying, but Marinaro's discovery of it is described in Charles Fox's *This Wonderful World of Trout.*

Advantages
- These flies all ride high, with the hook well out of the water
- Since they ride so lightly, they can be moved in a natural way by wind or the rod

Disadvantages
- Suitable only for the imitation of large flies, or for very high-

riding flies of medium size
- Hook is small in relation to the size of the fly (these can be considered big flies for small fish)
- Not realistic imitations of any quality except behavior
- Fragile
- Depend on unusually good hackles
- Worse-than-average hooking ability

Conclusions When big-hackle flies are needed, they may be needed badly. Most of the time, however, they are not very useful as imitative patterns. The exception is a variant with hackles only slightly oversize, which is widely useful.

Fore-and-Aft Fly

Fore-and-Aft Fly This design has a hackle at each end, the front one logically a little smaller than the rear. The shape is nothing like any single natural fly. The design is, however, a good imitation of two mating flies, in which case it is known as the knotted midge (see the later discussion on Black Gnats). Just as frequently, the design is used for Greendrakes and their spinners. In this application, good high-floating behavior is the main advantage of the fore-and-aft design. The best one can say for the shape of this fly is that it is not quite as unrealistic as a bushy palmer fly.

In my experience, the fore-and-aft design is as good for small midges and sedges as for mayflies and black gnats, although I have not seen this use noted elsewhere. American anglers might try a fore-and-aft fly when egg-laying sedges return to the water in the early evening.

Origin Several writers have mentioned the use of the fore-and-aft fly by British anglers on the Kennet in the 1930s. It is hard to believe that a dry-fly design so obvious and so useful did not get a chance earlier. I have seen a wet fore-and-aft from Ireland that dates well into the last century. I cannot fathom the reasoning behind a wet fly with this design, but it shows that the idea has been around for a long time. Similar wet flies are still used in the American West.

Tying Notes I have never been sure that trout get a close view of a fly's body when it is supported above the water, as with this design. On the other hand, I have also never been sure that trout do *not* see such a body, so I compromise by putting on one of the right color, but of light weight. A fly whose best feature is high-riding behavior should not be loaded down with heavy components. Hackles are the dominant feature of the fore-and-aft design and should be stiff and shiny. This seems more important than color or (within limits) size. The rear hackle should be tied shiny-side-forward and the front hackle reversed, so that the fibers of the two hackles tip away from each other. If a very small fly is wanted, however, only one good hackle is necessary. Tie it on dull-side-forward. Make two small turns at the rear of the body, one broad turn forward over the whole body, and two more turns at the head.

Advantages
- The advantages of the big-hackle flies mentioned earlier, plus better balance, more compact size, and slightly better hooking ability

Disadvantage
- Unrealistic shape, though the trout do not seem to mind this as much as humans

Conclusions When a really high-floating fly is needed, the fore-and-aft fly offers some advantages over the designs tied with a big hackle all in one spot.

Bent-Hackle Fly This is a strange one. It seems to violate all the rules for a high-riding fly. The hackle is soft and dense, but not heavily wound. It looks like a traditional wet fly and is difficult to float at all. But while it floats, it is right up high, with the hook far out of the water. The bent-hackle fly does a good job for sedges too. The natural that is being matched must be fairly large.

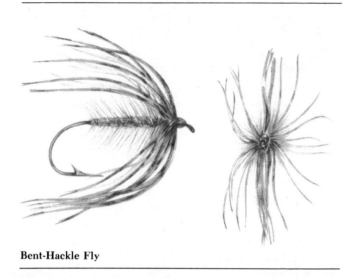

Bent-Hackle Fly

I use a Greendrake imitation with a size 12 hook and a much larger hackle. On one difficult Irish river, this is the only Greendrake design that has ever worked for me.

The mechanics of the bent-hackle fly must be clearly understood if the design is to be successful. A large, soft hackle—such as dyed French partridge—is wound on shiny-side-forward, supported by a small, stiff, cock's hackle out of sight behind the main hackle. The function of the stiff hackle is purely mechanical: it strengthens the middle of the soft hackle, while the soft tips bend backwards around the point of the hook. The fly floats on the bend of the soft hackle fibers. Nothing at all penetrates the surface film: something difficult to achieve with any other pattern. A good fly flotant helps to keep the soft fibers from soaking up water instantly. At best, however, the bent-hackle fly is suitable for only a few casts over a rising fish—but that should be enough. A similar effect can sometimes be achieved by using a long, thin-fibered, cock's hackle, with fibers much longer than normal. If the hackle does not go on just right, the fly will be useless. The body could be omitted entirely.

Angling literature is full of references to the fickle behavior of trout with regard to Greendrakes. Many of the traditional patterns featured soft hackles of French partridge, mallard breast, or some similar feather. I suspect that the fickle fancy of the trout could be explained in part by failure of the tyer to understand the correct design of the fly. The hackles cannot be expected to work properly by coincidence.

Origin The bent-hackle fly is another ancient wet-fly design gone dry. Big French partridge feathers are almost as traditional for Greendrake imitations as the duck feathers that gave the natural fly its common name. But I have rarely seen the big feathers tied in a way that seemed correct (to me). I suspect that there is a school somewhere in Britain that knows the design well, and it has long been used in France. One angler who seemed to understand it was an Irishman who gave me the idea. His flies looked odd even to other Irish fly-tyers, but he had no hesitation in proclaiming their superiority. His constant companion was a docile angler named Fred. Fred's role was to assent several dozen times a day when Partridge Hackle (as we came to know him) asked: "Isn't that right, Fred?" Fred never failed. The trout seldom did.

Tying Notes Light weight is important; if a tail and body are used at all, they should be sparse. Every attention should be devoted to getting the soft hackle to lie properly. The small supporting hackle can, if desired, be palmered over the body.

Advantages
- Dressing more dense than on other high-riding flies; otherwise the same advantages
- Good hooking qualities because of soft hackle
- No part of the fly penetrates the surface film
- Simple and cheap to tie

Disadvantage
- A bad floater, suitable only for a few casts before it needs drying

Conclusions Not a practical dressing for most purposes, but sometimes the best imitation of a large mayfly or sedge.

Low-Riding Flies

Low-riding designs are at the important dividing line between wet and dry flies. The soft-hackle fly, in particular, can be fished as a nymph. Low-riding flies are, however, for two distinct stages in the life of a mayfly: first when the dun hatches from the nymph, and second when the spinner (usually the female only) returns and dies on the water. The natural flies look quite different at these two times, and so should the artificials, although the shaped-hackle design described below can be pressed into double-duty. The hatching dun is typically bedraggled, with dense wings. The spinner usually has wings that are transparent. Very often the spinner is fully spent—with both wings caught in the surface film—but it can also be high-riding. The spent spinner is imitated by the first design below. The high-riding spinner can be well imitated by a plain hackle fly, a variant, a reverse-tied fly, or the fore-and-aft design. A half-spent spinner is easily made from the shaped-hackle fly design below.

Shaped-Hackle Fly This design is very widely used, for good reason. It is effective even for fishing blind on flat water. A great many materials other than shaped hackle can be used for spinner wings: hackle points, hair of several kinds, and, today, even synthetic yarn. Some are a little cheaper, easier to tie, or more visible. To my mind, none produces a fly as realistic as the original design. It is not necessary to use extremely stiff hackle, although it should be shiny and (for most mayflies) pale.

Origin John Henderson described the shaped-hackle design in Halford's *Dry-Fly Man's Handbook,* published in 1913. An article by Henderson in the *Flyfisher's Journal* of Summer 1970 pushes the origin back to 1907. In addition to the two flat bunched wings at the side, Henderson added a "head hackle" of partridge. This is often omitted but may be added to big mayfly imitations, to duplicate the prominent legs of the naturals and help in floating a heavy hook.

Marryat's spinners with hackle-point wings (as described by Halford in his *Floating Flies and How to Dress Them*, 1886) might be considered ancestors of the Henderson design. The wing of spread fibers, however, is better for realism as well as for durability.

Shaped-Hackle Fly

Tying Notes Make a good bed of tying thread, then wind a long hackle over about a third of the shank, leaving enough space in front for the head. Tie off the hackle. The head and hackle together will just about take up the front half of the shank. Now pull the hackle into *widely based* bunches, one at each side of the hook, and secure the fibers in their horizontal position with figure-eight turns of dubbed thread above and below the hook. Be careful not to let the figure-eights narrow the bases of the wings. Henderson, and more recently Marinaro, insist on a wide wing to represent the silhouette of the natural spinner.

The shaped-hackle design is one in which the tips of the hackle can, if necessary, be trimmed. If visibility is a problem, the hackle can be wound flat on the bottom only, leaving a fringe on top to protrude above the surface. (The design is then sometimes called a "half-spent.") The tail consists of a few stiff hackle fibers, which should be spread in a broad *V*. The abdomen can be a shiny fur or stripped quill. My Red Spinner uses Lunn's body of stripped and soaked red-hackle quill. The thorax is made of soft, dark, shiny, brown seal's fur from an old coat. The dubbing is spun on the thread and criss-crossed sparsely over the flattened hackle. If trout taking red spinners pass up this design and pattern, the angler can be almost sure that his presentation is at fault.

Advantages
- About as realistic a design as can be tied, both to humans and to trout
- Durable and fairly simple to make
- No scarce or expensive materials are needed
- Hooking qualities are especially good

Disadvantages
- Hard to see on the water
- Does not hide the hook (an almost unavoidable fault in a spinner imitation)

Conclusions While it is sometimes necessary to use several designs of duns, sedges, and other flies, I want no better spent spinner than this. Its only faults are those built into a spent-spinner imitation.

What may not be commonly known is that the shaped-hackle fly can also be a good design for hatching duns, which often get their wings caught in the surface film.

Parachute Fly In this design, the hackle is wound horizontally along the shank of the hook rather than in the normal vertical position. Usually the hackle is wound around the base of the wings and above the hook shank. The heavy hook then acts as the cargo of the hackle "parachute," almost ensuring that the fly will land upright. Formerly, Parachute Flies were tied on a special hook that had a small, vertical piece of wire sticking up above the shank.

The hackle was wound around this projection. Such special hooks are no longer available, unfortunately.

The Parachute Fly can still be tied without wings by winding the hackle around its own stem or a bit of nylon. So tied, the design is an excellent imitation of a small spinner, a hatching midge pupa, and probably many other low-floating insects. A creative Danish fly-tyer, Preben Torp Jacobsen, recommends such a fly for troublesome *Caenis* mayflies.

Parachute Fly

Origin Harold Smedley, in his book *Fly Patterns and Their Origins,* says that William A. Bush of Detroit applied for a patent on the parachute design in 1931. The fly was patented in the United Kingdom in 1933 and sold as a specialty of the Alexander Martin firm of Glasgow. Martin took the unusual step of fastening a small slip of paper with a patent number to the hook of each fly sold. I found three dozen of these flies in an old fly-box. Most are heavily dressed, with double quill wings pressed flat in the middle of a wide hackle. Hooks are large but well made.

In a 1949 book, Arthur Woolley showed Parachute Flies that look excellent for imitative purposes. Swisher and Richards revived American interest in the design in their book *Selective Trout,* published in 1971. It too gives the details of attractive imitative patterns.

The parachute design has, of course, been used by many other experimenters. The version I like has points of resemblance to Marinaro's Thorax Dun. The small parachute hackle helps greatly in cocking the fly and gives a good light pattern.

Tying Notes The hackle of the Parachute Fly should be small and sparse. So tied, it is a good representation of a mayfly's legs. Hackle color does not seem to matter greatly, since the wings are imitated separately. On the other hand, hackle stiffness is important: a soft hackle tied horizontally quickly becomes deformed from air resistance. Wings are another potential weak spot; the hackle squeezes them together at the base and tends to mat them when the fly gets wet. Hair wings are durable but heavy and often stiff. A fly tied of stripped hackle fibers is shown in the illustration. Before tying many flies with soft feather fibers, however, it is well to test one to make sure the wing holds its shape during fishing. If the fly-tyer is willing to take a little extra time, an unclipped hackle-point wing makes a realistic imitation that still behaves well.

The Parachute Fly balances best in the thorax style. The wing goes on first, well back on the body. The tail is second. A widespread tail of stiff hackle fibers helps to ensure good cocking. The abdomen is wound of lightly dubbed fur. The hackle is then tied on by the butt and wound, shiny side down, around the wings and as near to their base as possible. A thin thorax is then wound, usually of the same dubbing as the abdomen. If the body is not thin, it distorts the hackle.

Advantages:
- Very likely to land upright
- Clear wing outline
- Forms a light pattern on the water that is close to that of the natural dun's legs

Disadvantages
- Fragile. Neither wings nor hackle stand as much use as in a traditionally tied fly
- Somewhat fussy to tie, but not extremely difficult

Conclusions This fly will sometimes catch a trout that has rejected more conventional dressings. Because of its fragility, however, the sparse parachute dun may be more useful as a reserve than as a front-line soldier.

Upside-Down Variation The parachute design can be tied up-side-down, keeping the hook out of the water. C. F. Walker showed such a design and called it a "freak" in 1957. An article by Ron Cordes in the December 1973 *Fly Fisherman* inspired more enthusiasm. The "stalking fly" he illustrated was tied by H. F. Janssen and, I thought, the best-looking artificial dun I had ever seen. Its light pattern (with hackle underneath and hook up) was close to perfect.*

In the spring of 1974, some Irish trout liked the fly as well as I did. Better, in fact, because they did not get hooked. The stiff wings seemed to block the gape of the hook. Wings big enough to cock the fly also created an airfoil problem, twisting my leader just when a heavy trout was making his dozen rises for the day. Un-clipped hackle-tip wings were better, but I never did find wings that were tall and stiff enough to cock the fly against the weight of the hook, yet small and soft enough to hook trout reliably.

I still think the upside-down idea is important, but the only hook-up flies I am currently using are tied without wings on special hooks. They work reliably only in medium or long sizes. The Parachute Fly did, at least, help me to work out the next design, which has been more reliable.

<u>The Perfect Dun?</u> I hope readers will recognize that any writer who calls a fly "perfect" has his tongue firmly in his cheek, or ought to have. If past performance is any guide, I am likely to keep on modifying this design, and who knows what will seem perfect in another ten years? "Definitive" new flies have usually been short-lived, no matter who invented them.

It does happen that this is the best low-riding dun I know of in the medium sizes, which is saying something, since low-riding flies are usually the best of all floating designs in a difficult hatch of mayflies. This fly allows close imitation of every important feature of a dun: the wings, body, legs, and even the tails, if you insist. The body can represent either that of a hatching dun or one that is fully hatched. The wings are an important recognition feature and

---

*Since writing the above passage for the first edition, I have read *The Trout And The Fly*, by Brian Clarke and John Goddard. It is an important book and one that I like very much. The authors recommend an upside-down design identical to Janssen's, and this is one of very few points on which I cannot agree with them.

Perfect Dun

should be slightly exaggerated in size. The design is such that the wings present no problems in casting, hooking, or durability; and since they assist rather than impede the cocking of the fly, they may safely be made "too big." The hackle is durable, is well placed geometrically to hold the fly upright, and can be tied so sparsely as to represent legs realistically.

This design, like the Parachute Fly, can be tied upside-down, with hook-point riding upright. But hooking ability is still not good enough in the upside-down version.

Tied with hook-point down in the normal position, this design has better-than-average hooking ability. There is nothing at all to mask the point and no stiff materials to catch on the trout's mouth. There is no other imitation of a dun that I have so often removed from deep in a trout's mouth, although the Parachute Fly comes close. In addition to its good hooking qualities, trout apparently accept this design with confidence. On windy days when I have been forced to use heavy leaders, I have noticed that many trout have "missed" standard fly designs. A change to this one has resulted in solidly hooked fish.

Although I have not seen this fly described elsewhere, it borrows features from a great many others. I claim no original features, but I did work it out methodically, with a number of bad starts and half-successful experiments. The objective was to keep the strong points of the best designs while eliminating what seemed to me to be the significant faults. Now that I have arrived at a design I like, however, it seems so simple and logical that I feel sure someone else must have done the same thing with less fuss.

As a matter of interest, my starting point was the Thorax Dun, which had a number of good features: a sharp, dark wing outline, a fairly realistic light pattern, and a hackle placed well back on the body for balance. Sometimes trout would accept the thorax tie after rejecting other good duns, but I found the clipped wings troublesome, and the criss-crossed hackle did not always turn out right. Many good fly-tyers have turned to a Thorax Dun with hackles wound normally, then clipped on the bottom. This, however, does not give as good a light pattern as the original Marinaro design.

The no-hackle duns and the Barb-Wing work well in the smaller sizes. I like their wing outline and simplicity. They do not cock reliably, however. For medium-sized flies with prominent wings—which make cocking important—a hackle can be helpful.

The hackle of the Parachute Fly is well positioned for cocking. My next step was to try a number of variations on this theme, aiming at more durability. Most of the parachute variations were pretty good, but the hackle always tended to become deformed in use. If bunched fibers were used for the wing, the hackle around their base was likely to deform them also.

The Henderson bunched-wing spinner has long seemed ideal for realism, performance, and durability. Eventually it dawned on me that an upright wing could be added to this fly. The resulting design was an instant success, although a few refinements were necessary to increase its durability and performance. These are described below.

Tying Notes A detailed description of the tying method for this fly will be given in chapter 12. The main features are:

- A wing of untrimmed cock's hackle points (one or two pairs) placed well back from the eye of the hook, thorax-style. They should also slope slightly backwards. Duck breast feathers, rolled and divided, are another good choice. Flexibility and dark outline are important in the wings; exact color does not seem to be. The wing size may be exaggerated. For good cocking, the wing must be divided into a V. Photo-dyed duns may be used for the wings.
- A sparse hackle wound flat (on the bottom only) by a figure-eight of dubbed tying thread. The hackle should be so sparse as to represent only the legs of the natural. If anything, the lowest fibers of the hackle should be tilted slightly above horizontal, which again aids cocking
- A body of dubbing blended to the color of the natural. Trout are definitely sensitive to color here, since the body floats low
- A tail that is spread into a wide V and tipped slightly upright. Both features aid cocking

Advantages
- A sharp wing outline
- Realistic imitation of both the body and legs of the natural
- Reliable cocking
- Level riding (because the hackle is well placed to support the wings)
- Casts well
- Hooks extremely well (because all materials are soft and flexible)
- Fairly durable, though not as good in this respect as plain hackle flies

Disadvantages
- More difficult to tie than standard designs, since some care must be taken to get the wings and hackle set right (easier than patterns using clipped wings, however)
- Hook-point not concealed

Conclusions You will have to try this one and let me know whether or not my liking for it is sheer bias. Commercial tyers would probably have to charge more for it than for standard designs, but the good ones could afford to get it right. Please note that I do not look on this as any sort of all-purpose fly (the plain hackle design comes much closer to that) but as a very good one during a rise to medium-sized duns. For the smallest duns, see the next section.

The Barb-Wing Dun and Two No-Hackles "No-Hackle" flies have become popular for good reasons. They make excellent representations of small mayfly duns, and they use no expensive materials. They are difficult to overdress: an exaggerated wing may even help. Flies tied with deer-hair wings have, however, some disadvantages noted below; and quill wings have more. These prompted the Barb-Wing. It cannot logically be called a no-hackle fly, because it starts with an inexpensive hackle. When finished, however, the Barb-Wing is almost identical to the two no-hackles—in design terms.

Please note here that a hackle barb is exactly the same thing as a hackle fiber. I chose the shorter term because, in addition to saving a syllable, it is more accurate. The hackle barb is not likely to be confused with the barb on a hook. Barbs and barbules are commonly confused, however. Barbules are the fuzzy projections fringing the edges of the barbs of most feathers. Cocks' hackles do not have barbules except on the portion we call the "web," near the stalk at base of the feather.

Origin Flies tied only with wings are the most obvious of designs, and probably the oldest. The Spanish rely on them. The Gold-Ribbed Hare's Ear has long been valued as a no-hackle dry fly. In America, however, the popularity of no-hackle dries began with the work of Swisher and Richards. They redesigned the old fly so that it worked better than ever, using Marinaro's divided V-tail and "thorax" design. Quill wings were then added with an ingenious geometry that helped to cock the fly. Swisher and Richards also mentioned a "hair clump no-hackle." Slightly later, Caucci and Nastase developed the no-hackle hair-wing, which is easier to tie and more durable. It is best for slightly larger duns.

In working out the Barb-Wing, I was guided by the above flies and also by Roger Woolley's design, which in its day became popular because it avoided the problems of quill wings. (Angling repeats its cycles as fast as other human endeavors.) As far as I know, however, Woolley always used his clumped-hackle wing at the head of the fly and added a second hackle that was left full circle. In effect, Woolley's fly was the conventional design with an improved wing. The Barb-Wing uses a single hackle that is wound and clumped well back from the eye, thorax-fashion.

Tying Notes Since these designs have no normal hackle, they depend for balance mainly upon a wing that is tied in a pronounced V shape; the wing should originate low on the sides of the fly, not on the top. Swisher and Richards point out that this wedges the fly upright in the water. With quill wings, this V shape is not easy to achieve without splitting. Swisher and Richards now advocate the old-fashioned double quill wing to give more bulk after the wing splits (which it quickly does in fishing). Using deer hair, it is easier to achieve the correct V. The resulting fly is durable, attractive to fish, and popular. There are, however, problems inherent in deer hair. It is coarse, running from about .005" to .016" in diameter. The finest diameters (such as those from a deer's mask) tie up into an attractive fly, even in small sizes. Unfortunately, these hairs are heavy, and the fly sinks faster than most wet flies. The thicker hairs do float, because they are hollow.

At this point, however, keep in mind that stiffness increases with the *fourth* power of diameter. A fine deer hair of .005" diameter is, therefore, roughly forty times stiffer than an average hackle barb measuring .002". The hackle, clearly, is going to collapse more easily in the trout's mouth. Hackles also float better than fine deer's hair, are more durable, have more

No-Hackle Dun

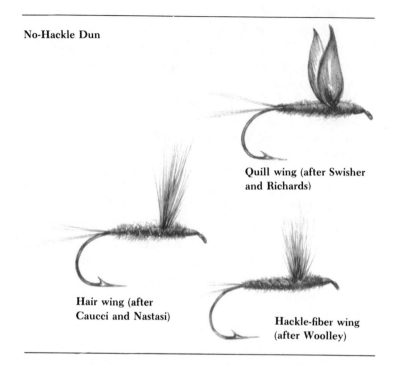

Quill wing (after Swisher
and Richards)

Hair wing (after
Caucci and Nastasi)

Hackle-fiber wing
(after Woolley)

sheen, and (least important) are available in more natural colors.

Hackles cost more than quill or feathers, so the barb-wing design may appeal less to professionals. It is easier to tie than the quill-wing and about as easy as the hair wing. Fly-tyers will find that it is almost impossible to tie the barb-wing so that it fails to fish well—at worst, it unravels into the full-circle hackle from which it began. Simply wind a cheap, oversized hackle on the hook, tie it off in the normal way, and then secure it in an upright V clump by figure-eight turns of the tying silk. The V should expand to between 90° and 120°.

All of these no-hackle designs also profit from a wide-spread tail for additional balance. Swisher and Richards tie it around a ball of dubbing; I prefer to tie the tail in first and secure it open with dubbed thread later.

Advantages

- Simple, cheap, and fast to tie (all three designs)
- Effective for small hatching duns (all three designs)
- Strong (deer-hair and clumped-hackle wings)

Disadvantages

- Fragile and hard to tie (quill wings only)
- Heavy and stiff (deer-hair wings only)
- May fail to cock, despite special wings and tail (all three designs)
- Absence of legs may be noticeable on larger duns
- Hard to see on the water
- Hook not concealed

Conclusions In my view, the quill-wing design is good for small duns (but not for the very smallest, like the *Caenis*). The deer-hair wing is coarse for small flies but effective in the medium sizes. It floats badly if made from deer face hair. The clumped-hackle design works in all sizes and is neither fragile nor heavy. If you tie a lot of small duns, you may find that this design is worth the price of the book. For medium-sized flies, however, I do not find any of these no-hackle flies quite as effective as the Perfect Dun, which adds a sparse outrigger of flattened hackle for balance.

Flies Intended to Sink—A Little or a Lot

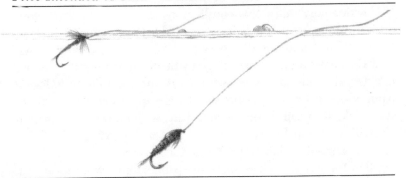

There are two reasons why the design of sunken flies is easier than that of dry flies. First, wet-fly components do not have to perform such difficult mechanical tasks as do dry-fly hackles, bodies, tails, and wings. Wet fly materials can therefore be chosen with less regard to lightness and water-resistance.

Second, trout do not seem as selective about deeply sunk flies. Please note that this is a relative statement; I have not said that selectivity disappears when the fly sinks. It does seem to diminish with depth. Selectivity appears most common with flies that are in, or just under, the surface film. Really high-floating dries do not seem to seem to induce much selectivity, and neither do the deepest nymphs.

It follows that we often cannot be rigorously sure what a trout thinks a deeply-sunk fly is when he takes it. I have listed all of these designs, shallow and deep, among the mayflies be-cause—well, because they had to go somewhere, and this is a book about imitative flies. But the trout seem to consider the deeply-fished flies generic. At least, the fish find them just as acceptable as caddis-flies, stoneflies, and various other things.

As a routine precaution, most of us try to make any fly look something like the natural, and with nymphs it is easy to get carried away. They invite "exact imitations." Being heavier than water, they will always sink, and having sunk, they will catch fish. Given a little more lead, they will get down to the trout's level even if they are made to bristle with natural-look-ing legs, tails, wing-pads, and eyeballs. These gorgeous cre-ations may even be as good as simple flies. They are seldom better. In a book that is based on the trout's opinion, I am reluctant to list designs that have not proven necessary.

The designs shown are durable, easy to tie, and attractive to trout. They can be modified to match almost any natural. The main modifications should be to behavior (especially rate of sinking and current-resistance), but size and color can ob-viously be changed too.

Stiff-Hackle Wet Fly Fly-tying manuals have often recommend stiff hackles from roosters for dry flies and supple hackles from hens for wet flies. Most of us ignore such advice. We use stiff hackles for both kinds of flies because we have roosters' capes lying around, and we are too stingy to throw them away when we've used up the best dry-fly feathers. The rejects are sparsely barbed, badly shaped, or just too big, but they are stiff and shiny. They nevertheless make good wet flies. It wouldn't be quite right to say that I used to feel guilty about this—a trout splashing around in the net can erase any amount of guilt—but I did wonder, in calmer moments, if I was doing something wrong.

Stiff-Hackle Wet Fly

It was the manuals that were wrong. They provided an example of the confusion that writers spawn when one repeats another's advice for generations without checking back to original sources, and their reasons. The source of the advice to use soft hackles seems to be clearly British. It would be difficult to unravel the thread back to one specific author—angling books so seldom confess their sources—but we might not go far wrong in focusing on W. C. Stewart. While flies with soft hackles were fished long before him, no other wet-fly specialist achieved such vast influence on so many generations of anglers (and writers).

Now, the important point about Stewart is that he fished upstream, and persuaded others to do likewise. In upstream (and
cross-stream) fishing, flies descend at about the same speed as
the current—perhaps a bit faster. Soft hackles are ideal under
these circumstances. They are dense, visible, and supple
enough to move even when the fly itself is moving very little,
in relation to the current.

When a fly is fished downstream, the problem is different.
For much of its course the fly must work against the current. If
the hackle is supple and the current strong, the hackle fibers
collapse backward. This is not to say that the soft-hackle fly
then fails: with hackle compressed, it looks something like a
nymph, and nymphs work when fished downstream. But the
compressed hackle does lose the mobility which it has when
fished as Stewart recommended. In his words, flies "dressed of
very soft feathers are more suitable for fishing up than fishing
down, as if drawn against the stream, it runs the fibers along-
side the hook, and all resemblance to a winged insect is de-
stroyed."

I have seen many American anglers fishing downstream with
wet flies. I have never seen one fishing traditional wet flies
upstream. Such anglers do exist: Jim Bashline is one of them,
and he has written about the technique in *Field & Stream*. But
I think we can take it—on the basis of my informal but prolonged stream census—that the downstream wet fly remains
vastly more common in this country.

This means that our traditional stiff-hackled wet flies remain
as useful as ever, though out of fashion. Some of them do (in
my view) have a design defect: they use wings of duck primaries or secondaries, which are easy to tie but have little action.
One solution is to use a wing of some material like woodduck
breast feathers or the secondaries of small birds—which are
much more flexible than duck. In larger flies, squirrel-tail is
good. The idea is to find materials that are neither limp nor
rigid. A cock's hackle is hard to beat, and I usually tie it full-
circle, with no wings at all, in the smaller wet flies.

Let me recommend that you add a smaller, stiff-hackled wet

fly to your leader next season whenever you fish some other fly down- or cross-stream. Put the little fly on as a dropper, two or three feet above your streamer, deep-fishing nymph, or whatever. Just do it routinely. There will be two effects. First, you may catch fish that would not have taken otherwise. Second, you will learn something about selectivity (or the absence thereof) in trout. If you like to believe that they are always selective, you may not enjoy finding out how often they take a little dropper fly that seems to imitate nothing and everything in nature: nothing specific and everything alive.

Origin See the comments under the dry hackle fly. The wet version is probably older than the dry, though British angling historian Jack Heddon has doubts about that.

Traditional American wet flies certainly had British and Irish origins. One logical source would have been the wet fly tied to fish downstream in running water, as Cutcliffe did it. His flies were much like those I use in Pennsylvania, but then my flies are modern. Old American wet flies look more like traditional lough flies. (The word is spelled loch if you are Scottish, but I am married to Ireland.) Our American ancestors did fish in the lough style, though few of us do it today.

Lough flies—notably big ones for the Green Drake—are sometimes tied with mallard flank feathers (which are semi-supple). Other non-poultry hackles are occasionally used, but for color, I think, rather than motion. Most lough flies are dressed with sparse but stiff cocks' hackles. These are the flies that look familiar to Americans. All are shallow-fishing wets, and the top dropper is often worked on the surface, where it takes more than its share of fish. The fly shown here is exactly the same as my favorite Irish light-and-motion design.

Tying Notes this fly moves a lot of water, which might make it suitable in large sizes for night-fishing. I don't do much of that and confine myself to medium sizes: say about 10 through 14, Redditch scale. The gape, however, should be ample. The Partridge Code A or Captain Hamilton seem ideal, in standard or heavy wire. Small double hooks also work well. Try a body of stiff guard hairs picked out through turns of tinsel. Perhaps any color would suit the fish, but there are two that please me: gold-ribbed hare's ear with furnace hackle and silver-ribbed black seal with black hackle. The hackle is wound at the shoulder and is always shiny-side-forward. Cutcliffe urges that it be "of a brilliant lustre, reflecting and sparkling in the light . . ."

Advantages
- Simple and sturdy.
- A good light-and-motion design.

Disadvantages
- Emotionally unsatisfying, if you like to know exactly what your fly imitates.
- Can be fished deep only if heavily weighted.

Conclusions The stiff-hackled wet fly fits the downstream method most of us use. The barbs of a cock's hackle provide mobility, even against the current. Their shine and translucency provide an illusion of life.

Please do not conclude, though, that stiff hackles are better than soft, or vice versa. The right hackle is the one that matches the fishing. It is easy to check: you just let the flies drift or swing in the current, as you will be fishing them, and watch their behavior. In Leisenring's words, "select a stiff, medium, or soft hackle according to the water to be fished."

Variation The woolly worm's palmer hackle makes it a separate design. The function, however, is much the same, with stiff hackle and furry body creating an appearance of life. In western lakes, a green-olive woolly worm with grizzly hackle usually works. Perhaps it panders to the trout's fantasy of a world-record scud. To watch this fly pulsating through clear mountain water is to understand the point about light and motion.

Soft-Hackle Fly This design's hackles usually come from wild birds: hen hackles can be used too but are not as dense. The supple, colorful fibers of game-bird feathers were intended to look like the wings of hatching flies, but they may also repre-

sent the legs of nymphs. I like to fish the fly dry—or damp—
and listed it with the dries in the first edition. I have now
moved it for easier comparison with the stiff-hackle wet fly,
which looks deceptively similar but (as already noted) is designed for use under different conditions.

Origin The earliest use of soft-hackled flies is probably impossible to pinpoint. It is certainly ancient. In reading authors
before W. C. Stewart, however, it is usually difficult to judge
how flies of all kinds were fished. Some earlier writers did fish
upstream and cross-stream—at least on occasion—and they
knew that their flies worked best as they drifted, drag-free, just
after they landed. Scholars still debate even the broadest point
of design: whether the early flies were wet or dry (in modern
terms). Feathers, furs, and silk were apparently chosen to imitate a particular insect—and imitation meant matching the
color.

Stewart broke the mold. He did not fuss over colors, but he
wanted the right behavior (not his term). He fished his wet flies
upstream whenever possible. And he thought through the
problems of design (my term again) as they bore on his method
of fishing. "An appearance of life," he wrote in 1857, "may be
much better accomplished by dressing the flies of soft materials, which the water can agitate . . ."

Though Stewart wanted few flies, writers before and after
him described many. Pritt's book is, to me, the most appealing
of all, though I suppose that we have to judge many of his
patterns as art forms, fashioned as much for humans as for
trout. Whichever the audience, the flies succeeded. At least
they were simple. Elegantly simple, or simply elegant. I admire baroque salmon flies, efficient dry flies—but the old soft-
hackle wet flies were in a class by themselves. A few turns of
straw-colored silk, then a feather from the outside of a male
dotterel's wing, and you had a fly of deadly beauty.

Soft-hackle wet flies compete with dry flies, in the sense that
both are likely to fish well under the same conditions: over
trout that are seen to be rising or are willing to rise, often in
shallow, fast streams. In the nineteenth century, anglers did

not generally know that dry flies would work in rocky streams. A few European anglers have still not figured this out. We learned about the versatility of dry flies early, in this country, and perhaps that is why the soft-hackle wet fly did not catch on here. But the soft-hackle fly also works well on the surface, and I probably use it most often that way. Skues brought the design to the attention of modern dry-fly and nymph fishers.

Tying Notes There are some special points in tying soft-hackle designs. If the fly is intended to spend most of its time afloat, a tail of stiff hackle fibers helps considerably. I also hackle a floating fly more fully than a sinking one, using up to three feathers if they are very thin.

As a rule, the best system is to tie the hackle feather in *by the tip*, wind the hackle, and then wind the tying thread through the hackle to reinforce it. Some big feathers lie best if tied in by the butt. Stewart's system makes the strongest fly: he ties on the feather by the tip, spins it around the waxed tying silk, and then winds the two together. J. R. Harris recommends a hatching Iron-Blue Dun with three small jackdraw throat hackles tied Stewart-wise on a true size 17 hook. Every fly-tyer should try this one before awarding himself a master's degree.

The behavior of soft hackles depends on their method of tying. (It is also true of stiff hackles, but to a lesser extent.) At one extreme are Stewart's "spiders," with hackles palmered sparsely over the body. No fiber is supported by any other, so each has maximum flexibility. When the hackle is wound at the shoulder, the fibers give each other some slight support, resisting the current better. The hackle is further propped up if the final whip-finish is tied *behind* it, as Skues recommended. A small ball of dubbing just behind the hackle gives a similar effect. The greatest support of all is provided by a small, stiff hackle wound behind the soft one. This works well for big dry flies; the design is discussed separately as the Bent-Hackle Fly.

Advantages
- Versatile. Excellent imitation of hatching duns and of many

other insects in the surface film, including midge and sedge pupae.
- Very good hooking qualities.
- Usually easy to tie (by the first method described).

Disadvantages
- Fibers collapse when fished downstream.
- Fragile.
- Some traditional feathers are scarce (but see chapter 12 for substitutes).

Conclusions Still an indispensable fly. When trout are taking something mysterious in or just under the surface film, this design is a good starting point. It will usually fool at least one fish for a stomach check.

Invisible-Hackle Fly

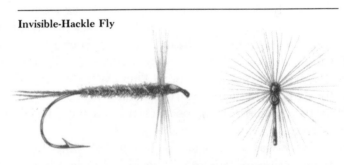

The Invisible-Hackle Fly The name of this fly (as in the case of the design that I have blushingly called the Perfect Dun) expresses good intentions rather than actual accomplishments. I certainly do not think that any fly is perfect, and I doubt that anything that can be tied on a hook is invisible to trout. (After all, they manage to feed on copepods.)

On the other hand, the hackle of this design is so sparse that I think it may be *functionally* invisible. The prominent body is the only feature of the fly that is intended to attract attention. The body represents a nymph that has moved to the surface preparatory to hatching, but that has not got its wing out. The hackle has the mechanical function of keeping the fly at the surface (if lightly greased) or letting it sink only slowly (if not greased). Since the hackle impedes sinking, this is not a good design for fishing deep.

Mechanically, the invisible-hackle fly serves almost the same purpose as the soft-hackle fly: both are wet flies in the old British sense, which in today's usage might translate as "near-surface flies." The old wet-fly fishermen considered such flies much different from sunken flies, which were fished deep.

The soft-hackle and invisible-hackle designs do not represent the same thing, however. The dense hackle of the former represents wings. The stiff, transparent hackle of the latter does not. The invisible-hackle design is therefore an artificial nymph in the strictest sense of the term.

The stiff-hackle and invisible-hackle designs differ only in degree, but they are fished very differently. The stiff-hackle fly is larger, thicker in hackle, bulkier and fuzzier in body. It is designed to be fished against the current. The invisible-hackle fly is designed to fish drag-free. The invisible-hackle design imitates a nymph; the soft-hackle, a dun; and the stiff-hackle, life in general but nothing in particular.

These differences go to the heart of the trout's interest— which is in the behavior of the fly. It would be impossible to tie flies which look much more distinctive than these three to humans, but which would not have the differences in behavior which matter to the trout.

Emerging insects are worth fussing over. Trout do.

Origin The invisible-hackle design resembles some of Skues' nymphs, although I use a wider hackle to support the fly close to the surface. Skues made beautifully neat bodies of dubbing with a bulge for wingpads; I try to get by with pheasant-tail herl. My starting point happened to be the Sawyer-type pheasant-tail nymph, which has an uncanny way of representing many naturals. The sparse hackle was added to keep the fly at the surface. Also, Sawyer ties his nymphs with wire; I naturally prefer thread for a fly that is intended to be fairly light.

Tying Notes For a fly intended to stay right in the surface film, stiff hackle fibers make the best tail. I normally prefer the tail to sink on this design, however, so I avoid stiff tail fibers. Sawyer's tail is simple and absorbent: he merely uses the short tips of the herls that will make the body.

I then spin the rest of the herls around a waxed thread (say orange, brown, or olive) and wind forward. A small wing pad can be wound with the darker butts of the herls. Rib the body with fine gold wire. Next, take *only two or three wraps* of a dun hackle. The color probably does not matter much, but a blue dun seems least visible. Again, if the fly is intended to stay right at the surface, a thicker hackle may be wound.

Other absorbent materials could be used for the body. Pale hare's ear fur, for example, makes a good light-colored nymph. But remember the principle: an absorbent body and tail to make the fly sink; a sparse but stiff hackle to make sure it does not sink far. The combination of opposed features accounts for the fly's effectiveness.

Advantages
- Easier to fish *barely* under the surface than any other design —an important point
- Simple, easy-to-make, and durable
- Cheap if a photo-dyed dun hackle is used (hackles dyed by older methods may show odd colors in the water)

Disadvantage
- Does not look very realistic to anyone except trout

Conclusions Next time you face a hatch of *Baetis* duns (for example), let your partner try his fanciest dun or nymph while you try this one in a true size 16 (Mustad 18 or 20). Then remember you owe me a beer.

I also have the impression that this fly has been effective as an imitation of sunken *Baetis* spinners. The point needs checking; I am not sure that I have encountered real selectivity to drowned spinners.

If fully greased, the invisible-hackle fly does a fair job for spent spinners on the surface. The shaped-hackle Henderson design is superior, however.

Finally, the invisible-hackle fly has been helpful on days when, in the absence of a hatch, trout are lying in shallow water and taking occasional nymphs. I have in mind the residents of a small

Montana spring creek. They are almost always in a "feeding" lie because the stream has few deep places for hiding. When not actually rising to a hatch, however, they are extraordinarily wary. Even the sound of a size 15 nymph hitting the water worries them. The invisible-hackle fly lands quietly and drifts at an appealing level. The fact that it rides so near the surface gives me a chance to see the rise and hook the fish.

This, then is one of those flies that may work when all else fails.

Deep-Sinking Nymph

Deep-Sinking Flies If there is such a thing as the standard American nymph design, the fly illustrated here must be close to it. I have purposely avoided the kind of tricky fly that distracts anglers from the real problem of deep-nymph fishing.

That problem is *behavior.* The most useful approach to solving it is to pick the kind of fly that will get down to the trout in the water you are going to fish and with the method you are going to use. Imitation of specific insects comes in a distant second.

The behavior of a deep-sinking fly boils down largely to the speed with which the fly sinks. In shallow or still water, a heavily weighted fly will not fish well; in fast water such a fly may be necessary. The right behavior is a function of size, weight, and the stiffness of the materials used. (Please see the end of chapter 6.) Size can be a little too big; color need not often be exact; and a long, thin shape imitates almost any mayfly (or stonefly) nymph well enough.

The fly in the illustration should be considered only a starting point in the middle of a range of variations. You might like to know that I tied it many seasons ago as a representation of the American March Brown *(Stenonema vicarium).* The natural is plentiful; the weighted artificial shown works well before the hatch. But I am not jumping to conclusions. The natural nymph is good at hiding, and while trout take it with enthusiasm, I doubt that they see it often enough to become selective.

The important thing is that this is a *medium-sized* fly intended to *sink fast*. It has only a soft beard or dubbing hackle to allow fast sinking. If the fly were large enough to carry a heavy weight, or if it did not need to sink fast, I would prefer a full-circle hackle. And if I could use a full-circle hackle, I would also omit the wing-cases. A beard-hackle fly looks bare without them, but the trout do not seem to mind. And the wing-cases are more fragile than they look.

Tying Notes When tying this fly, I like to have the natural at hand, preferably alive, in a little water in a white plate (Skues' advice). The new commercial plastic box with a five-power magnifying lens in the top is even better. Live observation allows one to note, for example, that *Stenonema* nymphs make good use of their conspicuous, stiff tails.

The shank of the hook is wrapped with waxed silk; the tail is then tied on and (optionally) spread. The abdomen is wound of tightly dubbed fur, such as a hare's mask. Herl spun around the thread is also good. Whatever the material used, it should be protected by a rib of wire or heavy thread wound in the opposite direction. The wing-case is made of several layers of stripped feather segments (dark turkey tail, for example). Tie one end of the rolled feather on very securely in front of the abdomen, then wind on a thorax of stiff dubbed fur. Pull the wing-cases forward over the thorax, tie them down firmly (they are slippery), and clip off the remaining feather. Saturate the wing-cases in cement: they wear faster than the rest of the fly.

Finish off with a thin beard hackle, or simply fray out the dubbing of the underside of the thorax. Omit the wing-case if a full-circle hackle is to be added.

Advantages
- Simple, cheap, easy to make, and durable
- Catches trout

Disadvantage
- Some humans feel more comfortable with an elaborate dress-ing

Conclusions We may all reach our own conclusions, since the trout show few clear preferences in deep nymphs. Before reject-ing the simple nymph, anglers might try fishing it on the same leader as a complicated dressing.

11 ❦ Designs for Caddis-Flies, Stoneflies, Midges, Terrestrials, and Black Gnats

CADDIS-FLY DESIGNS

In my experience, caddis-flies (sedges) are a little easier to imitate than mayflies. Most sedges are comparatively sturdy creatures, with thick bodies and heavy, mothlike wings. Fly-tying materials used need not be quite as delicate as with mayflies. For wings, deer hair is cheap and effective; the best hackles in scarce colors can be spared for other uses.

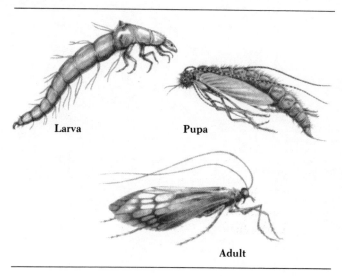

Larva   Pupa

Adult

Perhaps the biggest problem in tying caddis-fly imitations is that anglers lack detailed information on most individual species. With mayflies, we know more and have better traditional designs available.

Sedges can *sometimes* be imitated by a simple, two-dimensional, silhouette design, whereas mayflies (other than spent spinners) require imitation in three dimensions. When the two-dimensional caddis-fly works, it works very well. It is based on the fact that a quietly floating, newly hatched sedge has a sharp silhouette against the sky. The odd thing is that the silhouette sedge, for all its simplicity, was not worked out until a few years ago.

As a matter of convenience, anglers have often used just a few good general patterns of sedges; there are so many species that very few fishermen can identify them by name or carry imitations of each. It is pleasant to assume that trout cannot identify individual sedges either. But they can. Trout are, I think, just as selective to a pronounced hatch of sedges as to that of any other insect. If the artificial is a bushy one moving along the surface, color and shape probably do not mean much. Low-floating hatching sedge imitations require attention to all the qualities of careful fly design.

High-Floating Designs

Palmer Sedge This is one of the basic old designs, consisting of nothing but a body and a full-length hackle. Even the body is optional. Such a fly has always been hard to beat when a skittering sedge is needed. A wing is often added, and perhaps the best wing for light weight and durability is the traditional stripped-and-rolled section of a wing quill. Skues' Little Red Sedge is an excellent model of the winged palmer. The wing makes a more realistic

Palmer Sedge

Wingless

Winged (after Skues' Little Red Sedge. Note square-bend hook recommended by Skues)

silhouette, but its weight detracts slightly from the fly's ability to be moved along the surface of the water.

Origin The palmer wet fly is one of the oldest wet-fly designs, with its earliest origins impossible to trace (see the note on origin under hackle flies in chapter 10). Because the palmer design floats especially well, it must also have been among the first dry flies. Indeed, it is hard to sink any kind of unweighted palmer on the first few casts. Pulman gives admirable instructions for tying palmer flies, and one of them may well have given him the idea that led to the first detailed account of dry-fly fishing. In any case, the winged floating sedge with full body-hackle had apparently evolved from the wet fly before Halford came on the scene and published his first book of dry-fly patterns. Skues further spread the design's popularity. More recently, a pattern called the Henryville has been regionally popular in America.

Purists might object to using the term "palmer" to describe a caddis-fly, since a palmer was originally a caterpillar. Today, however, this is the common term for a fly with hackle wound all the way along the body.

Tying Notes The main feature of the palmer sedge is its hackles. For best behavior, they should be short in fiber, stiff, and shiny. These factors are more important than color. The hackles will stand up to casting best if they are wound dull-side-forward.

Start by winding a good bed of waxed silk thread from the front to rear of the hook. At the bend, fasten on a piece of gold or silver wire and tie in a long, short-fibered hackle. A red hackle is often used simply because it is easiest to find in top quality. Next, wind on a fuzzy body of dubbing (hare's ear is used in the illustration).

Wind the hackle forward to the front of the body and tie it off, then wind the ribbing wire forward in the *opposite* direction to secure the hackle doubly. I usually like two additional hackles at the head of the fly, one of them in some broken color like grizzly. If wings are wanted, tie them on after winding the body hackle and before putting on the head hackle. Skues' method of winging is durable: strip off almost all of the long fibers on the wing quill of a bird (such as a woodcock or hen). Roll the feather segment up carefully. Skues folded a landrail segment repeatedly into a compact, flat bundle, then tied it in on edge. The trimmed roots should be given a coat of cement before you tie in the front hackle.

Advantages
- Durable
- Simple to tie, especially if the wing is omitted
- Floats well and can be moved realistically on the surface
- Carries a large hook in relation to the fly size (good for big fish)

Disadvantage
- Works best as an imitation of a fully hatched sedge trying to get off the surface of the water (this is not usually as important as the hatching stage)

Conclusions Still an excellent fly under the right conditions, but not as widely useful as the low-floating designs given later. Trout learn to be wary of skittering sedges.

Deer-Hair Sedge This design is very much like the hair-wing sedge described in the section on low-floating designs below, but with some fibers of the hollow deer-hair wing pulled under the hook. The design can be overdone, but it is realistic if dressed with care. Floating ability is exceptional.

Fore-and-Aft Fly This has already been described in chapter 10. The design is more delicate than the heavily dressed palmer, but still floats well. I like it for the smaller skittering sedges and for those returning to oviposit.

Traditional Hackle or Winged Flies—Normal and Reversed

These designs are tied as described in chapter 10, but more heavily dressed throughout, so that they float high. The tail should be short, since natural sedges have none at all. Such traditional designs apparently evolved to imitate mayflies (see chapter 10), not sedges. In human eyes, resemblance to a caddis-fly is hard to see. Nevertheless, the trout will take these flies during a sedge hatch.

The American Adams pattern, for example, seems able to imitate either a mayfly or a sedge, with variations in the dressing. And when small pale sedges were hatching on the Firehole River, we used to get by with a size 18 (Mustad) Light Cahill—in the days before the jassid-type flat-wing sedge came along. Today I would have more confidence in a specific sedge design.

Compared to newer designs, the traditional dry fly, as normally dressed, has only the advantage of easy availability. Its disadvantages are:

- An unrealistic silhouette (bushy hackle and long tail)
- The hook-point lies underwater (unlike high-floating designs described previously)
- A small hook in proportion to the size of the total fly (because the tail must be counted as part of the body when imitating a natural that lacks a tail)

However, this design can easily be tied reversed, with the hackle at the bend of the hook and no tail (see chapter 10). Although the silhouette is still not much like that of a sedge, the behavior of the fly will now be good; there is no hook-point below the water to impede skittering or to distort the light patterns. When *small* natural sedges are being taken in motion, the reverse-tied fly may be the best choice of all. Other designs are either low floating or best in large sizes.

Leonard Wright's Caddis-fly Leonard Wright's thoughtful book, *Fishing the Dry Fly as a Living Insect,* has done much to make American anglers conscious of sedge fishing. He recommends a new design consisting of a body (which must be thin), a full hackle at the head of the fly only, and a long wing (extending well beyond the bend of the hook) of stiff hackle fibers. Points of support for the fly on the water are the bottom of the front hackle and the end of the long wing. The advantage is a silhouette that is more realistic than that of the palmer design, though less realistic than that of the low-floating designs shown next.

I have classified Wright's Caddis-fly as a high-floating design because it is intended to be moved along the surface. Unlike most of the other high-floating designs, however, this one carries its hook-point underwater. It also shares with the traditional hackle fly the disadvantage of carrying a hook that is relatively small in proportion to the size of the fly. (The Wright design uses a long wing for the same mechanical purpose as the tail on the Adams.) A small hook can be a problem where trout run large and strong, but it is rarely a factor in the waters of eastern America, where the fly was designed.

This design is original, and it makes an interesting compromise between the behavior of the high-floaters and the silhouette of the low-floaters. It also has the virtue of looking neat and attractive to us humans, which can inspire confidence.

Low-Floating Designs

Flat-Wing Sedge This design is simple and has proven to be highly realistic. The main feature is the wing, which is trimmed to represent the *V* shape of a natural sedge that has just hatched and is floating quietly down the surface of the water. The body and hackle form little more than a platform to support the wing.

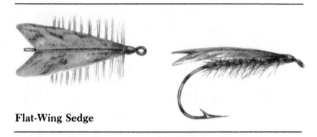

Flat-Wing Sedge

Origin Marinaro's Jassid is the ancestor of this and many other good flies. It might be more accurate to say that the Marinaro Jassid is the basic design and this a variation. Ernest Schwiebert was one of the first to use it, and he showed it to me.

Tying Notes Use a dubbed body (or omit it entirely in the smallest sizes). Wind one short-fibered hackle forward over the body from rear to front; clip off the top and bottom fibers (being careful to get the top ones off completely). To prepare the wing, take a wide, soft, dense feather, such as a body feather of quail, partridge, woodcock, or crow. Strip off the fluffy base and pull the feather forward through two fingers coated with cement (different cements are discussed in chapter 12). This narrows and thickens the feather, making it almost opaque. Tie it flat on top of the clipped hackle, being sure to catch a few fibers as well as the quill by the thread, for a stronger connection. A spot of cement may also be placed between the wing and the body. Alternatively, hackle at head only and roll the pre-clipped wing around the body in a tent shape.

Advantages
• Simple and cheap to tie
• Very effective; probably more realistic than any of its ancestors over the centuries

Disadvantages
• The wing is fragile
• The design is best in smaller sizes and is not recommended above size 14

Conclusions An important design, despite its fragility. British fly-tyers should look at this one carefully. I sometimes found it the best fly for the Irish Grey Flag, a day-hatching sedge.

Variation Larry Solomon recommends a flat wing of two hackle points instead of the trimmed feather. This variation is more durable, although the silhouette is not as sharp.

Hair-Wing Sedge This is an even more widely useful hatching design than the flat-wing sedge. The wing is an important feature and should be chosen for color, texture, and amount of flare when compressed. The body is also important, however, since it hangs down in the water below the wing.

Origin As a bass fly, the hair-wing sedge has been around for a long time. In 1940, by which time the design was well established, William Bayard Sturgis described it as a "moth." Some anglers must have used it in smaller sizes for trout fishing as well. (I have heard sedges described as "moths" in both America and Ireland; the insects look alike). Clipped deer-hair is unsuitable for small flies, so the switch to a dubbing body would have been inevitable.

Chauncy Lively tells me that he learned of the Hair-Wing sedge from Paul Young in the 1950s, by which time Young was cataloguing the design as a trout fly. I first saw the fly (courtesy of Sid Neff) in 1971.

Al Troth reports that he first used hair wings on sedges in 1958. He was attempting to match a specific hatch in Pennsylvania, but his fly developed into the design he calls the "Elk-Hair Caddis." It is now perhaps the best-known fly of its kind in America: first because it is a sound design, but also because

Hair-Wing Sedge

Troth takes uncommon care in choosing materials and tying each fly he sells. His design has a palmer hackle but is otherwise identical to what I have described, more generically, as the Hair-Wing Sedge. He considers that the main purpose of the hackle is to provide an illusion of motion, not flotation. (With or without hackle, the design floats mainly on its wing.) In my view, the addition of hackle is helpful in fast water—and Al lives in Montana, where there is plenty of that. In calmer streams I like the sharper silhouette provided by the version with no hackle.

Hair-wing flies had, of course, been used both wet and dry for years. The Trudes of western America were the best known, but there was some experimentation in England. G. E. M. Skues tried a squirrel-tail sedge wing in his last years, and liked it. Calftail hair remains very common in western America. Squirrel is also popular. Hair from every member of the deer family—elk, moose, antelope, as well as white-tail deer and others—is used. Since calf and squirrel hair do not flare much, their silhouette is different from that of deer hair.

Most of the early American hair-wing flies also used a collar hackle. I have shown one such design as a stonefly variation, though it could pass as well for a sedge.

Tying Notes Use a body of dubbing mixed for color. The body can be as thick as that of the natural. Secure the body with a rib of wire or thread. Choose the hair for the wing as carefully as the hackle for a dun, mixing if necessary. A non-flaring hair, such as that from a deer's face, floats poorly but makes a neat outline. A hollow hair with lots of flare floats better. (Wing materials are discussed in chapter 7.) Before tying on the hair, make a good bed of tying thread at the front of the body. Cement the bed, then tie the wing on very firmly, bringing it down to the middle of the body on each side.

This is one design for which strong nylon thread is a good idea. The amount of flare can be reduced, if necessary, by putting a loose wind or two behind the main winding after the wing is secure. Work more cement into the butts of the hair after trimming. A flared head (Muddler Minnow–style) is realistic and strong.

Advantages

- Strong, simple and cheap to tie
- Very effective when hatching sedges are being taken

Disadvantages

- Too coarse for flies smaller than a true size 14 (Mustad 16). Small sedges are better imitated with the flat-wing design described earlier

Conclusions If (heaven forbid) I could use only two designs for all my dry flies, one of them would be this (the other would be the plain hackle fly for mayflies). These days, I almost always start on a hatch of medium-to-large sedges with the hair-wing design, switching to the flat-wing model if necessary and to a skittering sedge if the fish are seen to take them.

This design works equally well for Alders, stoneflies, grasshoppers, and other large down-wing flies. When plenty of hollow hair is used and some of it is pulled under the hook, the design produces the high-floating deer-hair sedge mentioned earlier in this chapter. If the wing is tied high above the hook, the body hangs below the water and imitates a hatching pupa.

Caddis Pupae—and Larvae?

Pupa

Larva

When wary trout are taking pupae below the surface in slow-moving water, I have often failed completely. On other occasions, the old soft-hackle fly (see chapter 10) has worked, probably because I was able to imitate the behavior of the natural then hatching. When tying the soft-hackle fly for sedge pupae, however, the body should be made rough and heavy, especially toward the front. Legs and wing-cases can be added, but the fish do not seem to notice. Sometimes the fly can be fished with a pronounced drag. When the pupa starts to hatch at the surface, the deer-hair design described above works well.

For reasons given in chapter 2, I am not sure that trout and humans agree on what constitutes a larval imitation. But a fly with the shape and color of a larva can readily be made—out of dubbing, plastic or latex rubber—and the result will catch fish.

STONEFLY DESIGNS

Small stoneflies can require careful imitations. Witness the old North Country wet flies. As a floating fly, the small design in the illustration seems (to me) better than others I have tried.

Large stoneflies are a different problem. They have been important to me only in the northern Rockies. Trout take them as both

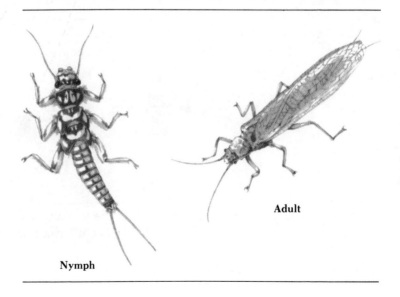

Adult

Nymph

nymph and ovipositing adult, but selective conditions are uncommon, perhaps because hatching adults are not accessible.

Of the thoughtful angler/fly-tyers I know, Scotty Chapman has been imitating large stoneflies twice as long as anyone else. Because he lives on the Yellowstone River where it leaves the park, his opportunities are exceptional. He has concluded that a simple peacock-bodied fly with a soft brown hackle makes the best large-stonefly nymph. It is tied in about size 10—much smaller than the natural Montana Salmon Fly. It does not look "realistic" in the fly-box, but it behaves well, and the peacock seems important. The large stonefly nymph invites "exact" imitations. They are also effective—especially at catching anglers.

The adult fly is more likely than the nymph to be available in quantities. Again, vast numbers of fussy imitations have been created. Most experienced anglers seem to settle on a single fly in a size much smaller than the natural. Scotty and many others favor the hair-wing Coachman. The fly does not appeal to me much, but it appeals to the fish. A hair-wing Royal Coachman seems to work too; the flash of red is thought by some to echo a feature of the natural.

Small Stonefly

A Small Stonefly The particular fly in the illustration represents a Yellow Sally, which is a medium-sized British and Irish stonefly. The design works well from about true sizes 8 through 14. It could be called a three-segment stonefly (see the tying notes below).

Like many of the medium and smaller stoneflies, the Yellow Sally comes down the water inconspicuously. For the trout, however, it makes a substantial morsel. They learn to look for it even though hatches are sparse. Where fish are rising occasionally at something puzzling, and where even one or two naturals have been spotted, the imitation is worth trying. On one hard-fished Irish river, this fly could be counted on for two or three fat May trout that had seemed invulnerable. The natural also has a convenient habit of moving about on bright, sunny days when other aquatic insects are taking a nap, and other anglers with them. My own tying of the Yellow Sally is influenced by Marinaro's Jassid design.

Tying notes The body has three segments—head, thorax, and abdomen—of approximately equal size. All are imitated by a fur dubbing (hare's mask dyed in picric acid and spun on yellow silk in this case). The abdomen is wound first and ribbed with dark brown, heavy silk thread. A short-fibered ginger hackle is then tied in by the butt. The thorax is wound and the hackle palmered over it, dull side forward. Then the hackle is clipped top and bottom. The wing is clipped from the webby part of a blue dun hackle dipped in picric acid. It is tied in flat over the body. If desired, two feathers, one on top of the other, can be used for the wing. Finally, the head is wound of the same dubbing. The design is reasonably easy to tie, since the wing does not need to be trimmed with care or tied upright. The hackle wing lasts longer than the soft-feather wing described for the flat-wing sedge.

Advantages

- Appears highly realistic to both fish and angler (except for that hook-point underwater)
- Requires only cheap materials
- Moderately simple to tie

Disadvantages

- Floats poorly, like the natural
- The natural fly is too scarce

Conclusions There are only a few fly designs that seem entirely satisfactory to me, and this is one of them.

A Large Stonefly This fly is like the hair-wing sedge described earlier, but tied in sizes and colors to match the natural. Flies as large as size 4 are used in western America, and anglers who have not seen the naturals should repress any tendency to giggle. Sizes

Large Stonefly

6 through 10 on long-shank hooks are normal. The long-shank (but not light) hook makes a good imitation.

Many fly-tyers like to add body or collar hackles, or both, to this fly to represent legs. The hackles may give the illusion of movement—worthwhile when ovipositing females are struggling on the water.

This fly appeals first because it is simple, second because it looks (to me) like a real stonefly with its wings in disorder, and third because it catches fish. But I do not suppose that it works better than other Salmon Fly designs, of which there are many.

Hard-to-Believe Stonefly
(Hair-Wing Coachman)

A Hard-to-Believe Stonefly (Hair-Wing Coachman) Well, this fly makes me question the wisdom of talking to trout. It just does not look right. But trout take it well when large stoneflies are common. The problem is that it is difficult to find a really selective rise to these flies. Lacking the kind of experience that is easily found with mayflies and sedges, I am not going to argue with the findings of the best western anglers I know.

My guess is that trout looking up at this fly focus on its peacock body, which hangs down in the water. The white wing must seem less conspicuous from below—with light shining through it—than from above. For the angler, the visibility of white is helpful. So is the ability of calftail to float. Western stonefly water is fast, dark, and turbulent.

Tying Notes Spin the peacock herl body on dark nylon thread for durability. Take care to tie the calftail wing in tightly, with a good cement: the hair is slippery. Brown hackle of any shade is wound over the cemented wing butt. A tail of golden pheasant tippet is often added, and it contributes a flash of color not far from that of the "salmon-fly."

Of course, the hair-wing Coachman (without the tail) may also be taken for a sedge or beetle. The trout don't say. But they do take it.

MIDGE (CHIRONOMID) DESIGNS

Trout can be selective to midges, but I have not had the opportunity to fish the *same* selective hatch for days in a row. This means

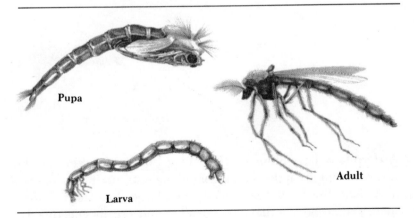

Pupa

Larva

Adult

that I have not been able to test midge designs as carefully as those for other aquatic insects. One of the designs described below usually works if I have it in the right size and roughly the right color.

For river midges, the size is likely to be very small and the color green-olive. For lake midges, all bets are off.

In both rivers and lakes, remember that the usual rise looks as if it were to a floating fly but is in fact to a pupa suspended just under the surface.

Midge Pupa

Midge Pupa

<u>Midge Pupa</u> For these insects, I have usually managed to get by with a small hackle fly, about a true size 17 or 18 (20 or 22 if Mustad). A very small, soft, non-poultry hackle seems to work best, but a small cock's hackle is also acceptable. The hackle has two functions. Much the most important is to keep the fly suspended in the surface film. To this end, the hackle is coated lightly with line grease rubbed on the fingertips. The body is left to hang down, as in the natural pupa. Some fishermen dress pupae "reversed," with the hackle at the bend. In this case, however, the tip of the leader must be pulled under water, and I think the fly is less likely to float in a natural position.

The second purpose of the hackle is to imitate the pupa's gills. These are pale, so I start with a grizzly hackle, a small pale feather from the neck of a thrush, or something similar. But I have no indication that this function of the hackle is very important for small river midges. For big lake chironomids, it might be better to use a piece of white synthetic yarn, as Frank Sawyer does. He recommends passing the leader clear through the eye of the hook and tying it around a short piece of "white nylon wool." The fly is thus free to turn around the leader. As my own contribution, I am tempted to recommend the small feather from the ear of a young, albino hooded crow. Probably no one but me has such a creature for a pet, so I could make the rest of you feel inadequate if I were not such a decent type.

The body of the pupa should be wound well around the bend of the hook. Fur works as well as anything, but it should be dubbed thinly and tightly, then ribbed with a dark thread or wire. If desired, the body can be made larger at the head, but I doubt that the fish will care.

This may seem a rather primitive midge pupa, and so it is. If it fails, one should certainly try a different imitation.

The low-riding midge adult also seems to be taken well for a pupa, although its resemblance to a natural pupa is remote. A small, wingless parachute design makes a good pupa but is a bit difficult to tie. Some anglers like to float pupae with a deer-hair head, but it is too coarse for all but the largest of these imitations.

Adult Midges

Low-Riding Midge Although I intended this fly to look like a fully hatched midge, it is accepted equally well for a pupa, as noted above. The fly tends to float on the wing, and the hanging body must look like a hatching pupa.

The design is the Henderson flat-wing spinner, with two hackle-point wings added in imitation of the natural midge.

Low-Riding Midge

Tying Notes First wind a thin body (abdomen) of dubbing or even waxed tying silk. Tie the wing on flat over the abdomen. (The prettiest wing is of hackle fibers or points, but a section of feather stripped from the quill of a small bird is easier to tie. Such a feather-section should be rolled two or three times.) When the wing is secure and cemented, a pale cock's hackle is wound two or three turns, then flattened into two bunches, one on either side of the hook. The thorax is made by winding lightly dubbed thread in figure-eight turns to spread and secure the hackle bunches. This is the same system used for tying spinner wings.

Advantages
* A realistic design to both trout and humans
* Hooks remarkably well, considering its small size

Disadvantage
* A bit fussy to tie in the usual small sizes

Conclusions This has been my most effective midge, but for those who find the tying too much work, a plain hackle pattern may work as well.

A High-Floating Midge Try the fore-and-aft design described in chapter 10. It rides high and flat, just like a fully hatched midge. This fly has worked for me on a few occasions. Stomach checks, however, showed that more pupae were being taken.

TERRESTRIAL DESIGNS

In his little book entitled *Silk, Fur and Feather*, Skues called these "casualty flies." The name seems better than "terrestrials," since many of the insects we are talking about are hardly earthbound. A wingless ant is a genuine terrestrial, but many other nonaquatic insects get to the water by their wings.

However, the name "terrestrial" has stuck. (It would be nice to think that "silk, fur, and feather" are also around to stay. In another few years, someone could write a fly-tying manual called *Nylon, Vinyl, and Polypropylene.*)

An infinite number of terrestrial insects can, of course, be imitated, and some of the most creative recent work has been done with terrestrials. It is even possible that we are getting a little carried away. In our recent fervor for imitative flies, we Americans have tied a "realistic" imitation of almost everyting, like an entomologist collecting minor mutations and fixing them under rows of pins. Trout can be as selective to terrestrials as to anything else, when there is a steady flow of one kind, but this does not happen quite as often as with aquatic flies.

The designs below are important. There are other designs of occasional usefulness, like the inchworm, but I would be inclined to try an ant before most of them.

Ant

This is the crawling ant, not the winged variety, but hackle-tip wings can easily be added if the angler thinks the trout might know the difference. The crawling ant is the most important summer fly on many streams in eastern America. I have often enough risen at five in the morning, made a bad job of the *Tricorythodes* hatch, and redeemed myself in the heat of the day with a relatively vast black ant in a true size 16. One of the nicest things about this design is that a small fly will float an ample hook, and fool trout in the process.

In Ireland, on the other hand, the crawling ant has been useless for me. There is apparently not enough heat to get many of them into the water. In England, where there is a bit more heat, the crawling ant is said to be useful on occasion.

Origin The ant has been imitated for a long time, usually in winged form, but few insects have been so badly caricatured by

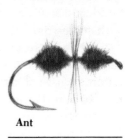

Ant

the fly-tyer. The problem, no doubt, is that fly-tying techniques evolved to imitate very different insects. Halford's ant was absurd: just a mayfly with steatopygia. Ronalds' was a little better back in 1836, but like many old fishermen, he relied on herl of the peacock and ostrich. This can be made to work after a fashion, but herl will not create the little round lumps characteristic of the ant's body. Except for wing color, Aldam's ant is virtually a Royal Coachman, and in fact Theodore Gordon thought the Royal Coachman an ant imitation. None of this, however, gets us much nearer the origin of the good floating ants in use today.

Roger Woolley (first published in 1932) is always sound, and his ant has a promising body: two lumps of tying silk with a shiny coating of lacquer (celluloid varnish). This gives the right shape, but is heavy and suitable only for a wet fly, which is what Woolley intended. Woolley also uses traditional hackle and upright wings, which would not be good for floating patterns.

The first book I have seen with a really good floating ant is Vince Marinaro's *A Modern Dry-Fly Code.* He prefers dyed nylon or horsehair for the body but gives dubbing as an option. The hackle is put on between the two lumps of the body, which is ideal for both imitation and floating qualities. Marinaro considers the shape extremely important and tells me that he got it from a wet, Woolley-style ant. In my view, his changes amount to a new design.

Tying Notes Choose both tying thread and a soft, shiny dubbing in colors to match the natural. Wind a large lump of dubbing at the rear of the fly, then leave a *long,* narrow waist. Wind a small sparse hackle—only two or three turns—at the waist. Some tyers flatten the hackle as in a spent spinner, but this requires some extra turns of thread and enlarges the waist. I simply leave the hackle full-circle—but small. Wind, in front of the hackle, a lump of the same dubbing used for the rear body, and then finish off the fly. Hackle-point wings can be added either at the hackle or the head. Horsehair makes a body that looks shiny and realistic to humans, but is harder to use than dubbing and heavier.

Advantages
- Simple and cheap to tie, and durable
- Accepted very readily by trout

- Good hooking qualities
  Disadvantages
- Modest floating qualities
- Low visibility

Conclusions The disadvantages are inevitable in any good ant but present no great problem in flat, low water, where ants are normally used. This is an excellent design.

The Jassid

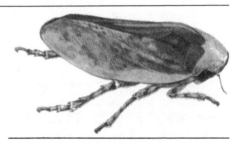

The Jassid design is important for two reasons. First, like the ant, it is a good choice when trout are rising to an assortment of small terrestrials on a hot summer day. There are times in eastern America when only the Jassid seems to work.

Second, the design has led the way to many other good flies that show a small, sharp silhouette to the trout: beetles and small sedges, for example (both mentioned elsewhere). It is thus of historical importance.

Origin This fly was worked out by Vincent Marinaro and first described in 1950 in his *A Modern Dry-Fly Code.* The jassid insect, however, was imitated much earlier. Ronalds gives a good illustration of it, calling it a Wren Tail or Frog Hopper. The artificial he recommends is wet instead of dry, vastly too big, of the wrong shape, and not a very good color. I have no doubt that Ronalds' fly caught fish, because it is a very fair representation of a Blue-Winged Olive nymph, which is active at the same time of the year as the jassid. As far as I am aware, no one described a good jassid design before Marinaro. His design would scarcely have been practical, for that matter, in the days before .004-inch nylon tippets and hooks in Redditch sizes 17 to 19 (Mustad 20 to 24). Hall's

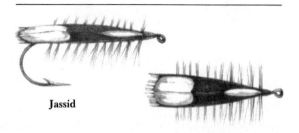

Jassid

pike-scale Black Gnat can be considered an ancestor, and Mottram's No. 3 Reed Smut was getting quite close. Mottram's design, however, used an abdomen of ostrich herl, which does not provide a good support for the flat wing.

Tying Notes The tying method has already been described under the flat-wing sedge. For the tiny jassid, however, the body must consist either of bare tying thread or thread with a minuscule amount of dubbing. Marinaro considered color unimportant, since the color of the natural fly varies widely. He recommended a single jungle-cock eye feather for the back. Jungle cock is good—being nearly opaque with a pale dot for visibility—but there is no need to use a feather that is now so scarce. These days, fly-tyers use all kinds of small feathers stiffened by cement. My favorite combination is tied with bright green nylon thread, a thin dubbing of bright but pale green, a light-colored hackle, and a wing of white feather (cemented).

The advantages and disadvantages of the basic design have been described under the flat-wing sedge. In the small hook used for the original Jassid, the fly is a little more durable than in the larger sizes.

Beetles

One realistic floating beetle imitation is simply a big jassid with an opaque, double wing. As in the case with the jassid, Marinaro was the first to describe this fly. He recommended using two layers of jungle-cock eye-feathers for the wing, but almost any dense feather works, if strengthened by glue. The neck of a cock pheasant (the common ringneck) provides good feathers. The shiny,

dark, metallic green feathers are suitable for dark beetles, and the dark-tipped reddish feathers are Skues' recommendation for the soldier beetle. (I skin out pheasant capes just like those of a chicken.) For black beetles, crow feathers are good.

This flat-wing beetle is useless as a wet fly. It will therefore never replace the traditional three-dimensional beetle of the Coch-y-Bondhu type, with a thick herl body and a small, sparse, full-circle hackle. The traditional beetle is an excellent "bug" that also works for trout that have never seen a beetle. The traditional design is an effective dry fly as well, and it is durable if the herl is spun on tying silk (see chapter 3).

Another floating beetle can be readily made of deer hair. Just take a large bunch of hollow body hair dyed approximately the right color. Tie it all the way along the shank of the hook, binding it firmly from the eye to the bend with strong nylon thread. The tips of the hair should be at the eye of the hook, and a substantial length of unused hair should protrude beyond the bend when the body has been completed. Then wrap the thread back up to the eye of the hook over the body, grasp the loose end of the hair, and bend it forward over the body. Tie the loose end down at the eye and clip off the bits of hair that protrude over the eye. The hair

Flat-Wing (after Jassid)

Coch-y-Bondhu

that now forms the back can be fanned out to form a realistic beetle silhouette. This fly is cheap and unsinkable. Commercial tyers especially like it.

A Grasshopper

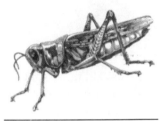

Recent designs for grasshoppers—or at least for floating grasshoppers—seem better than the Joe's Hopper I grew up with. The modern work may have begun on the Pennsylvania spring creeks; Ernest Schwiebert's LeTort Hopper started something. Some designs are made entirely of deer hair; some have dubbing bodies, full-circle hackles, and wings of pheasant "church window" feathers; one is even made from the hollow section of a large quill. The design illustrated is simply the hair-wing sedge in different form.

As with the sedge, hair for the grasshopper's wing should be chosen for physical properties; strength, suppleness, and limited flare. Any of the usual deer-hair browns work fine for color. For the body, try more deer-hair tied flat along the shank and doubled back on itself for a second layer. A ribbing of tying thread holds the whole thing in place. It floats well, and trout like it. The fly in the color plate was tied this way by Al Troth of Dillon, Montana.

Another good body is made of dubbed hare's ear fur dyed yellow in picric acid, also with a ribbing. Using dubbing, it is easy to match the color of real grasshoppers along the stream. Perhaps this is worth doing occasionally. (I doubt that the trout care, but they do seem to find a lot of excuses for rejecting grasshoppers.)

Grasshopper

I don't know exactly when the moth/sedge design was pressed into use as a hopper, but Chauncy Lively tells me that he was using it by the mid-'sixties. I think he had much to do with developing the attractive folded-hair body. In his articles for *Pennsylvania Angler*, he also extended the use of deer-hair bodies to several other terrestrials, including the Carpenter Ant.

BLACK GNATS

The name "Black Gnat" has, historically, been used to describe three different British insects that look much alike but vary in size and habits (see chapter 3). The size of these naturals varies greatly, but most species are small and some are tiny, with a body color that is near enough to black. In honor of tradition, I use crow herl for the body of my small spent flies, and this gives a realistic off-gray. If I had only black dubbing available, however, I would use it with confidence.

Grey Dusters and other fancy patterns have been recommended for the Black Gnat, but they do not work as well as small, realistic imitations. It seems to me that the only reason for using large, fancy flies is inability to fish sufficiently fine. J. C. Mottram advanced interesting dressings as far back as 1915, but he was very much the exception. His patterns, unfortunately, featured bodies of black wool, which is not a very good material, and black ostrich herl, which is worse. I like to think that he would be interested in these new designs.

Black Gnat

Single Fly—Spent or Hatching This design has already been described as the low-riding midge. For use as a Black Gnat, make the abdomen of two or three strands of crow herl spun around black thread. For a wing, use either hackle fibers or the tips of the same crow feather that furnished the body. These shade into a gray much like the natural's wing and work well, even though the hackle fibers have more shine. The hackle is black and flattened, Henderson-style. The thorax dubbed over it is dyed beaver or some other fine fur.

I never fish this fly without thinking of the dear old boys who saw no need to strike their trout. Trout may take the spent Black Gnat with an almost invisible sip, then reject it with unbelievable speed. I have seen a good angler taken and rejected without even knowing it. For me to stand any chance of hooking the trout, I have to wade very close and fish a tight line. One Irish angler says that because the trout does not close its mouth on the fly, he always strikes up rather than sideways. (I am doubtful, but cannot disprove the idea.) The strike must be as gentle as it is quick, because any leader above .005 inch is too heavy.

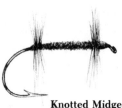

Knotted Midge

Knotted Midge This is a standard pattern for mating gnats, and a very good one. It is, of course, simply the fore-and-aft fly described earlier. I find it best with two black hackles, though a grizzly or badger is sometimes recommended for one end. A neat body can be made of black herl or beaver dubbing. These insects, however, have an abundance of shiny wings and legs sticking out at all angles. A rough body of seal's fur seems most realistic. The usual size of the knotted midge is about a true 14.

Black Gnat, clumped

Clumped Gnats The clumped gnat is simply a blob of stiff black seal's fur on a relatively large hook—a true 12 or 14. Where trout are used to seeing an orgy of insects coming down the water in a clump, this shapeless design seems to work best of all. I do not think Halford would have fancied it.

Another Variation A plain hackle fly also works for a black gnat, but I recommend that it be tied reverse-style, with the hackle at the bend of the hook. This design (described in chapter 10) does a better job of supporting a relatively big hook, which is needed when big trout are taking small flies.

12 ᵗᵗ *Notes on Fly-Tying*

Or How to Talk to Trout
Without Using an Interpreter

ᵗᵗ ᵗᵗ ᵗᵗ American fishermen interested in imitative flies always seem to start tying their own. They have to. No reflection on the professionals: the best of them in this country have been first class for a long time, and the new crop is as good as the old boys. Fly-tying is in part a labor of love for them—speaking now of the creative angler/fly-dressers like my friend Ted Godfrey, who is doing fascinating new things with hair "hackles." Most of the tyers in the biggest commercial operations seem to be performing a mechanical job. Even so, they acquire a manual facility beyond us amateurs.

I cannot bring myself to tie more than a dozen flies at a sitting, and even they are likely to be of two or three different patterns. The professionals tie dozens at a time. To do it efficiently, they must settle on standard patterns, and that is half of the problem. Even such plausible-*sounding* patterns as Blue-Winged Olive are not likely to be effective for the naturals you will see on your next trip to the stream. In Ireland and England, it has been known for half a century that a fly which looks blue-winged and olive does not always work during a Blue-Winged Olive hatch (chapter 1).

The other half of the problem is that big commercial operations, understandably, prefer materials that are fast and inexpensive. That Blue-Winged Olive in the shop may have a body of fake fur, a dyed dun hackle, and a flabby wing of turkey fibers. The thing will catch fish—almost anything will sometimes—but I cannot easily think of a less promising imitative fly.

You can afford the best materials for your own flies. And you can make changes whenever the trout mutters disapproval. If you tie only three or four flies at a time, some of them will be clumsy, because you will not have time to figure out the most efficient way to use your materials. But you will be surprised at how little the trout care if your flies' wings are a millimeter too far back. At least you will be talking to the trout in his own language. If you buy your flies, you will be dealing through an interpreter, and he may not know the language of *your* trout.

The previous chapters show some easy designs to tie, and they are often better than the difficult ones. The important thing is to be able to tie flies at all. In earlier centuries, every competent fisherman carried his "book" of silk, feathers, hooks, and scraps of dubbing.

Imitative flies still do not require a vast kit for tying; and in fact the big, showy ones are hard to use as well as to carry. The kit that must be transported in a station wagon is aimed at impressing other anglers, not trout. By carrying small pieces of fur and trimmed necks, you can easily get everything you need in a kit measuring about ten-by-seven-by-five inches. This is roughly the size of the old British and Irish models I have seen. Nothing like them is on the market at the moment, so I have to use a back-up kit plus a small one that is always with my fishing gear. The big kit is a ladies' cosmetic case salvaged from a junk shop; it is about a foot square and eight inches deep. The small kit measures only six inches long by four inches high by two-and-one-half inches thick, fully stuffed. It is very well made of pigskin. It has a box for tools and thread, six envelopes for other materials, an end pocket in the actual pigskin, two parchment envelopes (with six pockets in each) which I sewed up myself for dubbing, and a sturdy strap around the whole thing. The kit carries the old American "Commonsense" label.

Some strong-minded anglers can actually tie imitations while the trout are rising to an unexpected hatch. My nerves would never stand this. Far better to keep plugging away with the best imitation at hand, hoping to catch at least the village idiot for an inventory of his diet. But it is perfectly practical to tie up a fly or two over lunch, while the kettle is coming to a boil over a pine fire. It goes without saying that properly regulated fishing expeditions have meals scheduled to avoid the rise. My best ideas come after breakfast, with the sun's new light on my vise, yesterday's lessons still fresh, and today ahead.

In a sense, most of this book has been about fly-tying, but it has not said much about how to begin doing it. I have been afraid that the technical details of how to spin dubbing and so forth would distract attention from the important things—the means of imitating the living insects upon which trout feed. The market is already flooded with good mechanical books on fly-tying that give no real idea of the principles of imitation. This one may, perhaps, have erred in the opposite direction. By way of compensation, a few instructions are given below, on the off chance that the book winds up in the hands of a sailor who is shipwrecked on an island where there are lots of trout and nothing else to do.

Most anglers outside desert islands probably have six fly-tying manuals. Of the older books, the most interesting is Roger Woolley's *Modern Trout Fly Dressing*, which badly needs a reprint and some good editing. William B. Sturgis' *Fly-Tying* is even better on some of the details, and is outstanding for clear illustrations, but it lacks Woolley's knowledge of insects. There are undoubtedly good modern manuals that I have not seen, but I can recommend Richard W. Talleur's *Mastering the Art of Fly-Tying* (Harrisburg: Stackpole, 1979).

Fly-Tying Materials

Hooks The hook is the most important and most neglected part of the fly, so chapter 5 is devoted to hook design and function. After the hook is chosen and mounted in the vise, it should be examined for defects (such as an open eye), tested for temper (by pushing the eye to one side), and sharpened. A thin tool is needed to sharpen a small hook-point on three sides. Probably the best file for this is a new kind made of artificial abrasives coated on a thin metal strip. The old Arkansas stone is more gentle but cannot be made quite thin enough.

Some hooks are so soft that they will actually squeeze down under the jaws of the vise. In this case, throw out the hooks rather than change the vise.

If the vise grips the hook by the point, a breakage may result. A grip at the bend avoids this problem and leaves room for sharpening.

Tying Thread There is much room here for personal preference. For me, nothing winds as nicely as good silk. When wet, silk also turns into realistic colors. I like the old Pearsall's Gossamer so much that I cannot understand why no economic czar has abolished it yet. By using it, one can also duplicate old patterns, since approximately the same colors have been available for generations.

Gossamer does have three problems. First, it is not as strong as nylon thread, and so I use nylon for hair-wing flies. (Nymo winds much like heavy silk and comes in good colors.)

Second, silk darkens when wet, so nylon is better where a vivid body is needed (the bright green jassid, for example).

Third, Pearsall does not make a silk fine enough for flies below about size 16 or 18. For these, I like a silk sold in the United States in 8/o size. It can be used to tie a neat dry fly even in the large sizes, but it comes, unfortunately, only in white and black. As a personal matter, it seems to me that extra-fine silk on normal-size flies leads to sloppy practice. When 8/o silk is used on a size 14 fly, it is easy to fall into the habit of making a dozen wraps where two would have done.

The most useful colors are white (which turns neutral on the fly), yellow, primrose, green-olive, hot orange, brown, pale brown (or ash), purple, red, and black.

Where silk is needed for the bodies of small flies, tying silk is usually better than floss.

Wax A few fly-tyers now omit the use of wax on thread, especially in America. Some nylon thread works well unwaxed; modern cements and techniques have reduced the need for the old, sticky waxes to hold materials securely.

The proper wax, however, is easy to use and still has virtues. It protects against fraying, helps prevent rot and rust, helps in spinning tight dubbing, and maintains the tension of the wraps even if pressure is relaxed during the tying. The wax also gives a good idea of the color the thread will assume when wet.

It took me a while to find a mixture I liked for pre-waxing whole spools of thread. In the end, the best base seemed to be pure beeswax, which is not as gummy as most others. I melt it in a small tin set into hot water, then add enough artists' turpentine to keep the mixture from building up too heavily as I dip the spools of thread into it. The wax must be kept warm and the consistency of the wax-turpentine mixture must be adjusted as the job goes on, but start with about half beeswax and half turpentine. The wax soaks deeply into the thread and saves waxing with every individual fly. The only disadvantage of the method comes in very hot American weather, when the spool can be a little sticky. Good beeswax has very little color and does not seem to turn the silk any darker than it is when soaked in water.

Dubbing It is easier to get exact body colors by mixing fur than by any other method, and the trout seem to like the results. Skues suggested that mixed colors were even more effective than those dyed to shade. This certainly seems true in hackles, and mixed colors in bodies are at worst no disadvantage. The easiest method of mixing dubbing and checking the result is described in chapter 8. For really careful imitations, the mixing must be done with the natural as a model: neither patterns nor pre-mixed dubbing are much of a help. The very best result comes when the fly-materials book is used at streamside to match a freshly hatched natural fly.

Furs should be picked for sheen, diameter, texture, and the right length. My practice (which I have not seen described in these terms elsewhere) is to collect small-animal skins that have shiny guard-hairs of the right length and consistency. Guard-hairs seem to have more sheen and life than soft underfurs. Additional sheen can be added by mixing in some stiff seal's fur.

Examples of the right guard-hairs are those from the hare's ear and mask, from mole, otter, and marten, and from some squirrels and some mice. Muskrat guard-hair is good for big nymphs. Fox and wildcat guard-hairs do not look as good to me but catch fish well enough. Wire fences provide unwashed wool that is easier to collect than the stuff that a tup finds indispensable. Some cattle fur is good, too, but coarse. Dyed beaver is a bit limp but takes color well and is useful for binding fur mixtures. Mole fur soaked in picric acid gives a good dark olive; a hare's mask in the same acid gives almost every necessary yellow.

It is worth ribbing a dubbed body counterclockwise with wire (for protection and sparkle), with a dark silk (for protection and a segmented effect), or with silk of the same color (for protection only).

There are so many complicated instructions for spinning dubbing that one must suppose many fly-tyers have trouble with the process. For small flies, the simplest method also happens to be the neatest: fluff out a very small amount of dubbing and spread it right on the tying silk, tapering the body as desired. Now spin the dubbing and silk counterclockwise till the fibers are tight. Wind the spun dubbing with fingers (not hackle pliers) to maintain a tight twist. A little practice will produce neat bodies, as tight as you want them. Stiff seal's fur will need the help of a sticky wax or glue on the thread.

Other Body Materials Options for other body materials are discussed in chapter 8.

Wings Options for wings are described in chapter 7. See also chapters 6, 10, and 11.

Hackles In addition to their function of imitating wings, hackles are the most convenient material we have for building high-riding behavior into a fly. (Some hairs are a fair substitute.) Before picking the hackles for a new imitation, therefore, it is always necessary to think about the level at which the fly is intended to float. If the hackle is omitted entirely or flattened on the bottom, the fly must float low. It will also float low if a soft, dense hackle, such as a feather from a small bird or hen, is used without waterproofing. See the notes on tying soft-hackle flies in chapter 10.

British anglers have available a wide body of written knowledge on the usefulness of different soft hackles. (See, for example, Aldam, Pritt, Edmonds and Lee, and Skues.) Americans have never done much with their own birds. The following list may therefore be useful.

Bobwhite Quail There is variation in the feathers of individual bobwhites, but you can find very nice brown feathers speckled with black on the back of the bird. They resemble the well-known feathers of the English partridge but are finer in both quill and fiber, and are not quite as brown. Skues complained that partridge was too brown for his Blue-Winged Olive nymphs. I wish I could send him some bobwhite feathers to use in the chalkstreams of the Elysian Fields. Down here, bobwhite works for true Blue-Winged Olive nymphs and many others.

Gambel's Quail This little desert bird has some of the most attractive blue-dun body feathers imaginable, a few of them finely speckled. They are just right for hatching duns. The scaled quail also has nice blue feathers, but with a small black tip. If desert quail were native to Yorkshire, there would be dozens of traditional patterns using their feathers.

Ruffed Grouse Every ruffed grouse seems different, but all have feathers which are a bit large and fragile for fly-tying. You can, however, find a few nice, small brown feathers on the neck. A few feathers on the upper wing resemble dark red-grouse feathers. Ruffed-grouse tail feathers can be used for the rolled wings of sedges.

Snipe The American Wilson's snipe seems identical to the European common snipe. This means that both the quill feathers and the small feathers on the wing are very useful for rolled wings and soft hackles, respectively. The feathers on top of the rump can be used for March Browns. We Americans use the term "jacksnipe" for the common snipe, and have no equivalent to the European jacksnipe, which (I think) has even finer feathers than the common snipe.

Woodcock American woodcock have some feathers that are

quite different from their European counterparts, even though the two species look similar superficially. American woodcock feathers, with more gray, look the better to me. It is possible to find small feathers above and below the wing which are close to those on the European bird and could be used for hackles on the same patterns.

Pheasant The Chinese ringneck pheasant in America is virtually the same as the bird now common in England and Ireland. The center tail feathers provide excellent herls. The hen wing-quills are useful for the wings of flies like the traditional March Brown. The neck of the cock has fair small feathers for beetles. Ned Maguire told me that he once found a pheasant tail with a pronounced olive cast, and I have been looking ever since.

Crow The crow has good body feathers (when reinforced with cement) for flat-wing sedges and beetles. The quill feathers make an attractive dark (not quite black) herl. As far as I know, we have in America no equivalent to the European jackdaw with its pale-gray neck feathers.

Starling I cannot say anything else good about this bird, but almost every feather is useful for fly-tying, if you get a good specimen. Shoot half a dozen out of a winter flock and skin the best one or two. There are good black hackles, very reasonable eye feathers (a jungle-cock substitute), useful quills, and a variety of different small feathers on the wings and body. See the English books mentioned above for details. Chetham noted the use of starling for wings back in 1681.

Wren You could be lynched for shooting a wren in America, but if one happens to commit suicide on your car radiator grille, the tail and inner secondaries are like those of the European bird—which is to say outstandingly good for soft hackles.

Blackbirds These are often a pest in America. Their feathers are entirely different from those of the European species and not nearly as useful; the American birds have only some small black feathers which are almost too soft. On the other hand, I should like to get my hands on an American robin. It is a little lighter in color than a hen European blackbird but otherwise similar (even to the song).

Oddments Have a good look at any small bird that expires within your reach. One year I got my best trout on the yellow feather of an Irish goldfinch wound hackle-wise. It made a marvelous Yellow May. I have been trying to get my hands on wings of the American clapper and king-rails, which appear to be a little more red than the traditional land-rail.

<u>Tails</u> The main function of tails is mechanical: to assist floating patterns of mayflies in landing upright, cocking correctly, and floating well. (Other commonly imitated flies do not have tails.) A stiff tail is especially useful on a soft-hackle mayfly that is intended to float. ("Stiff," however, is a relative term in fly-tying. A really stiff, bulky tail gives a most unrealistic appearance and light pattern; it also impedes hooking.) Approximately six to twelve hackle fibers should be used, and they should be divided into a widespread *V* shape. Vince Marinaro started the popularity of the widely spread tail. His method of tying it is excellent, although I prefer a different one, described below.

You can still get an argument over the angle of the tail: up, down, or horizontal? This is an important part of the dry fly's geometry, and I don't recall seeing it explained in design terms.

Those are the only terms that matter. The Tail does *not* seem very noticeable to the trout, unless you make it so thick that it becomes a sort of extended body. You can use any color, divide the tail or leave it in one bunch, even put a tail on flies that shouldn't have it—like the black gnat—and the trout won't pay much attention.

But the tail will markedly affect the way the fly lands and floats. Some fly-tyers like to tip the tail down, hoping that it will elevate the hook off the water. This might work if the fly could be placed on the water by hand, carefully, in exactly the desired position. In fishing, however, the down-tipped tail turns the fly over on its back. You don't want this, clearly, if the fly has wings in the normal position. For winged flies, rock the tail slightly *upwards* and divide it. This makes the fly much more likely to cock.

On the other hand, if you are fishing with a plain hackle fly, a sharply down-tipped tail will often land the fly with hook up, out of the water. This is the simplest of hook-up designs, and perhaps the best—though the hook won't always land just as you want it.

The point to remember is that the tail is an airfoil, not a static display. The V-tail makes an airfoil that is twice as good as the clumped tail. You can check out the design of a tail by dropping the fly on the table—even without a leader—from an altitude of a foot or more. Flies that cock well when you do this will probably cock on the stream.

Some hairs have about the same stiffness and diameter as hackle fibers. These can be used for tails if preferred, but they offer no special advantages. The usual deer body hair is too coarse for tails, and it is worth repeating that deer mask hair sinks like wire.

Cements, Varnishes, and Lacquers The most widely used of these mixtures is celluloid-based and is variously known as head cement and head lacquer (in America), or as celluloid varnish in England. It dries quickly and gives a shiny finish if enough is used. If thinned, it penetrates a little. If thick, it can be used to coat a thread in order to hold stiff dubbing. (Wax is better for this, however.)

For a really durable fly, one of the best potions is artists' varnish, which is sold in convenient small bottles as rod varnish. It soaks in deeply, but takes a long time to dry and can discolor light materials.

Flat clipped wings (as on the Flat-Wing Sedge) should be reinforced with some cement. The old celluose lacquer works after a fashion. Modern vinyl cement is better. Strongest of all is Pliobond, which dries to a flexible, rubber-like coating. Unthinned, it is also good for patching waders and coating line-to-leader splices.

Fly-Tying Tools

Vises The Thompson Model A was the first modern vise to become popular. It must have made a vast difference to fly-tyers when it came on the market around the turn of the century: its cam-actuated lever worked quickly and positively, unlike the thumbscrews of older vises. I bought my first Model A in the 'fifties and still use it for big flies. Even with "midge" jaws, however, my version does not hold small hooks without slippage—and I use small hooks most of the time.

Eventually I treated myself to an HMH "Spartan" vise designed by Bill Hunter, and regretted having waited so long. The jaws are very carefully machined. The smallest of them make it a pleasure to tie tiny flies. The vise as a whole is compact, fitting neatly in my larger traveling kit, but not my streamside kit. Several other beautiful vises are now on the market; I have not had the opportunity to test them. Good machining cannot be cheap.

For the streamside kit, I am still using a pin vise. It is not good, but it is cheap and small. I admire people who can tie flies with the hook in their fingers, but they cannot handle really small hooks. Even with a hand-held vise, the flies I dress are rougher than ones tied with a bench vise, but there is no difference in their effectiveness.

Of strictly hand-held vises, the neatest I have seen is an old one made of greenheart and owned by J. R. Harris. You might think that wood could not stand the strain of holding a small steel hook tightly, but it does, and the jaws of this one are unmarked after two generations of use.

Bobbins There are three methods of keeping fly-tying silk tight after fastening on materials: sticky wax, knots (half-hitches), and a weight on the end of the thread. When tying a fly with a hand-held vise, the best solution is probably to add a half-hitch after every operation. When a bench-mounted vise is used, however, the weight system is simple and effective; and when a bobbin provides the weight, it is also economical of thread and fast in use. There is obviously a good deal of room for individual preference in these matters, but the only bobbin that ever seemed just right to me is a simple one now being sold in America. The initials "FM" (for Frank Matarelli) are stamped on the frame. The thread tube lasts a long time and is easier on silk than the slightly rough skin of my fingertips. The bobbin can thus be used for fast winding, though fingertip tension is best for delicate operations. The frame of the Matarelli bobbin can be bent to put the right tension on any thread spool, but I like to rewind most of my large American spools onto wooden Pearsall's spools, which take up less space. A small electric drill does the job in no time.

Oddments For small flies, the hackle pliers should not be too heavy, or delicate feathers may break. If the ends of the jaws are sharp, they may be rounded off with a fine stone. Otherwise, the only requirement is that the loop in the base of the pliers be large enough to admit the index finger, since this is the easiest way to wind a hackle properly on edge. One also needs a very fine pair of scissors, preferably with curved blades, for cutting feathers and silk, and a heavier pair for coarse bunches of hair. A large needle stuck into a cork makes a bodkin that will stand on end without tipping over and can be used to plug the cement bottle. Three or four such bodkins allow flies to be dried with a needle in the hook eye, so that cement cannot plug it. A small modelmaker's knife is easier to use than a razorblade and can be sharpened at will on a hard Arkansas stone. A hook sharpener, ten-power magnifier, and a bottle for insects completes the kit.

Step-by-Step Instructions

The fly described here is the one I have lightly called the Perfect Dun, since its tying requires most of the operations necessary for any fly. Variations are described in the "Tying Notes" sections for each design described in the previous two chapters.

Begin by placing the natural fly in front of you. Daylight or a good artificial light (very much second best) should be abundant. This is the most important step of all. Pictures in books are not good enough, though an artificial fly that is known to be a correct imitation serves well as a model. Nymphs taken from a trout's stomach should be put in water in a white dish (courtesy of Mr. Skues again). For floating flies, a live model is much better. Its belly will have to be seen, so place it in a small, transparent plastic box.

1. Secure the hook as shown and sharpen the point on three sides with a fine abrasive strip or Arkansas-stone needle.

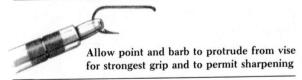

Allow point and barb to protrude from vise
for strongest grip and to permit sharpening

2. Start the silk slightly behind the eye of the hook by winding it over itself. Most fly-tyers prefer to wind clockwise (over the hook shank and back under it), but the important thing is to wind in the same direction all the time. (The main exception, which is explained later, is the rib.) Then wind the thread far enough back over itself to make a good base for the wings. Cut off the loose end.

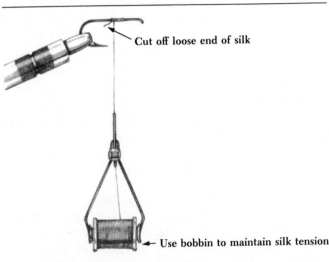

Cut off loose end of silk

Use bobbin to maintain silk tension

3. Pick two (optionally four) large straight hackles for wings. (This is a good way to use up those extra-large feathers.) Cut about an inch off the tips of each. Place the two tips together, shiny-side-inwards, so that they will naturally flare outward when placed on the fly. Strip some of the fibers from the base, but do not strip quite to the point where the feather will be tied in. Leaving a few fibers along with the quill makes a stronger wing, though one that is less neat.

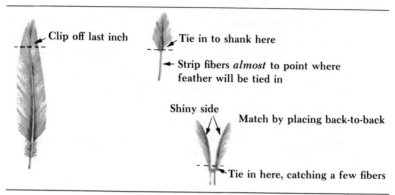

Clip off last inch

Tie in to shank here

Strip fibers *almost* to point where feather will be tied in

Shiny side

Match by placing back-to-back

Tie in here, catching a few fibers

4. Hold the tips of the wings with your left hand and place the butts vertically over the shank of the hook, just forward of the middle of the shank. The first two wraps of thread must go in front of the wing on the top of the hook and behind the wing stub on the bottom of the hook. This will tip the wings slightly back, in the normal mayfly position—which is also a good position for cocking the fly. (When making the first wraps around wings of any kind, hold the wings tightly, with your left thumb and forefinger, where they join the shank, pulling the wraps down through your fingers. This maintains tension and keeps the wings from shifting around.)

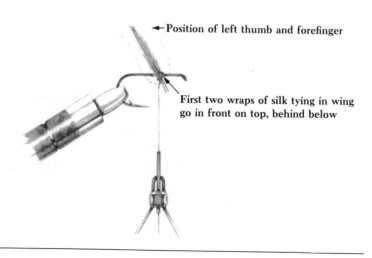

Position of left thumb and forefinger

First two wraps of silk tying in wing go in front on top, behind below

5. Now bend the stubs of the wings back along the shank, tie them down, and cut them off. The bend in the quill of the wing feather will prevent the wings from collapsing in use. You should further prop the wings up with one turn of silk behind them and, later, with two turns of the wound hackle. As a matter of curiosity, I tried a number of methods before finding that this one holds the wings securely at a slightly tipped-back angle. Then, on re-reading Skues' *Side-Lines, Side-Lights, and Reflections,* I saw that this was the system originally worked out by Marryat for winging some of the first dry flies.

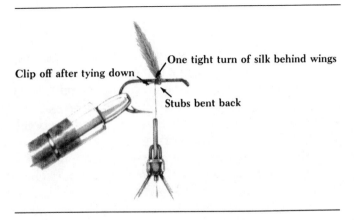

Clip off after tying down

One tight turn of silk behind wings

Stubs bent back

6. Checking the wings: this system will not always prevent a hackle-tip wing from twisting slightly out of a perfect plane when viewed from above. But fortunately, in a soft feather of this kind, a slight twist will not cause any casting problems. You should be sure, however, that the wings are not lopsided when viewed from the *front* of the fly. This could make the fly cock badly. The length of the wings can be varied greatly, but start with wings that are long—about equal to the total length of the hook. Long wings tied in this way will assist cocking and may attract the notice of trout.

Check wing lineup from above. Slight twist does not matter

Imaginary vertical line should bisect angle between wings when viewed from front

7. Wind the thread back a short distance behind the wings, then catch the stubs of several tail fibers which you have already cut to proper length. Wind the thread over the stubs and back to the point at which you will wish to begin the rear end of the body of the fly. Now separate the tail-fiber stubs into a wide *V* and secure each leg of the *V* with one wrap of silk.

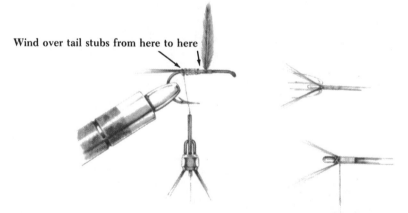

Wind over tail stubs from here to here

Tail stubs separated and held in place with one wrap each

8. Spin the dubbing onto the silk *very* sparsely, especially at the rear. Tighten by spinning the silk and dubbing together between your fingers, as described earlier in the chapter.

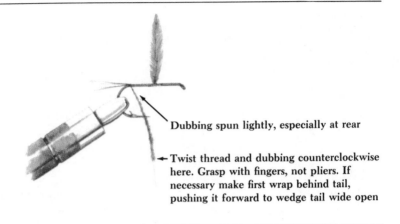

Dubbing spun lightly, especially at rear

← Twist thread and dubbing counterclockwise here. Grasp with fingers, not pliers. If necessary make first wrap behind tail, pushing it forward to wedge tail wide open

9. Make a wrap of thinly dubbed silk behind the tail to wedge it wide open. Then make one wrap in front of the tail. Now catch the end of the ribbing under the dubbed silk and wind the thread forward to a position just behind the wings, giving the dubbed silk an extra twist when necessary to keep it firm. With experience, your dubbing will run out when the body approaches the wings.

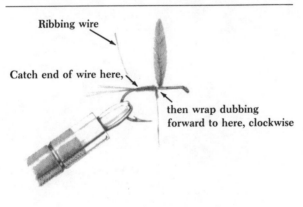

Ribbing wire

Catch end of wire here,

then wrap dubbing forward to here, clockwise

10. Wind the ribbing wire forward counterclockwise (against the direction of the body) to secure the dubbing more firmly and give a segmented effect. Tie off the ribbing behind the wings with two

wraps of silk; then break the ribbing wire off by bending it. This leaves a small rough end that will not pull out.

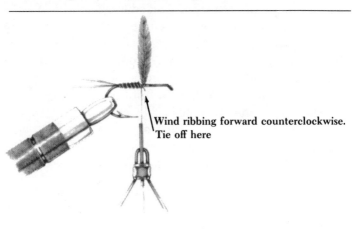

Wind ribbing forward counterclockwise. Tie off here

11. The hackle will almost certainly hold securely and wind correctly if you prepare it by a method I have not seen described elsewhere. First, cut it off with about one-quarter inch of extra stem. Strip off about a dozen fibers on the side that will be *underneath* as you wind the hackle; *clip off* only four or five fibers on

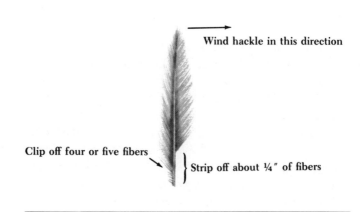

Wind hackle in this direction

Clip off four or five fibers

Strip off about ¼" of fibers

the side that will be on top. Hold the hackle against the hook to see the direction of winding. For this design, you can wind the hackle shiny-side-forward if needed for good sheen and color.

12. Choose a hackle (one only for this design) with fibers shorter than the wing and about the length of the fly's entire body. Fix the feather so that the point is away from you, the stem is on top of the hook, and the hackle is in front of the wings. With your fingers, wind one turn of the hackle in front of the wings, then fasten a hackle plier on the tip of the hackle feather. Wind two more turns tightly behind the wings, then one final turn in front. Tie the hackle off securely and half-hitch your silk.

**Wind one turn of hackle in front of wing, two turns in back, one more in front
Tie off with half-hitch**

13. You may now wish to turn the hook over in the vise, at least for the first few flies you tie. Flatten the hackle underneath the hook and hold it with one figure-eight turn of thread. Try to spread the hackle fibers widely. Now spin a little dubbing on the thread, again very lightly, and make one more figure-eight turn to hold the hackle flat. This will give a dubbed and slightly thickened thorax, as in the natural fly. Make sure that the hackle fibers are horizontal, or slightly above horizontal, for best cocking and floating of the fly. *This design floats low and depends on a flat hackle that is almost as sparse as a mayfly's legs.*

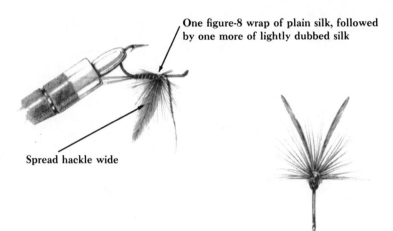

One figure-8 wrap of plain silk, followed by one more of lightly dubbed silk

Spread hackle wide

From front, fly should look like this

14. Wind the rest of the dubbing forward to a position just behind the eye of the hook. The thorax, or portion of the body in front of the wings and hackle, should be only about half as long as the portion to the rear (the abdomen). Finish off with a whip finish, which is faster and neater than half-hitches, as well as more durable. Theodore Gordon called half-hitch finishes "the lazy man's makeshift." Unfortunately, it seems impossible to teach the fast whip-finish method except by personal instruction. You can, however, do a good slow job by just laying the loose end of the silk back along the hook and winding its own loop over it for about five turns. Insert a needle in the loose loop to maintain tension while pulling the finish tight.

15. Apply a drop of cement to the head of the fly and also to the butt of the tail and the base of the wings. (If the body were of a hard material, you might wish to coat the whole thing, at some increase in weight.) Dry the fly on a needle to keep the eye clear.

16. Show it to a trout.

Afterword

🪰 🪰 🪰 In Portugal it begins early. An ancient alarm clock emits a death rattle in the dark. Windows clank open somewhere in the house. This is not my best time of day and I am wondering why we need fresh air, because the stones in the walls have leaned on each other for three centuries without caulking and the wind has been whistling through all night. Also there is a reminder of fermented grape juice at the back of my tongue. I'll not swear it's the world's best red wine, as I did at dinner.

Portuguese women start even faster than their men. Because I am a foreigner and soft, everyone knows I need food before sunup. They have already taken a clay jar to the well for water, and to a little pan of it they've added garlic, olive oil, eggs, and what's left of yesterday's bread. The soup tastes like it ought to be good for me. The bread is still the world's best. It is to be used up before today's sourdough finishes rising and gets shoved into the earthen oven, which is already being heated by a fire of grapevine trimmings. The men drink a cup of bitter coffee with raw brandy. Then they pretend not to be amused while I feed myself for fifteen minutes. Only when I start moving toward last night's walnuts and figs do they hustle me out the door.

The day is feeling more promising. For one thing, it has formally arrived, with an orange-peel of sun giving the houses their only touch of color. The streets, if you can call them that, are of granite stones too, and they clamber around houses piled together at random. Nothing wider than a burro will ever get through.

Chickens scatter in front of us. Everyone gives us a courteous *"bom dia,"* and no one older than five stares at the American who is a foot too tall and dressed in a funny vest full of pockets. The smell is of woodsmoke and damp nanny-goats.

About now I discover that we did not rise early for the fishing. The object is to get to the market before all the good stuff is gone. A trout is only possible; an appetite is inevitable. And starvation is not part of our program.

We need lean meat from a pig fed on chestnuts, then a braid of garlic, another of onions, a sack of oranges, and some big cans of chick-peas. We also get lucky and catch a fine, thick, salt-dried codfish. I'm bargaining for a chicken at the counter of a woman whose underpinnings are wrapped in about five yards of black skirt. The hen I want is much thinner than its owner and has perfect honey-dun hackles. Naturally I am pretending to admire a big white rooster instead. When the price stays high, I offer to settle in disgust for the scrawny little honey-dun. All this gets me the hackles for only 20 percent more than they would have cost if I had not been wearing the opulent fishing vest.

You need this information to understand fishing in Portugal, which is as much gustatory as piscatory.

Eventually my host gets me pointed for the river. I am to hike a half-hour along the top of a canyon and then cut down to the stream along the trail to an abandoned water-mill. Can't miss it. In forty-five minutes, though, I am still walking along the top, and then someone appears. She is a woman with a little boy about the age of my own, but this one looks listless. He sits with his mother. She supervises three cows trying to find a living among half-burned gorse and rock-roses and wild lavender. She has a peeled orange in her lap and offers it to me as if she had a bushel: "Would you care for some?" I try to decline with equal courtesy. An orange would be good after the taste of gorse ashes, but it looks like her only lunch. She is ready to pick up the child and escort me to the river trail. I convince her that I can find it, and a quarter-hour still further along I do.

Scrambling down the canyon, there is another taste in the back of my mouth: fear. Montana has bigger cliffs but Portugal's are meaner. They get in position between the time I fish down in the morning and the time I head home in the evening. With the sun gone this evening and the partridges calling in the rock-roses, I may be hanging onto the face of a very big piece of rock while small ones flake off, take hundred-foot bounces, and send up gouts of water from the river down there. That was okay in college, with ropes when I fell and girls to show off for. Here the partridges would not miss me.

In Portugal, however, the alternative to climbing is to abstain from fishing, and if you believe that that is a choice you would hardly have stayed with this book till the end.

Nowhere else do trout have to put up with quite as much. The Mondego is the longest river in the country and the best I know for trout. It heads up here in the Range of the Stars. In the trouty part it is one long freestone gorge, with murderous floods in the winter and only a few stagnant pools in summer. Fish are sought with wet flies, hardware, worms, grasshoppers, live nymphs, maggots, dynamite, and poison. Trout may be legally killed at nineteen centimeters—seven-and-a-half inches—and the twelve-centimeter variety is usually accorded honorary legality. Their worst defect is tasting delicious. They are the quickest fish I know. They are slender but strong, like a sea trout. They are survivors, like their countrymen. The Portuguese have been fighting off the Spanish for eight hundred years, during part of which time the Spaniards had the best infantry in the world. Not many trout streams discourage Portuguese fishermen.

I cannot outrun or outclimb them. Carlos Pereira will cover twice as much river in a day, but then he's younger. Adriano Cancela will cover half again as much, but then he's older. I do have a secret weapon: the dry fly. It is slower to fish, but the trout have never seen one.

The dry fly does not always work. The best time is late March and early April, which is about equivalent to early May in Virginia or July in Yellowstone. Then there are some fair hatches of sedges, empid flies, and mayflies. (The March Browns may even appear in March.) A hatch will bring fish up everywhere along the river in numbers that testify to the survival ability of the European brown trout. But they have learned to feed without showing more than a furtive dimple. Just a chub? My dun floats over the spot, winks out, and suddenly a bright little trout is splashing around. Usually, he does not say much except "What happened?"

One of last season's problems was striking fast enough. I tried to solve it with a nine-foot carbon-fiber rod, a four-weight line, and a long tippet, not too light. Even then I had to keep a short line and concentrate as hard as if I were nymphing. A longer line would give better floats and bring up more trout, but half of them would get rid of the fly before I could get the slack out.

When the water is high and clear, the river can be fished almost everywhere, but usually with three wet flies downstream. This does not work often. When it does the trout hate themselves for being had so easily. They shrug—which is awkward for a trout—and say, "To hell with you."

The interesting part comes a little later in the season, when the water is low but still fresh. The hatches are over except for a short burst after sunset. Once last year I went all day with only three decent fish—meaning eight-inchers—and then caught eight more after sundown, as fast as I could dry the fly. Wet flies and spinning lures failed for everyone that time. The trout did not know what to make of a floating mayfly with a hook in it. There was little time for conversation, but I distinctly heard one nine-inch giant mutter "That was pretty tricky."

By the end of the season, quite a few of the Portuguese trout had made their opinions heard over the rush of water. They taught me about Matching the Water.

They wanted a match for the hatch too, more or less, but they were not inclined to spend all day discoursing on the body color of Blue-Winged Olives.

The message finally reached me on that day of the half-hour hike that lasted an hour. Three miles of hard fishing had yielded not one keeping-size trout. I gave up by another decayed old water-mill, where a sandy point stuck out in a narrow riffle. The sand was shaded by old pines and carpeted by their needles. A rest seemed like as good an idea as any other I'd had all day. The needles smelled like Yellowstone, and the water near my ear sounded just like my old home-stream there. Maybe the trout started whispering when they thought I was asleep. Maybe I was.

Anyhow, half an hour later I knew I should fish back to my starting point with a Yellowstone dry fly: the old Coachman with a white calftail wing tied low along the body. It was in a very small size, but it looked content bobbing along. Come to think of it, the only flies on the water had been some little black gnats. The peacock body came close to theirs.

In that same riffle, one of the whispering trout came howling after my fly. He got it, too. "Why now?" I asked him, "when you guys have been ignoring me all day."

"What's it worth to you?" he asked. That's a rough translation from Portuguese. It was the second time I'd heard the phrase that day, the first being from the fat lady who sold me the honey-dun hen—at her price. So we were in for some negotiating.

I dipped the net back in the water to keep its tenant fresh. Can't rush these things. "What will you take?"

"Well," he answered, "I'd hate to die a virgin. Got stuck in a hole that almost dried up last summer and the snakes chased me for three months. I wasn't up to spawning. Tell you what . . . but give me a drink first."

The net dipped again. I was careful to keep it folded over with the trout trapped in the bottom. He was not the kind from whom I would have bought a used car.

"Here's the deal," he resumed. "You put me back and I'll stick my head out and tell you how to catch another half dozen."

"The snakes got all of 'em but you." I yawned. "And you'd make a nice ten inches with your jaw stretched out a little."

"You're a hard man," sighed the trout. "Tell you what. I'll talk in the net, and I promise by the Mermaid to take that fly of yours again next spring, assuming I manage to leave some heirs."

"It's a deal."

"Okay," he rattled on, before I could change my mind. "You fish only water that looks like this riffle: just over your knobby knees with a nice bit of chop to kill the glare. No deep spots for those worm fishermen. Deep enough for me. Lots of bugs drifting down from the shallows. And that bug of yours was bouncing around so much that it looked real good. Next place is half a kilometer up, just below the footbridge."

The trout went back chuckling. He probably thought I didn't know he had sworn off black gnats. The fish below the bridge was easy to locate, and then I hiked along with an eye out for other spots where a dry fly would bounce like a cheerleader. Or like a dry fly in Montana. Those spots were a long way apart. Maybe it's no great triumph to come up with a system that requires passing up most of the trout in the river: there were only some two hundred feet of the good stuff in three miles. But I found my way over or around the cliffs and was looking for more water to match my fly when a violent thunderstorm spoiled the evening rise. Back at the car I had a trout for my baby fisherman, two for his mother, and two for me. That's enough.

There should be a way to catch some of the trout in the other 15,640 feet. For the short time that remained in the season, I experimented with the peculiar Portuguese wet flies. They worked —sometimes—in the deep holes under mill-dams and around big boulders. Nothing worked on the flats that are traditionally considered "dry-fly water." In July, just before the water got too hot to be fished at all, a few trout did come to tiny upstream nymphs. That was in water too calm for dry flies and too shallow for three wets. Perhaps the answer is an old fly book with a whole series of leaders ready to go, flies and all, for matching every piece of water. Otherwise the time saved from hiking would be lost tying knots.

Mr. Halford did not like "fishing the water." If he is still paying attention, his verdict on Matching the Water may have been summed up in that thunderstorm. But my new idea has kept me tying flies in the off-season. For all the days I have spent fishing "blind" on rapid streams, it had never occurred to me to articulate a system for each new stretch.

So there is next season's problem: it's not the biggest in the world, but it's available. To solve it there is at least one fast-talking trout looking out for a counterfeit Black Gnat. He'll get a little pale mayfly spinner. I have not identified the species yet, but they lay their eggs on bouncy water of an April evening.

Thank the Lord for next season.

Bibliography

Bibliographies are intended to serve different purposes. At worst, they are lists of books that have not been read but which—the new author hopes—will add a bit of literary class by association. At best, every book in a bibliography has been studied for some particular kind of information, and the bibliographic entry may even be annotated.

The following bibliography merely records books that I have searched for the facts and origins of concepts mentioned in the text. Undoubtedly I have missed much, but readers will know where I have looked. Not every book consulted is listed, but most of those that are listed have made some contribution, often minor.

The editions consulted are important. For example, my third edition of Pulman has the famous reference to what sounds like dry-fly fishing; earlier editions do not. But my first edition of Davy lacks information on optics which is said to be in the second edition. Occasionally—as in the case of the revolutionary Ronalds—I have noted that there is a first edition much earlier than mine.

I have omitted many magazine articles and a number of scientific papers that were not published in book form. The most useful magazines have been *The American Fly Fisher, Fly Fisherman, Trout and Salmon,* and the *Flyfisher's Journal.* (I had only occasional copies of the British publications.)

Several criticisms of my list might be made.

First, American authors are not strongly represented until 1950. This is because the book focuses on imitative flies. We Americans got a late start in that field, and there is no disguising it.

Second, there are no footnotes, and I have not been able to weave enough credits into the text. By way of example, I did not record that Alexander Mackintosh gave a very modern description of mixing dubbing, and testing it for color, back in 1821 (though not with a blender). Third, I have not had access to many of the very scarce (and expensive) early editions.

But I shall be content if the approach used here commends itself to other angling writers. The approach is simply to give credit where credit is due. This is not original; in most fields of scholarship, anything else would be called plagiarism. We fly-fishers now have a literature that deserves respect. The most sincere kind of flattery is neither plagiarism nor adulation. It is credit extended openly.

Aldam, W. H. *A Quaint Treatise on "Flees, and the Art a Artyfichall Flee Making," by an Old Man.* London: Day, 1876.

Allan, P. B. M. *Trout Heresy.* London: Allan, 1937.

Allen, Richard K., and George F. Edmunds. "A Revision of the Genus *Ephemerella." Miscellaneous Publications of the Entomological Society of America,* 1965. A number of other papers in this series were also consulted.

The American Fly Fisher (periodical). Manchester, Vermont: Museum of American Fly Fishing. All issues 1974 through 1977 consulted.

Barker, Thomas. *Barker's Delight: Or, The Art of Angling.* London: 1659 (facsimile reprint of second edition by Scholars' Facsimiles and Reprints).

Bergman, Ray. *Just Fishing.* London: Hutchinson, 1932.

————. *With Fly, Plug, and Bait.* New York: Morrow, 1947.

Brooks, Charles E. *Nymph Fishing for Larger Trout.* New York: Crown, 1976.

[Brown, John J.] *The American Angler's Guide.* New York: Burgess, Stringer & Co., 1845.

Burns, Eugene. *Advanced Fly-Fishing.* Harrisburg, Pennsylvania: Stackpole, 1953.

Burrard, Gerald. *Fly Tying: Principles and Practice.* London: Jenkins, 1940.

Caucci, Al; and Bob Nastasi. *Hatches.* New York: Comparahatch, 1975.

Cholmondeley-Pennell, H. *Fishing—Salmon and Trout.* London: Longmans, 1885.

Collin, J. E. *British Flies: Empididae,* 3 volumes. Cambridge, England: Cambridge University Press, 1961.

Connett, Eugene V., III. *My Friend the Trout.* Princeton: Van Nostrand, 1961.

Cotton, Charles. *See* Walton, Izaak.

Cross, Reuben R. *The Complete Fly Tier.* New York: Freshet, 1971. First edition, 1936.

Cutcliffe, H. C. *The Art of Trout Fishing on Rapid Streams.* London: n.d. First edition, 1863.

[Davy, Sir Humphrey.] *Salmonia.* London: Murray, 1828.

Du Bois, Donald. *The Fisherman's Handbook of Trout Flies.* New York: Barnes, 1960.

Dubravius, Jan. *A New Booke of Good Husbandry.* 1599. Gainesville, Florida: Scholars' Facsimiles and Reprints, 1962.

Dunne, J. W. *Sunshine and the Dry Fly.* London: Black, 1924.

Durnford, Richard. *The Diary of a Test Fisherman, 1809–1819.* Winchester, England: Warren, 1911.

Edmonds, Harfield H., and Norman N. Lee. *Brook and River Trouting.* Bradford, England: [1916].

Edmunds, George F., Jr, Steven L. Jensen, and Lewis Berner. *The Mayflies of North and Central America.* Minneapolis: University of Minnesota Press, 1976.

Fedden, Romilly. *Golden Days From the Fishing Log of a Painter in Brittany.* London: Black, 1919.

Flick, Art. *New Streamside Guide.* New York: Crown, 1969.

Fox, Charles K. *This Wonderful World of Trout.* New York: Freshet, 1971.

Francis, Francis. *A Book on Angling.* London: Longmans, Green & Co., 1885.

Gingrich, Arnold. *The Fishing in Print.* New York: Winchester, 1974.

Goddard, John. *Trout Fly Recognition.* London: Black, 1966.

———. *Trout Flies of Stillwater.* London: Black, 1969.

Greene, H. Plunket. *Where the Bright Waters Meet.* London: Allan, 1936.

Grey, Sir Edward. *Fly Fishing.* London: Dent, 1907.

Halford, Frederic M. *Floating Flies and How to Dress Them.* London: Sampson Low, Marston, Searle, and Rivington, 1886.

———. *Dry-Fly Fishing in Theory and Practice.* London: Sampson Low, Marston, Searle, and Rivington, 1889.

———. *Dry-Fly Entomology,* Vol. II. London: Vinton, 1902.

———. *Modern Development of the Dry Fly.* London: Routledge, 1910.

———. *The Dry-Fly Man's Handbook.* London: Routledge, 1913.

Harding, E. W. *The Flyfisher and the Trout's Point of View.* London: Seeley, 1931.

Hardy's Anglers' Guide (and catalogue), 1898 and subsequent.

Harris, J. R. *An Angler's Entomology.* London: Collins, 1970. First edition, 1950.

Henderson, William. *My Life as an Angler.* London: Satchell, 1880.

Herbert, Henry William (Frank Forester). *Fish and Fishing of the United States.* London: Bentley, 1849.

Hewitt, Edward R. *Hewitt's Nymph Fly-Fishing.* New York: Marchbanks, 1934.

_____. *A Trout and Salmon Fisherman for Seventy-five Years.* New York: Scribners, 1950.

Hills, John Waller. *A History of Fly-Fishing for Trout.* London: Allan, 1921.

_____. *River Keeper.* London: Geoffrey Bles, 1947.

Jackson, John. *The Practical Fly-Fisher.* London: Farlow, 1862.

Jennings, Preston J. *A Book of Trout Flies.* New York: Derrydale, 1935.

Keene, J. Harrington. *Fly-Fishing and Fly-Making.* New York: Judd, 1887.

Keene, John H. *Fishing Tackle.* London: Ward, Lock & Co., n.d.

Kingsley, Charles. "Chalk-Stream Studies." In *Prose Idylls.* London: Macmillan, 1891.

Kite, Oliver. *Nymph Fishing in Practice.* London: Jenkins, 1963.

La Branche, George M. L. *The Dry Fly and Fast Water.* New York: Scribner's, 1914.

Leisenring, James E. *The Art of Tying the Wet Fly* (as told to V.S. Hidy). New York: Dodd, Mead, 1941.

Leiser, Eric. *Fly-Tying Materials.* New York: Crown, 1973.

Leonard, J. Edson. *Flies.* New York: Barnes, 1950.

Leonard, Justin W. and Fannie A. *Mayflies of Michigan Trout Streams.* Bloomfield Hills, Michigan: Cranbrook Institute of Science, 1962.

Lewis, Philip A. *Taxonomy and Ecology of Stenonema Mayflies.* Cincinnati, Ohio: U.S. Environmental Protection Agency, 1974.

Macan, T.T., and C. Joan Worthington. *A Key to the Adults of the British Trichoptera.* Ambleside, Westmorland, England: Freshwater Biological Association, 1973.

Macan, T. T., and E.B. Worthington. *Life in Lakes and Rivers.* London: Collins, 1951.

Mackintosh, Alexander. *The Modern Fisher; or, Driffield Angler.* Derby, England: Henry Mozley, 1821.

Marinaro, Vincent. *A Modern Dry-Fly Code.* New York: Crown, 1970. First edition, 1950.

_____. *In the Ring of the Rise.* New York: Crown, 1976.

Markham, Gervase. *The Pleasures of Princes.* 1614. Gainesville, Florida: Scholars' Facsimiles and Reprints, 1962.

McClane, A. J. *The Practical Fly Fisherman.* New York: Prentice-Hall, 1953.

McClelland, H. G. *The Trout Fly-Dresser's Cabinet of Devices.* London: Fishing Gazette, 1927. First edition, 1898.

McDonald, John. *Quill Gordon.* New York: Knopf, 1972.

Menzies, W. J. M. *Sea Trout and Trout.* London: Arnold, 1936.

Mottram, J. C. *Fly-Fishing: Some New Arts and Mysteries.* London: The Field, n.d. Second edition, 1921.

Needham, Paul R. *Trout Streams.* New York: Winchester, 1969.

O'Gorman. *The Practice of Angling, Particularly as Regards Ireland.* Dublin: Curry, 1845.

Overfield, T. Donald. *G. E. M. Skues: The Way of a Man With a Trout.* London: Benn, 1977.

Prime, W. C. *I Go A-Fishing.* London: Sampson Low, Marston, Low, and Searle, 1873.

Pritt, T. E. *North-Country Flies.* London: Sampson Low, Marston, Searle, and Rivington, 1886.

Pulman, G. P. R. *The Vade-Mecum of Fly-Fishing for Trout.* London: Longmans, 1851.

Reid, John. *Clyde-Style Flies.* Newton Abbot, England: David & Charles, 1971.

Rennie, James. *Alphabet of Scientific Angling.* London: Orr, 1833.

Ritz, Charles. *A Fly-Fisher's Life.* New York: Holt, 1959.

Ronalds, Alfred. *The Fly-Fisher's Entomology.* London: Longmans, 1868. First edition, 1836.

Sargent, Walter. *The Enjoyment and Use of Color.* New York: Dover, 1964.

Sawyer, Frank. *Nymphs and the Trout.* London: Black, 1970. First edition, 1958.

Schwiebert, Ernest G., Jr. *Matching the Hatch.* New York: Macmillan, 1955.

_____. *Nymphs.* New York: Winchester, 1973.

Scotcher, George (c. 1809). *The Fly Fisher's Legacy.* Reprinted with notes by Jack Heddon. London: Honey Dun Press, 1974.

Scott, Genio C. *Fishing in American Waters.* New York: Harper, 1869.

Secombe, Joseph. *Discourse at Ammauskeeg-Falls.* 1739. Reprinted. Boston: Kneeland & Green, 1892.

Shipley, William. *Fly Fishing.* Edited by Edward Fitzgibbon. London: Simpkin, Marshall & Co., 1838.

Skues, G. E. M. *Minor Tactics of the Chalk Stream.* London: Black, 1924. First edition, 1910.

————. *The Way of a Trout With a Fly.* London: Black, 1928.

————. *Side-Lines, Side-Lights, and Reflections.* London: Seeley, [?1932].

————. *Nymph Fishing for Chalk Stream Trout.* London: Black, 1939.

————. *Silk, Fur and Feather.* Beckenham, Kent, England: The Fishing Gazette, 1950.

————. *Itchen Memories.* London: Jenkins, 1951.

————. *Angling Letters.* Edited by C. F. Walker. London: Black, 1956.

Smart, John. *The British Simulidae.* Ambleside, Westmorland, England: Freshwater Biological Association, 1944.

Smedley, Harold H. *Fly Patterns and Their Origins.* Muskegon, Michigan: Westshore, 1950.

Smith, Jerome V. C. *Natural History of the Fishes of Massachusetts, Embracing a Practical Essay on Angling.* 1833. Reprinted. New York: Freshet Press, 1970.

Solomon, Larry, and Eric Leiser. *The Caddis and the Angler.* Harrisburg, Pennsylvania: Stackpole, 1977.

Sosin, Mark, and John Clark. *Through the Fish's Eye.* New York: Harper & Row, 1973.

Stewart, W. C. *The Practical Angler.* Edinburgh: Black, 1857.

Sturgis, William Bayard. *Fly-Tying.* New York: Scribner's: 1940.

Swisher, Doug, and Carl Richards. *Selective Trout.* New York: Crown, 1971.

Taverner, Eric. *Trout Fishing from All Angles.* London: Seeley, Service, 1929.

Taverner, Eric, and John Moore. *The Angler's Week-End Book.* London: Seeley, Service, n.d.

Theakston, Michael. *British Angling Flies.* Revised and annotated by Francis Walbran. Ripon, England: n.d. First edition, 1853.

Tod, E. M. *Wet-Fly Fishing.* London: Sampson Low, Marston and Co., 1903.

Turing, H. D. *Trout Problems.* London: Black, 1948.

Wade, Henry. *Rod-Fishing in Clear Waters.* London: Bell and Daldy, [c. 1860].

Walker, C. F. *Chalk Stream Flies.* London: Black, 1953.

————. *Fly-Tying as an Art.* London: Jenkins, 1957.

Walker, Charles Edward. *Old Flies in New Dresses.* London: 1898.

Walker, Richard. *Fly Dressing Innovations.* London and Tonbridge: Benn, 1974.

Walton, Izaak, and Charles Cotton. *The Compleat Angler.* Edited by George W. Bethune. London: 1891.

Wells, Henry P. *Fly-Rods and Fly-Tackle.* London: Sampson Low, Marston, Searle, and Rivington, [*c.* 1890].

Webster, David. *The Angler and the Loop Rod.* Edinburgh: Blackwood, 1885.

Wetzel, Charley. *The Art of Fly Tying.* Doylestown, Pennsylvania: Noll, 1966. First edition, apparently 1936.

Wheatley, Hewett. *The Rod and Line.* London: 1849.

Williams, A. Courtney. *A Dictionary of Trout Flies.* London: Black, 1950.
———. *Angling Diversions.* London: Jenkins, n.d.

Woolley, Arthur. *Thoughtful Practice with a Dry Fly.* London: Redman, 1949.

Woolley, Roger. *Modern Trout Fly Dressing.* Kent, England: The Fishing Gazette, 1950. First edition, 1932.

Wright, Leonard M. Jr. *Fishing the Dry Fly as a Living Insect.* New York: Dutton, 1972.

Index

absorbency of materials, 119–20
action, behavior distinguished
    from, 32–33
Adams fly, 218, 219
airfoil problem, upright wings and,
    129
Air Net, 46
Aldam, W. H., 17
alders, 62–64, 127
American Fly Fisher, The
    (periodical), 115
ants, 63
    designs, 232–34
aphids, 65
aquatic insects
    behavior of. *See* behavior of
        natural flies
    direct observation of, 46
    obtaining specimens of, 45–47
    pictures of, 45
    stages in life of, 43–44
art, fly tying as, xiv–xv, 166
artificial flies. *See also* dry flies; fly
        tying; wet flies; *specific topics*
    rank-order of features of, 30–33

Baetis (mayfly), 47, 112. *See also*
        Large Dark Olive; Small Dark
        Olive
    duns, 210
    rhodani, 48
    spinners, 50, 51, 210
    vagans, 48
Baigent, William, 182–83
bank fishing, 76–77
Barb-Wing Dun, 195, 197–200
Bashline, Jim, 203
beard hackle, 122

beetles, 37–39, 63, 124, 235–37
    black, 37, 38
    flat-wing silhouette, 38–39
behavior imitation, 19
    "action," distinguished from
        "behavior," 32–33
    color perception of trout and,
        142–43
    exaggerations in, 31
    importance of, 25, 27, 30–32
    weight-size-materials
        relationship, 121–22
behavior of natural flies, 37–65
Bent-Hackle Fly, 180, 185–87
Bergman, Ray, 115, 162, 182
Berner, Lewis, 47
Bibio species, 59
big-hackle fly, 181–84
birds. *See* feathers; *specific birds*
Black Beetle, 37, 38
blackbirds, 130, 249
Black Gnat, 12, 27, 29, 59–60, 64,
    124, 152, 235
    clumped, 240
    designs, 238–41
    knotted midge, 240
    Mottram, 125–26
    Pike-Scale, 125
    single fly, spent or hatching,
        239–40
Black Woolly Worms, 57
Blue Quill, 162, 172
Blue-Winged Olives, 12–15, 27,
    149, 154, 156, 234, 242–43
    trout's description of, 136–37
Boaze, Raleigh, 52
bobbins, 252–53
bobwhite quail, 248